T0181481

Multimedia Systems and Applications

Series editor
Borko Furht, Florida Atlantic University, Boca Raton, USA

More information about this series at http://www.springer.com/series/6298

Jenny Benois-Pineau • Patrick Le Callet
Editors

Visual Content Indexing and Retrieval with Psycho-Visual Models

 Springer

Editors
Jenny Benois-Pineau
LaBRI UMR 5800, Univ. Bordeaux,
  CNRS, Bordeaux INP
Univ. Bordeaux
Talence, France

Patrick Le Callet
LS2N, UMR CNRS 6004
Université de Nantes
Nantes Cedex 3, France

Multimedia Systems and Applications
ISBN 978-3-319-86224-8   ISBN 978-3-319-57687-9   (eBook)
DOI 10.1007/978-3-319-57687-9

Printed on acid-free paper

This Springer imprint is published by Springer Nature
The registered company is Springer International Publishing AG
The registered company address is: Gewerbestrasse 11, 6330 Cham, Switzerland

We dedicate this book to our colleagues and friends, bio-physicists and neuroscientists. Aymar, Daniel, Mark. . . Thank you for our fruitful discussions on physiology and biological control of Human Visual System.

Preface

Since the early ages of Pattern Recognition, researchers try to make computers imitate the perception and understanding of visual content by humans. In the era of structural pattern recognition, the algorithms of contour and skeleton extrapolation in binary images tried to link missing parts using the principle of optic illusions described by Marr and Hildreth.

Modeling of Human Visual System (HVS) in perception of visual digital content has attracted a strong attention of research community in relation to the development of image and video coding standards, such as JPEG, JPEG2000, and MPEG1,2. The main question was how strongly and where in the image the information could be compressed without a noticeable degradation in the decoded content, thus ensuring quality of experience to the users. Nevertheless, the fundamental research on the borders of signal processing, computer vision, and psycho-physics continued and in 1998 has appeared the model of Itti, Koch and Niebur which has become the most popular model for prediction of visual attention. They were interested in both pixels-wise saliency and the scan-path, "static" and dynamic components. A tremendous amount of saliency models for still images and video has appeared during 2000 ties addressing both "low-level", bottom-up or stimuli-driven attention and high-level,"top-down", task-driven attention.

In parallel, content-based image an video indexing and retrieval community (CBIR and CVIR) has become strongly attached to the so-called "salient features", expressing signal singularities: corners, blobs, spatio-temporal jams in video. Using the description of the neighbourhood of these singularities, we tried to describe, retrieve and classify visual content addressing classical tasks of visual information understanding: similarity search in images, recognition of concepts, objects and actions. Since a few years these two streams have met. We are speaking today about "perceptual multimedia", "salient objects", and "interestingness" and try to incorporate this knowledge into our visual indexing and retrieval algorithms, we develop models of prediction of visual attention adapted to our particular indexing tasks... and we all use models of visual attention to drive recognition methods.

In this book we tried to give a complete state of the art in this highly populated and exploding research trend: visual information indexing and retrieval with psycho-visual models. We hope that the book will be interesting for researchers as well as PhD and master's students and will serve as a good guide in this field.

Bordeaux, France   Jenny Benois-Pineau
Nantes, France   Patrick Le Callet
March 2017

Acknowledgements

We thank the French National Research Network GDR CNRS ISIS for the support of scientific exchanges during our Workshops, and Souad Chaabouni and Boris Mansencal for their technical help in preparation of the manuscript of the book.

Contents

Contributors

Chokri Ben Amar REGIM-Lab LR11ES48, National Engineering School of Sfax, Sfax, Tunisia

Jenny Benois-Pineau LaBRI UMR 5800, Univ. Bordeaux, CNRS, Bordeaux INP, Univ. Bordeaux, Talence, France

Adrian G. Bors Department of Computer Science, University of York, York, UK

Lilian Calvet Simula Research Laboratory, Fornebu, Norvége

Axel Carlier IRIT, UMR 5505, Université Toulouse, Toulouse, France

Souad Chaabouni LaBRI UMR 5800, Univ. Bordeaux, CNRS, Bordeaux INP, Univ. Bordeaux, Talence, Cedex, France

Vincent Charvillat IRIT, UMR 5505, Université Toulouse, Toulouse, France

Frédéric Comby LIRMM, CNRS/Univ. Montpellier, Montpellier, France

Mihai Gabriel Constantin LAPI, University Politehnica of Bucharest, Bucharest, Romania

Vincent Courboulay L3i - University of La Rochelle, La Rochelle, France

Claire-Hélène Demarty Technicolor R&I, Rennes, France

Thanh-Toan Do Singapore University of Technology and Design, Singapore, Singapore
University of Science, Ho Chi Minh City, Vietnam

Michael Dorr Technical University Munich, Munich, Germany

Ngoc Q.K. Duong Technicolor R&I, Rennes, France

Christine Fernandez-Maloigne Xlim, University of Poitiers, CNRS, Poitiers, France

Syntyche Gbehounou Jules SAS, Blagnac, France

Pierre Gurdjos IRIT, UMR 5505, Université Toulouse, Toulouse, France

Bogdan Ionescu LAPI, University Politehnica of Bucharest, Bucharest, Romania

Pol Kennel IMFT, INPT/Univ. Toulouse, Toulouse, France

Patrick Le Callet LS2N, UMR CNRS 6004, Université de Nantes, Nantes Cedex 3, France

François Lecellier Xlim, University of Poitiers, CNRS, Poitiers, France

Karam Naser LS2N, UMR CNRS 6004, Polytech Nantes, University of Nantes, Nantes Cedex, France

Wei Tsang Ooi School of Computing, National University of Singapore, Singapore

Alex Papushoy Department of Computer Science, University of York, York, UK

William Puech LIRMM, CNRS/Univ. Montpellier, Montpellier, France

Arnaud Revel L3i - University of La Rochelle, La Rochelle, France

Vincent Ricordel LS2N, UMR CNRS 6004, Polytech Nantes, University of Nantes, Nantes Cedex, France

Mats Sjöberg Helsinki Institute for Information Technology HIIT, Department of Computer Science, University of Helsinki, Helsinki, Finland

Thierry Urruty Xlim, University of Poitiers, CNRS, Poitiers, France

Eleonora Vig German Aerospace Center, Oberpfaffenhofen, Germany

Hanli Wang Department of Computer Science and Technology, Tongji University, Shanghai, China

Akka Zemmari LaBRI UMR 5800, Univ. Bordeaux, CNRS, Bordeaux INP, Univ. Bordeaux, Talence, Cedex, France

Visual Content Indexing and Retrieval with Psycho-Visual Models

Patrick Le Callet and Jenny Benois-Pineau

Abstract The present chapter is an introduction to the book. The subject we propose has seen an exploded interest since last decade from research community in computer vision and multimedia indexing. From the field of video quality assessment where models of Human Visual System (HVS) were generally used to predict where humans will foveate and how will they perceive the degradation, these methods moved to classical Image and Video Indexing and retrieval tasks, recognition of objects, events, actions in images and video. In this book we try to give the most complete overview of the methods for visual information indexing and retrieval using prediction of visual attention or saliency. But also consider new approaches specifically designed for these tasks.

1 From Low to High Level Psycho Visual Models: Perceptual Computing and Applications

Along the last two decades, perceptual computing has emerged as a major topic for both signal processing and computer science communities. Taking care that many technologies produce signals for humans or process signals produced by humans, it is all the more important to consider perceptual aspects in the design loop. Whatever the uses cases, perceptual approaches rely on perceptual models that are supposed to predict and/or mimic some aspects of the perceptual system.

Such models are not trivial to obtain. Their development implies a multidisciplinary approach, in addition to signal processing of computer science encompassing neurosciences, psychology, physiology to name few. Perceptual modeling depends on the ability to identify the part of the system under study. In the case

P. Le Callet (✉)
LS2N UMR CNRS 6004, Université de Nantes, Nantes Cedex 3, France
e-mail: patrick.lecallet@univ-nantes.fr

J. Benois-Pineau
LaBRI UMR 5800, Univ. Bordeaux, CNRS, Bordeaux INP, Univ. Bordeaux, 351, crs de la Liberation, F33405 Talence Cedex, France
e-mail: jenny.benois-pineau@u-bordeaux.fr

© Springer International Publishing AG 2017
J. Benois-Pineau, P. Le Callet (eds.), *Visual Content Indexing and Retrieval with Psycho-Visual Models*, Multimedia Systems and Applications, DOI 10.1007/978-3-319-57687-9_1

of visual perception, sub-part of human visual system are easier to identify than some others, especially through psychophysics. With such approaches, relatively sufficient models have been successfully developed, mainly regarding "low level" of human vision. First order approximation for contrast perception such as Weber's law is a good and classic example, but we have been able to go much further, developing models for masking effects, color perception, receptive fields theory. In the late 1990s, there were already pretty advanced and practical perceptual models suitable for many image processing engineers. Most of them, such as Just Noticeable Difference (JND) models, are touching the visibility of signals and more specifically the visual differences between two signals. This knowledge is naturally very useful for applications such as Image quality prediction or image compression.

For years, these two applications have constituted a great playground for perceptual computing. They have probably pushed the evolution of perceptual models along the development of new immersive technologies (increasing resolution, dynamic range . . .), leading not only to more advances JND models [19] but also to explore higher levels of visual perception.

Visual attention modeling is probably the best illustration of this trend, having concentrating massive efforts by both signal processing and computer science the last decade. From few papers in the mid 2000s, it is now a major topic covering several sessions in major conferences. High efforts on visual attention modeling can be legitimated also by applications angle. Knowing where humans are paying attention is very useful for perceptual tweaking of many algorithms: interactive streaming, ROI compression, gentle advertising [17]. Visual content indexing and retrieval field is not an exception and a lot of researchers have started to adopt visual attention modeling for their applications.

2 Defining and Clarifying Visual Attention

As the term *Visual Attention* has been used in a very wide sense, even more in the community that concerns this book, it requires few clarification. It is common to associate visual attention to eye gaze location. Nevertheless, eye gaze location do not necessarily fully reflect what human observers are paying attention to. One should first distinguish between overt and covert attention:

- **Overt attention** is usually associated with eye movements, mostly related to gaze fixation and saccades. It is easily observable nowadays with eye tracker devices, which record gaze tracking.
- **Covert attention**: William James [13] explained that we are able to focus attention to peripheral locations of interest without moving eyes. Covert attention is therefore independent of oculomotor commands. A good illustration is how a driver can remain fixating road while simultaneously covertly monitoring road signs and lights.

Even if overt attention and covert attention are not independent, over attention has been from far much more studied mostly because it can be measured in a straightforward way by using eye-tracking techniques. This is also one of the reasons why the studies of computational modeling of visual attention are tremendously focused on overt attention. In that sense, visual attention is often seen in a simplified manner as a mechanism having at least the following basic components: (1) the selection of a region of interest in the visual field (2) the selection of feature dimensions and values of interest (3) the control of information flow through the network of neurons that constitutes the visual system; the shifting from one selected region to the next in time.

An important classification for Visual content indexing and retrieval field implies to distinguish between endogenous and exogenous mechanisms that drive visual attention. The **bottom-up** process is passive, reflexive, involuntary also known as exogenous as being driven by the signals, while the **top-down** process is active and voluntary and referred as endogenous attention. Attention can consequently either be task driven (Top-Down attention modeling) or feature driven (Bottom-Up attention modeling). The former is reflexive, signal driven, and independent of a particular task. It is driven involuntarily as a response to certain low-level features: motion, and in particular sudden temporal changes, is known to be dominant features in dynamic visual scenes whereas color and texture pop-outs represent the dominant features in the static scenes. Top-down attention, on the other hand, is driven by higher level cognitive factors and external influences, such as, semantic information, contextual effects, viewing task, and personal preference, expectations, experience and emotions. It is now widely known in the community that top-down effects are an inherent component of gaze behavior and these effects cannot be reduced or overcome even when no explicit task is assigned to the observers.

2.1 Interaction Between the Top-Down and Bottom-Up Attention Mechanisms

Itti et al. [12] describe the neurological backbone behind the top-down and bottom-up attention modeling as natural outcomes of the Inferotemporal cortex and Posterior parietal cortex based processing mechanisms respectively.

Whatever of the considered neurological model, it is more important in most usage of them, to appreciate the relative weights to be used or the mechanisms of interaction between these top-down and bottom-up approaches. Schill et al. [27] highlighted that humans gaze at regions where further disambiguation of information when required. After the gaze is deployed towards such a region, it is the bottom-up features which stand up by feature selection that helps achieve this goal. The work in [23] also highlights some important aspects of free-viewing in this regard, where the variation of the relative top-down versus bottom-up weight $\lambda(t)$ was examined as a function of time. While attention was initially found to be strongly bottom-up driven, there was a strong top-down affect in the range of 100–2000 ms. Later however the interaction between the two processes reach an equilibrium state.

2.2 The Concept of Perceived Importance/Interest: A Visual Attention Concept for Visual Content Indexing and Retrieval

From the application angle addressed in this book, it is desirable to get some models of visual attention. Despite their common goal of identifying the most relevant information in a visual scene, the type of relevance information that is predicted by visual attention models can be very different. While some of the models focus on the prediction of saliency driven attention locations, others aim at predicting regions-of-interest (ROI) at an object level.

Several processes are thought to be involved in making the decision for an ROI, including, attending and selecting a number of candidate visual locations, recognizing the identity and a number of properties of each candidate, and finally evaluating these against intentions and preferences, in order to judge whether or not an object or a region is interesting. Probably the most important difference between eye movement recordings and ROI selections is related to the cognitive functions they account for. It is very important to distinguish between three "attention" processes as defined by Engelke and Le Callet [6]:

- Bottom-up Attention: exogenous process, mainly based on signal driven visual attention, very fast, involuntary, task-independent.
- Top-down Attention: endogenous process, driven by higher cognitive factors (e.g. interest), slower, voluntary, task-dependent, mainly subconscious.
- Perceived Interest: strongly related to endogenous top-down attention but involving conscious decision making about interest in a scene.

Eye tracking data is strongly driven by both bottom-up and top-down attention, whereas ROI selections can be assumed to be mainly driven by top-down attention and especially perceived interest. It is the result of a conscious selection of the ROI given a particular task, providing the level of **perceived interest or perceptual importance**. Consequently, from a conceptual point of view, it might interesting to distinguish between two different types of perceptual relevance maps of a visual content: Importance versus Salience maps. While Salience refers to the pop-out effect of a certain feature: either temporally or spatially, importance maps indicates the perceived importance as it could be rated by human subjects. A saliency map is a probabilistic spatial signal, that indicates the relative probability with which the users regard a certain region. Importance maps on the other hand could be obtained by asking users to rate the importance of different objects in a scene.

2.3 Best Practices for Adopting Visual Attention Model

As stated before, the terms visual attention and saliency can be found in literature with various meaning. Whatever models adopted, researchers should be cautious and check if the selected model is designed to meet the requirements of the targeted application. Moreover, one should also carefully verify the data on which models have been validated. In the context of Visual content indexing and retrieval applications, models touching concepts related to top down saliency, ROI and perceived interest/importance seem the more appealing. Nevertheless, while practically useful, it is very rare that these concepts are explicitly refereed as such, including some of the chapters in this book. The careful reader should be able to make this distinction when visual attention is concerned.

3 Use of Visual Attention Prediction in Indexing and Retrieval of Visual Content

Modeling the selective process of human perception of visual scenes represents an efficient way to drive the scene analysis towards particular areas considered 'of interest' or 'salient'. This is why it has become a very active trend in visual information indexing and retrieval [9]. Due to the use of saliency maps, the search for objects in images is more focused, thus improving the recognition performance and additionally reducing the computational burden. Even more, saliency methods can be naturally applied to all models which have been used up to now in these tasks, such as Bag-of-Visual-Words (BoVW) [25], sliding window approaches for visual object recognition [2, 31], image retrieval [4] or action recognition [32]. Saliency maps are used for generation of "object proposals" for recognition of objects in images and video with Deep Convolutional Neural Networks [5]. Hence in this book we give a large overview of the use of different visual attention models in fundamental tasks of visual information indexing: image and video querying and retrieval, action recognition, emotional analysis, visualization of image content. Models of visual attention, such as the one proposed by Itti et al. [12], Harel's graph implementation [10] are frequently used in literature for computing saliency maps. Nevertheless, as a function of target application and visual task, new forms of saliency can be predicted. Recently, the notion of saliency has been extended to the "interestingness" of visual content [24]. The latter can be understood globally for images and video fragments or locally, in which case it roughly delimits the area in image plane, where the objects of interest can be situated. This notion is also addressed in the present book.

We start with introduction of perceptual models in the problem of visual information retrieval at quite a general level. Visual textures represent areas in images which appears to be uniform from the perspective of human perception. It is difficult to speak here about salient areas, as this is the case in structural visual scenes with objects of interest. In chapter "Perceptual Texture Similarity for Machine Intelligence Applications" the authors are interested in how perceptual models can help in similarity matching of textures. The chapter reviews the theories of texture perception, and provides a survey about the up-to-date approaches for both static and dynamic textures similarity. The authors target video compression application.

In chapter "Deep Saliency: Prediction of Interestingness in Video with CNN" the authors propose a first approach to the prediction of areas-of-interest in video content. Deep Neural Networks have become winners in indexing of visual information. They have allowed achievement of better performances in the fundamental tasks of visual information indexing and retrieval such as image classification and object recognition. In fine-grain indexing tasks, namely object recognition in visual scenes, the CNNs have to evaluate multiple "object proposals", that is windows in the image plane of different size and location. Hence the problem of recognition is coupled with the problem of localization. In [8] a good analysis of recent approaches for object localization has been proposed, such as "regression approaches" as in [1, 28], and "sliding window approaches" as in [29] when the CNN processes multiple overlapping windows. The necessity to classify multiple windows makes the process of recognition heavy. The authors of Girshick et al. [8] proposed a so called Region-based convolutional network (R-CNN). They restrict number of windows using "selective search" approach [31] thus the classifier has to evaluate a limited number of (2K) "object proposals". Prediction of the interestingness of windows is another way to bound the search space. This prediction can be fulfilled with the same approach: a deep CNN trained on the ground truth of visual saliency maps build upon recorded gaze fixations of observers in a large-scale psycho-visual experiment.

In chapter "Introducing Image Saliency Information into Content Based Indexing and Emotional Impact Analysis" the authors are interested in the influence of pixel saliency in classical image indexing paradigms. They use the BoVW paradigm [22] which means building of image signature when selecting features in image plane, quantizing them with regard to a built dictionary and then computing the histogram of quantized features. The authors predict visual saliency of image pixels with Harel's model [10]. They compute a dense set of local image features by four methods: (1) Harris detector [11], (2) Harris-Laplace detector [18], (3) Difference-of-Gaussians (DOG) used in [16] to approximate Harris-Laplace detector and (4) Features from Accelerated Segment Test (FAST) detector [26]. They define "saliency" features on the basis of underlining saliency map. They experimentally show that when filtering out salient features, the drop of image retrieval accuracy is almost four times stronger compared to the removal of "non-salient" features. Such a study on a publicly available databases is a good experimental witness of the importance of saliency in selection of content descriptors and thus justifies the general trend.

Chapter "Saliency Prediction for Action Recognition" develops on the same idea. Here the problem of action recognition in video content is addressed. In order to reduce computational burden, the authors propose a non-uniform sampling of features accordingly to the saliency maps build on the gaze fixations available for a public Hollywood dataset. They follow the standard (improved) Dense Trajectories pipeline from [33–35]. Based on optical flow fields, trajectories are computed first, and then descriptors are extracted along these trajectories from densely sampled interest points. These descriptors comprise the shape of the trajectory, Histogram of Gradients (HOG), Histogram of Optical Flow (HOF), and Motion Boundary

Histograms (MBH). In order to exclude irrelevant trajectories corresponding to the background they compensate motion along the video sequence. Based on the a priori knowledge of video scenes they exclude detected humans from this compensation. Following the objective of selection of action-salient features, they compute several saliency maps. First of all, the central bias saliency map is computed. It expresses Buswell's central bias hypothesis that humans fixate the center of an image [3] or a video frame, and thus in video production the most important objects are situated in the center of video frames in footage. Then they compute an empirical saliency maps identifying smooth pursuit gaze fixation. These saliency maps are specifically relevant to the action recognition as humans perform smooth pursuit movement accommodating to the moving objects. Finally, an analytical saliency map using 2D +t Hessian is computed. Pruning of features is proposed considering Weibull distribution on saliency measures of computed maps. Their detailed studies on the Hollywood2 dataset convincingly show that using saliency—based pruning of features in a classical BoVW with Fisher encoding indexing scheme improves with regard to the base line when a smaller amount of descriptors is used.

In chapter "Querying Multiple Simultaneous Video Streams with 3D Interest Maps" the interestingness of an object in a visual scene is defined by the user. The method is designed for the selection of the best view of an object-of-interest in the visual scene in real-time when a 3D reconstruction of the scene is available. The user selects the region-of-interest on his/her mobile phone, then the 2D ROI is back-projected on a 3D view of the video scene which is obtained from independent cameras. The objects of interest are found inside a projection cone in a 3D scene and the view with the highest entropy is selected expressing the best contrasts in video. The framework is different from a classical Content-Based Image Retrieval schemes. It is designed for real-time and real-life scenarios where the quality of the video being captured in a querying process with the mobile phone can be very poor. Hence the intervention of the user is necessary do delimit the "saliency", which is region/object-of-interest in this case.

While in chapter "Querying Multiple Simultaneous Video Streams with 3D Interest Maps" the entropy is used for selection of the best view of the object-of-interest, in chapter "Information: Theoretical Model for Saliency Prediction—Application to Attentive CBIR" the authors propose an information—theoretical model of saliency itself. The novelty of the proposed work is to present an application of Frieden's well established information framework [7] that answers to the question: how to optimally extract salient information based on the low level characteristics that the human visual system provides? The authors integrate their biologically inspired approach into a real-time visual attention model and propose an evaluation which demonstrates the quality of the developed model.

Chapter "Image Retrieval Based on Query by Saliency Content" is devoted to the study on how the introduction of saliency in image querying could improve the results in terms of information retrieval metrics. They propose a Query by Salience Content Retrieval (QCSR) framework. The main parts of the QCSR system consist of image segmentation, feature extraction, saliency modelling and evaluating the distance in the feature space between a query image and a sample image from the given pool of images [21]. The authors proposed to consider saliency of images at two levels: the local level is the saliency of segmented regions, the global level is the saliency defined by image edges. For querying image database they select salient regions using underlying Harel's (GBVS) saliency map [10]. To select salient regions to be used in a query the authors use the statistics which is a mean saliency value across a region. Salient regions are selected accordingly to the criterion of retrieval performance by thresholding of its histogram for the whole image partition. The authors use various thresholding methods including the well-known Otsu's method [20]. The querying is fulfilled by computation of Earth Mover Distance from regions of Query Image and the Database Image with saliency weighting. The global saliency expressed by the energy of contours is also incorporated into the querying process. They conduct multiple tests on CORELL 1000 and SIVAL databases and show that taking into account saliency allows for better top ranked results: more similar images are returned at the top of the rank list.

In chapter "Visual Saliency for the Visualization of Digital Paintings" the authors show how saliency maps can be used in a rather unusual application of visual content analysis, which is creation of video clips from art paintings for popularization of cultural heritage. They first built a saliency map completing Itti's model [12] with a saturation feature. Then the artist is selecting and weighting salient regions interactively. The regions of interest (ROIs) are then ordered accordingly to the central bias hypothesis. Finally, an oriented graph of salient regions is built. The graph edges express the order in which the regions will be visualized and the edges of the graph are weighted with transition times in the visualization process set by the artist manually. Several generated video clips were presented to eight naive users in a psycho-visual experiment with the task to score how the proposed video animation clip reflects the content of the original painting. The results, measured by the mean opinion score (MOS) metric, show that, in case of four-regions visualization, the MOS values for randomly generated animation clips and those generated with proposed method differ significantly up to 12%.

Finally, chapter "Predicting Interestingness of Visual Content" is devoted to the prediction of interestingness of multimedia content, such as image, video and audio. The authors consider visual interestingness from a psychological perspective. It is expressed by two structures "novelty-complexity" and a "coping potential". The former indicates the interest shown by subjects for new and complex events and the latter measures a subject's ability to discern the meaning of a certain event. From the content-driven, automatic perspective, the interestingness of content has been studied in a classical visual content indexing framework, selecting the most relevant image-based features within supervised learning (SVM) approach [30]. Interestingness of media content is a perceptual and highly semantic notion that remains very subjective and dependent on the user and the context. The authors address this notion for a target application of a VOD system, propose a benchmark dataset and explore the relevance of different features, coming from the most popular local features such as densely sampled SFIT to the latest CNN features extracted from fully connected layer fc7 and prob features from AlexNet Deep CNN [14]. The authors have conducted the evaluation of various methods for media content interestingness assessment in the framework of the MediaEval Benchmarking Initiative for Media Evaluation [15]. In this evaluation campaign 12 groups were participating using prediction methods from SVM to Deep NNs with pre-trained data. The conclusion of the authors are that the task still remains difficult and open as the highest Mean Average Precision (MAP) metric values for image interestingness was 0.22 and for video interestingness it was only 0.18.

References

1. Agrawal, P., Girshick, B., Malik, J.: Analyzing the performance of multilayer neural networks for object recognition. In: Computer Vision - ECCV 2014–13th European Conference, Zurich, September 6–12 (2014), Proceedings, Part VII, pp. 329–344 (2014)
2. Alexe, B., Deselaers, T., Ferrari, V.: Measuring the objectness of image windows. IEEE Trans. Pattern Anal. Mach. Intell. **34**(11), 2189–2202 (2012)
3. Buswell, G.T.: How People Look at Pictures. University of Chicago Press, Chicago, IL (1935)
4. de Carvalho Soares, R., da Silva, I.R., Guliato, D.: Spatial locality weighting of features using saliency map with a BoVW approach. In: International Conference on Tools with Artificial Intelligence, 2012, pp. 1070–1075 (2012)
5. de San Roman, P.P., Benois-Pineau, J., Domenger, J.-P., Paclet, F., Cataert, D., de Rugy, A.: Saliency driven object recognition in egocentric videos with deep CNN. CoRR, abs/1606.07256 (2016)
6. Engelke, U., Le Callet, P.: Perceived interest and overt visual attention in natural images. Signal Process. Image Commun. **39**(Part B), 386–404 (2015). Recent Advances in Vision Modeling for Image and Video Processing
7. Frieden, B.R.: Science from Fisher Information: A Unification, Cambridge edn. Cambridge University Press, Cambridge (2004)
8. Girshick, R.B., Donahue, J., Darrell, T., Malik, J.: Region-based convolutional networks for accurate object detection and segmentation. IEEE Trans. Pattern Anal. Mach. Intell. **38**(1), 142–158 (2016)
9. González-Díaz, I., Buso, V., Benois-Pineau, J.: Perceptual modeling in the problem of active object recognition in visual scenes. Pattern Recogn. **56**, 129–141 (2016)
10. Harel, J., Koch, C., Perona, P.: Graph-based visual saliency. In: Advances in Neural Information Processing Systems, vol. 19, pp. 545–552. MIT, Cambridge (2007)
11. Harris, C., Stephens, M.: A combined corner and edge detector. In: Proceedings of the 4th Alvey Vision Conference, pp. 147–151 (1988)
12. Itti, L., Koch, C.: Computational modelling of visual attention. Nat. Rev. Neurosci. **2**(3), 194–203 (2001)
13. James, W.: The Principles of Psychology. Read Books, Vancouver, BC (2013)
14. Jiang, Y.-G., Dai, Q., Mei, T., Rui, Y., Chang, S.-F.: Super fast event recognition in internet videos. IEEE Trans. Multimedia **177**(8), 1–13 (2015)
15. Larson, M., Soleymani, M., Gravier, G., Jones, G.J.F.: The benchmarking initiative for multimedia evaluation: MediaEval 2016. IEEE Multimedia **1**(8), 93–97 (2017)
16. Lowe, D.G.: Distinctive image features from scale-invariant keypoints. Int. J. Comput. Vis. **60**, 91–110 (2004)
17. Le Meur, O., Le Callet, P.: What we see is most likely to be what matters: visual attention and applications. In: 2009 16th IEEE International Conference on Image Processing (ICIP), pp. 3085–3088 (2009)
18. Mikolajczyk, K., Schmid, C.: Indexing based on scale invariant interest points. In: Proceedings of the 8th IEEE International Conference on Computer Vision, vol. 1, pp. 525–531 (2001)

19. Narwaria, M., Mantiuk, K.R., Da Silva, M.P., Le Callet, P.: HDR-VDP-2.2: a calibrated method for objective quality prediction of high-dynamic range and standard images. J. Electron. Imaging **24**(1), 010501 (2015)

20. Otsu, N.: A threshold selection method from gray-level histograms. IEEE Trans. Syst. Man Cybern. **9**(1), 62–66 (1979)

21. Papushoy, A., Bors, G.A.: Visual attention for content based image retrieval. In: 2015 IEEE International Conference on Image Processing, ICIP 2015, Quebec City, QC, 27–30 September 2015, pp. 971–975

22. Philbin, J., Chum, O., Isard, M., Sivic, J., Zisserman, A.: Lost in quantization: Improving particular object retrieval in large scale image databases. In: 2008 IEEE Computer Society Conference on Computer Vision and Pattern Recognition (CVPR 2008), Anchorage, Alaska, 24–26 June 2008

23. Rai, Y., Cheung, G., Le Callet, P.: Quantifying the relation between perceived interest and visual salience during free viewing using trellis based optimization. In: 2016 International Conference on Image, Video, and Multidimensional Signal Processing, vol. 9394, July 2016

24. Rayatdoost, S., Soleymani, M.: Ranking images and videos on visual interestingness by visual sentiment features. In: Working Notes Proceedings of the MediaEval 2016 Workshop, Hilversum, 20–21 October 2016, CEUR-WS.org

25. Ren, X., Gu, C.: Figure-ground segmentation improves handled object recognition in egocentric video. In: IEEE Conference on Computer Vision and Pattern Recognition (2010)

26. Rosten, E., Drummond, T.: Fusing points and lines for high performance tracking. In: Proceedings of the IEEE International Conference on Computer Vision, vol. 2, pp. 1508–1511 (2005)

27. Schill, K., Umkehrer, E., Beinlich, S., Krieger, G., Zetzsche, C.: Scene analysis with saccadic eye movements: top-down and bottom-up modeling. J. Electron. Imaging **10**(1), 152–160 (2001)

28. Sermanet, P., Eigen, D., Zhang, X., Mathieu, M., Fergus, R., LeCun, Y.: Overfeat: integrated recognition, localization and detection using convolutional networks. CoRR, abs/1312.6229 (2013)

29. Sermanet, P., Kavukcuoglu, K., Chintala, S., LeCun, Y.: Pedestrian detection with unsupervised multi-stage feature learning. In: 2013 IEEE Conference on Computer Vision and Pattern Recognition, Portland, OR, June 23–28, pp. 3626–3633 (2013)

30. Soleymani, M.: The quest for visual interest. In: ACM International Conference on Multimedia, New York, pp. 919–922 (2015)

31. Uijlings, J.R.R., Van de Sande, K.E.A., Gevers, T., Smeulders, A.W.M.: Selective search for object recognition. Int. J. Comput. Vis. **104**(2), 154–171 (2013)

32. Vig, E., Dorr, M., Cox, D.: Space-Variant Descriptor Sampling for Action Recognition Based on Saliency and Eye Movements, pp. 84–97. Springer, Firenze (2012)

33. Wang, H., Schmid, C.: Action recognition with improved trajectories. In: Proceedings of the IEEE International Conference on Computer Vision (2013)

34. Wang, H., Kläser, A., Schmid, C., Liu, C.-L.: Action recognition by dense trajectories. In: Proceedings of the IEEE Conference on Computer Vision and Pattern Recognition (CVPR), pp. 3169–3176. IEEE, New York (2011)

35. Wang, H., Oneata, D., Verbeek, J., Schmid, C.: A robust and efficient video representation for action recognition. Int. J. Comput. Vis. 219–38 (2016)

Perceptual Texture Similarity for Machine Intelligence Applications

Karam Naser, Vincent Ricordel, and Patrick Le Callet

Abstract Textures are homogeneous visual phenomena commonly appearing in the visual scene. They are usually characterized by randomness with some stationarity. They have been well studied in different domains, such as neuroscience, vision science and computer vision, and showed an excellent performance in many applications for machine intelligence. This book chapter focuses on a special analysis task of textures for expressing texture similarity. This is quite a challenging task, because the similarity highly deviates from point-wise comparison. Texture similarity is key tool for many machine intelligence applications, such as recognition, classification, synthesis and etc. The chapter reviews the theories of texture perception, and provides a survey about the up-to-date approaches for both static and dynamic textures similarity. The chapter focuses also on the special application of texture similarity in image and video compression, providing the state of the art and prospects.

1 Introduction

Textures are fundamental part of the visual scene. They are random structures often characterized by homogeneous properties, such as color, orientation, regularity and etc. They can appear both as static or dynamic, where static textures are limited to spatial domain (like texture images shown in Fig. 1), while dynamic textures involve both the spatial and temporal domain Fig. 2.

Research on texture perception and analysis is known since quite a long time. There exist many approaches to model the human perception of textures, and also many tools to characterize texture. They have been used in several applications such

K. Naser (✉) • V. Ricordel
LS2N, UMR CNRS 6004, Polytech Nantes, University of Nantes, Rue Christian Pauc, BP 50609, 44306 Nantes Cedex 3, France
e-mail: karam.naser@univ-nantes.fr; vincent.ricordel@univ-nantes.fr

P. Le Callet
LS2N UMR CNRS 6004, Université de Nantes, Nantes Cedex 3, France
e-mail: patrick.lecallet@univ-nantes.fr

© Springer International Publishing AG 2017
J. Benois-Pineau, P. Le Callet (eds.), *Visual Content Indexing and Retrieval with Psycho-Visual Models*, Multimedia Systems and Applications,
DOI 10.1007/978-3-319-57687-9_2

Fig. 1 Example of texture images from VisTex Dataset

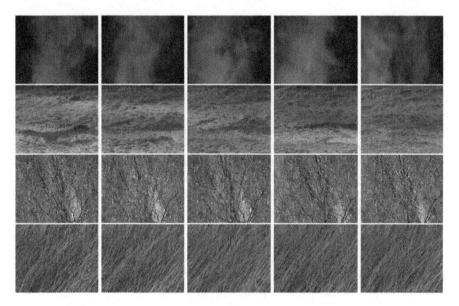

Fig. 2 Example of dynamic textures from DynTex Dataset [93]. *First row* represents the first frame, and *next rows* are frames after respectively 2 s

as scene analysis and understanding, multimedia content recognition and retrieval, saliency estimation and image/video compression systems.

There exists a large body of reviews on texture analysis and perception. For example, the review of Landy [57, 58] as well as the one from Rosenholtz [98] give a detailed overview of texture perception. Besides, the review of Tuceryan et al. in [117] covers most aspects of texture analysis for computer vision applications, such as material inspection, medical image analysis, texture synthesis and segmentation. On the other hand, the book Haindl et al. [45] gives an excellent review about modeling both static and dynamic textures. A long with this, there are also other reviews that cover certain scopes of texture analysis and perception, such as [29, 62, 88, 124, 135].

This chapter reviews an important aspect of texture analysis, which is texture similarity. This is because it is the fundamental tool for different machine intelligence applications. Unlike most of the other reviews, this covers both static and dynamic textures. A special focus is put on the use of texture similarity concept in data compression.

The rest of the chapter is organized as follows: Sect. 2 discusses about the meaning of texture in both technical and non-technical contexts. The details of texture perception, covering both static texture and motion perception, are given in Sect. 3. The models of texture similarity are reviewed in Sect. 4, with benchmarking tools in Sect. 5. The application of texture similarity models in image and video compression is discussed in Sect. 6, and the conclusion is given in Sect. 7.

2 What is Texture

Linguistically, the word texture significantly deviates from the technical meaning in computer vision and image processing. According to Oxford dictionary [86], the word refers to one of the followings:

1. *The way a surface, substance or piece of cloth feels when you touch it*
2. *The way food or drink tastes or feels in your mouth*
3. *The way that different parts of a piece of music or literature are combined to create a final impression*

However, technically, the visual texture has many other definitions, for example:

- *We may regard texture as what constitutes a macroscopic region. Its structure is simply attributed to pre-attentive patterns in which elements or primitives are arranged according to placement order* [110].
- *Texture refers to the arrangement of the basic constituents of a material. In a digital image, texture is depicted by spatial interrelationships between, and/or spatial arrangement of the image pixels* [2].
- *Texture is a property that is statistically defined. A uniformly textured region might be described as "predominantly vertically oriented", "predominantly small in scale", "wavy", "stubbly", "like wood grain" or "like water"* [58].
- *We regard image texture as a two-dimensional phenomenon characterized by two orthogonal properties: spatial structure (pattern) and contrast (the amount of local image structure)* [84].
- *Images of real objects often do not exhibit regions of uniform and smooth intensities, but variations of intensities with certain repeated structures or patterns, referred to as visual texture* [32].
- *Textures, in turn, are characterized by the fact that the local dependencies between pixels are location invariant. Hence the neighborhood system and the accompanying conditional probabilities do not differ (much) between various image loci, resulting in a stochastic pattern or texture* [11].
- *Texture images can be seen as a set of basic repetitive primitives characterized by their spatial homogeneity* [69].
- *Texture images are specially homogeneous and consist of repeated elements, often subject to some randomization in their location, size, color, orientation* [95].

- *Texture refers to class of imagery that can be characterized as a portion of infinite patterns consisting of statistically repeating elements* [56].
- *Textures are usually referred to as visual or tactile surfaces composed of repeating patterns, such as a fabric* [124].

The above definitions cover mostly the static textures, or spatial textures. However, the dynamic textures, unlike static ones, have no strict definition. The naming terminology changes a lot in the literature. The following names and definitions are summary of what's defined in research:

- Temporal Textures:

  1. They are class of image motions, common in scene of natural environment, that are characterized by structural or statistical self similarity [82].
  2. They are objects possessing characteristic motion with indeterminate spatial and temporal extent [97].
  3. They are textures evolving over time and their motion are characterized by temporal periodicity or regularity [13].

- Dynamic Textures:

  1. They are sequence of images of moving scene that exhibit certain stationarity properties in time [29, 104].
  2. Dynamic textures (DT) are video sequences of non-rigid dynamical objects that constantly change their shape and appearance over time[123].
  3. Dynamic texture is used with reference to image sequences of various natural processes that exhibit stochastic dynamics [21].
  4. Dynamic, or temporal, texture is a spatially repetitive, time-varying visual pattern that forms an image sequence with certain temporal stationarity [16].
  5. Dynamic textures are spatially and temporally repetitive patterns like trees waving in the wind, water flows, fire, smoke phenomena, rotational motions [30].

- Spacetime Textures:

  1. The term "spacetime texture" is taken to refer to patterns in visual spacetime that primarily are characterized by the aggregate dynamic properties of elements or local measurements accumulated over a region of spatiotemporal support, rather than in terms of the dynamics of individual constituents [22].

- Motion Texture:

  1. Motion textures designate video contents similar to those named temporal or dynamic textures. Mostly, they refer to dynamic video contents displayed by natural scene elements such as flowing rivers, wavy water, falling snow, rising bubbles, spurting fountains, expanding smoke, blowing foliage or grass, and swaying flame [19].

- Texture Movie:

  1. Texture movies are obtained by filming a static texture with a moving camera [119].

- Textured Motion:

  1. Rich stochastic motion patterns which are characterized by the movement of a large number of distinguishable or indistinguishable elements, such as falling snow, flock of birds, river waves, etc. [122].

- Video Texture:

  1. Video textures are defined as sequences of images that exhibit certain stationarity properties with regularity exhibiting in both time and space [42].

It is worth also mentioning that in the context of component based video coding, the textures are usually considered as details irrelevant regions, or more specifically, the region which is not noticed by the observers when it is synthesized [9, 108, 134].

As seen, there is no universal definition of the visual phenomena of textures, and there is a large dispute between static and dynamic textures. Thus, for this work, we consider the visual texture as:

A visual phenomenon, that covers both spatial and temporal texture, where spatial textures refer to homogeneous regions of the scene composed of small elements (texels) arranged in a certain order, they might exhibit simple motion such as translation, rotation and zooming. In the other hand, temporal textures are textures that evolve over time, allowing both motion and deformation, with certain stationarity in space and time.

3 Studies on Texture perception

3.1 Static Texture Perception

Static texture perception has attracted the attention of researchers since decades. There exists a bunch of research papers dealing with this issue. Most of the studies attempt to understand how two textures can be visually discriminated, in an effortless cognitive action known as pre-attentive texture segregation.

Julesz extensively studied this issue. In his initial work in [51, 53], he posed the question if the human visual system is able to discriminate textures, generated by a statistical model, based on the kth order statistics, and what is the minimum value of k that beyond which the pre-attentive discrimination is not possible any more. The order of statistics refers to the probability distribution of the of pixels values, in which the first order measures how often a pixel has certain color (or luminance value), while the second order measures the probability of obtaining a combination of two pixels (with a given distance) colors, and the same can be generalized for higher order statistics.

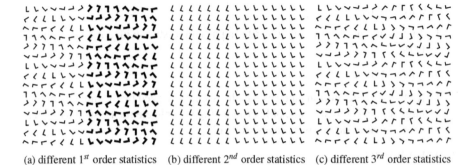

(a) different 1ˢᵗ order statistics   (b) different 2ⁿᵈ order statistics   (c) different 3ʳᵈ order statistics

Fig. 3 Examples of pre-attentive textures discrimination. Each image is composed of two textures side-by-side. (**a**) and (**b**) are easily distinguishable textures because of the difference in the first and the second order statistics (resp.), while (**c**), which has identical first and the second but different third order statistics, is not

First, Julesz conjectured that the pre-attentive textures generated side-by-side, having identical second order statistics but different third order and higher, cannot be discriminated without scrutiny. In other words, textures having difference in the first and/or second order statistics can be easily discriminated. This can be easily verified with the textures given in Fig. 3. The textures are generated by a small texture element (letter L) in three manners. First, to have different the first order statistics, where the probability of black and while pixels is altered in Fig. 3a (different sizes of L). Second, to have difference in second order statistics (with identical first order statistics) by relatively rotating one texture to the other. Third, to have difference in third order statistics (with identical first and second order statistics) by using a mirror copy of the texture element (L). One can easily observe that conjecture holds here, as we just observe the differences pre-attentively when the difference is below the second order statistics. Several other examples can be found in [53] to support this conjecture.

However, it was realized then it is possible to generate other textures having identical third order statistics, and yet pre-attentively discriminable [54]. This is shown in Fig. 4, in which the left texture has an even number of black blocks in each of its 2×2 squares, whereas the left one has an odd number. This led to the modified Julesz conjecture and the introduction of the texton theory [52]. The theory proposes that the *pre-attentive texture discrimination system cannot globally process third or higher order statistics, and that discrimination is the results of few local conspicuous features, called textons.* This has been previously highlighted by Beck [8], where he proposed that the discrimination is a result of differences in first order statistics of local features (color, brightness, size and etc.).

On the other side, with the evolution of the neurophysiological studies in the vision science, the research on texture perception has evolved, and several neural models of human visual system (HVS) were proposed. The functionality of the visual receptive field in [48], has shown that HVS, or more specifically

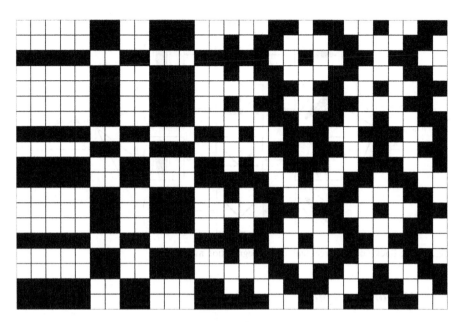

Fig. 4 Example of two textures (*side-by-side*) having identical third order statistics, yet preattentively distinguishable

the visual cortex, analyzes the input signal by a set of narrow frequency channels, resembling to some extent the Gaborian filtering [94]. According, different models of texture discrimination have been developed, based on Gabor filtering [85, 118], or difference of offset Gaussians [65], etc. These models are generally performing the following steps:

1. Multi-channel filtering
2. Non linearity stage
3. Statistics in the resulting space

The texture perception models based on the multi-channel filtering approach is known as back-pocket model (according to Landy [57, 58]). This model, shown in Fig. 5, consists of three fundamental stages: linear, non-linear, linear (LNL). The first linear stage accounts for the linear filtering of the multi-channel approach. This is followed then by a non-linear stage, which is often rectification. This stage is required to avoid the problem of equal luminance value which will on average cancel out the response of the filters (as the filters are usually with zero mean). The last stage refers to us as pooling, where a simple sum can give an attribute for a region such that it can be easily segmented or attached to neighboring region. The LNL model is also occasionally called filter-rectify-filter (FRF) as how it performs the segregation [98].

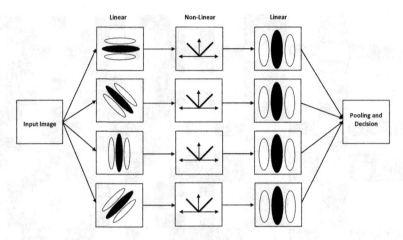

Fig. 5 The Back-pocket perceptual texture segregation model [57]

3.2 Motion Perception

Texture videos, as compared to texture images, add the temporal dimension to the perceptual space. Thus, it is important to include the temporal properties of the visual system in order to understand its perception. For this reason, the subsection provides an overview of studies on motion perception.

The main unit responsible for motion perception is the visual cortex [40]. Generally, the functional units of the visual cortex, which is responsible for motion processing, can be grouped into two stages:

1. **Motion Detectors**

    The motion detectors are the visual neurons whose firing rate increases when an object moves in front of the eye, especially within the foveal region. Several studies have shown that the primary visual cortex area (V1) is place where the motion detection happens [20, 83, 102, 116]. In V1, simple cells neurons are often modeled as a spatio-temporal filters that are tuned to a specific spatial frequency and orientation and speed. On the other hand, complex cells perform some non-linearity on top of the simple cells (half/full wave rectification and etc.).

    The neurons of V1 are only responsive to signal having the preferred frequency-orientation-speed combination. Thus, there is still a lack of the motion integration from all neurons. Besides, the filter response cannot cope with the aperture problem. As shown in Fig. 6, the example of the signal in the middle of the figure shows a moving signal with a certain frequency detected to be moving up, while it could actually be moving up-right or up-left. This is also true for the other signals in the figure.

2. **Motion Extractors**

    The motion integration and aperture problem are solved at a higher level of the visual cortex, namely inside the extra-striate middle temporal (MT) area. It

Fig. 6 Examples of the
aperture problem: *Solid arrow*
is the detected direction, and
the *dotted arrow* is the other
possible directions

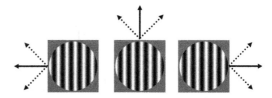

is generally assumed that the output of V1 is directly processed in MT in a feed-forward network of neurons [83, 90, 99, 102]. The velocity vectors computation in the MT cells can be implemented in different strategies. First, the intersection of constraints, where the velocity vectors will be the ones that are agreed by the majority of individual motion detectors [10, 102, 105]. Other than that, one can consider a maximum likelihood estimation, or a learning based model if the ground truth is available. An example of this could be MT response measured by physiological studies [83], or ground truth motion fields such as [15, 68].

It is worth also mentioning that there are other cells responsible for motion perception. For example, the medial superior temporal (MST) area of the visual cortex is motion perception during eye pursuit or headings [41, 87]. Another thing, the above review is concerning the motion caused by a luminance traveling over time, which is known as the first order motion. However, there exist the second and third order motion which are due to contrast moving and feature motion (resp.). These are outside the scope of this chapter, as they are not directly related to the texture perception.

3.3 Generalized Texture Perception

Up to our knowledge, a perceptual model that governs both static and dynamic textures doesn't not exist. The main issue is that although extensive perceptual studies on texture images exist, the texture videos have not been yet explored.

Looking at the hierarchy of the visual system in Fig. 7, we can differentiate two pathways after V1. The above is called the dorsal stream, while the lower is called the ventral stream. The dorsal stream is responsible for the motion analysis, while the ventral stream is mainly concerned about the shape analysis. For this reason, the dorsal stream is known as the *"where"* stream, while the ventral is known as the *"what"* stream [40].

One plausible assumption about texture perception is that texture has no shape. This means that visual texture processing is not in the ventral stream. Beside this, one can also assume that the type of motion is not a structured motion. Thus, it is not processed by the dorsal stream. Accordingly, the resulting texture perception model is only due to V1 processing. That is, the perceptual space is composed of proper modeling of V1 filters along with their non-linearity process. We consider this type of modeling as **Bottom-Up Modeling**.

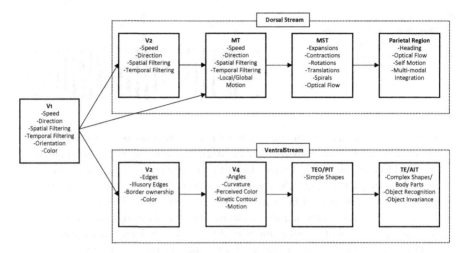

Fig. 7 Hierarchy of the human visual system [91]

On the other hand, another assumption about the texture perception can be made. Similar to Julesz conjectures (Sect. 3.1), one can study different statistical models for understanding texture discrimination. This includes either higher order models, or same order at different spaces. One can also redefine what is texton. These models impose different properties about the human visual system that don't consider the actual neural processing. We consider this type of modeling as **Top-Down Modeling**.

4 Models for Texture Similarity

Texture similarity is a very special problem that requires a specific analysis of the texture signal. This is because two textures can look very similar even if there is a large pixel-wise difference. As shown in Fig. 8, each group of three textures has overall similar textures, but there is still a large difference if one makes a point by point comparison. Thus, the human visual system does not compute similarity using pixel comparison, but rather considers the overall difference in the semantics. For this reason, simple difference metrics, such mean squared error, can not accurately express texture (dis-)similarity, and proper models for measuring texture similarity have always been studied.

This is even more difficult in the case of dynamic textures, because there exists a lot of change in details over time, the point-wise comparison would fail to express the visual difference. In the following subsections, a review of the existing texture similarity models is provided, covering both static and dynamic textures.

Fig. 8 Three examples of
similar textures, having large
pixel-wise differences. These
images were cropped from
dynamic texture videos in
DynTex dataset [93]

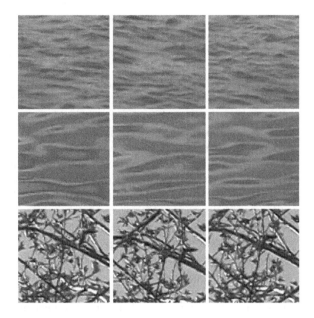

4.1 Transform Based Modeling

Transform based modeling has gained lots of attention in several classical as well
as recent approaches of texture similarity. This is because of the direct link with
the neural processing in the visual perception. As explained in Sect. 3, both neural
mechanisms of static texture and motion perception involve kind of subband filtering
process.

One of the early approaches for texture similarity was proposed by Manjunath
et al. [67], in which the mean and standard deviation of the texture subbands
(using Gabor filtering) are compared and the similarity is assessed accordingly.
Following this approach, many other similarity metrics are defined in a similar way,
using different filtering methods or different statistical measures. For example, the
Kullback Leiber divergence is used in [25] and [26]. Other approach is by using
the steerable pyramid filter [101] and considering the dominant orientation and
scale [69].

Knowing the importance of subband statistics, Heeger et al. proposed to synthesize textures by matching the histogram of each subband of the original and
synthesized textures. To overcome the problem of irreversibility of Gabor filtering,
they used the steerable pyramid filter [101]. The resulting synthesized textures were
considerably similar to the original, especially for the case of highly stochastic
textures. The concept has also been extended by Portilla et al. [95], where larger
number of features defined in the subband domain are matched, resulting in a better
quality of synthesis.

The significance of the subband statistics has led more investigation of texture similarity in that domain. Recently, a new class of similarity metrics, known as structural similarity, has been introduced. The structural texture similarity metric (STSIM) was first introduced in [137], then it was enhanced and further developed in [138, 140] and [64]. The basic idea behind them is to decompose the texture, using the steerable pyramid filter, and to measure statistical features in that domain. The set of statistics of each subband contains the mean and variance. Besides, the cross correlation between subbands is also considered. Finally, these features were fused to form a metric, that showed a high performance in texture retrieval.

The filter-bank approach, which was applied for static textures, has been also used in dynamic texture modeling by several studies. However, the concept was used in a much smaller scope compared to static textures. In [103], three dimensional wavelet energies were used as features for textures. A comparison of different wavelet filtering based approaches, that includes purely spatial, purely temporal and spatio-temporal wavelet filtering, is given in [30].

A relatively new study on using energies of Gabor filtering is found in [39]. The work is claimed to be inspired by the human visual system, where it resembles to some extent the V1 cortical processing (Sect. 3).

Beside this, there exist also other series of papers, by Konstantinos et al. [21, 22], employed another type of subband filtering, which is the third Gaussian derivatives tuned to certain scale and orientation (in 3D space). The approach was used for textures representation recognition and also for dynamic scene understanding and action recognition [23].

4.2 Auto-Regressive Modeling

The auto-regressive (AR) model has been widely used to model both static and dynamic textures, especially for texture synthesis purposes. In its simplistic form, AR can be expressed in this form:

$$s(x, y, t) = \sum_{i=1}^{N} \phi_i s(x + \Delta y_i, y + \Delta y_i, t + \Delta t_i) + n(x, y, t) \qquad (1)$$

Where $s(x, y, t)$ represents the pixel value at the spatio-temporal position (x, y, t), ϕ_i is the model weights, $\Delta x_i, \Delta y_i, \Delta t_i$ are the shift to cover the neighboring pixels. $n(x, y, t)$ is the system noise which is assumed to be white Gaussian noise.

The assumption behind AR is that each pixel is predictable from a set of its neighboring spatio-temporal pixels, by the means of weighted summation, and the error is due to the model noise $n(x, y, t)$. An example of using model for synthesis can be found in [4, 12, 55].

The auto-regressive moving average (ARMA) model is an extension of the simple AR model that is elegantly suited for dynamic textures. It was first introduced by Soatto and Dorreto [29, 104] for the purpose of dynamic texture recognition. The ARMA model is mathematically expressed in this equation:

$$x(t + 1) = Ax(t) + v(t)$$
$$y(t) = \phi x(t) + w(t)$$

(2)

Where $x(t)$ is a hidden state and $y(t)$ is the output state, $v(t)$ and $w(t)$ are system noise (normally distributed) and A, ϕ are the model weights as in AR. The output state is the original frame of the image sequence. Comparing Eq. (2) with Eq. (1), it is clear that the model assumes that the hidden state $x(t)$ is modeled as an AR process, and the observed state is weighted version of the hidden state with some added noise.

Both AR and ARMA can be directly used to measure texture similarity by comparing the model parameters. In other words, the parameters can be considered as visual features to compare textures and express the similarity. This has been used in texture recognition, classification, segmentation and editing [27, 28]. Other than that, it has been extended by several studies to synthesize similar textures. For example, by using Fourier domain [1], by including several ARMA models with transition probability [59], using higher order decomposition [18] and others [35, 131].

Although there is no direct link between the texture perception and the auto-regressive models, we can still interpret its performance in terms of Julesz conjectures (Sect. 3.1). The assumption behind these models is that textures would look similar if they are generated by the same statistical model with a fixed set of parameters. While Julesz has conjectured that the textures look similar if they have the same first and second order statistics. Thus, it can be understood that these models are an extension of the conjecture, in which the condition for similarity is better stated.

4.3 Texton Based Modeling

Recalling that textons are local conspicuous features (Sect. 3.1), a large body of research has been put to define some local features that can be used to measure the texture similarity. One of the first approaches, and still very widely used, is the local binary pattern approach (LBP) [84]. This approach is simply comparing each pixel with each of its circular neighborhood, and gives a binary number (0–1) if the value is bigger/smaller than the center value. The resulting binary numbers are gathered in a histogram, and any histogram based distance metric can be used.

The approach has gained a lot of attention due to its simplicity and high performance. It was directly adopted for dynamic textures in two manners [136]. First, by considering the neighborhood to be a cylindrical instead of circular in the case of Volume Local Binary Pattern (V-LBP). Second, by performing three orthogonal LBP on the *xy*, *xt* and *yt* planes, which is therefore called Three Orthogonal Planes LBP (LBP-TOP).

Several extensions of the basic LBP model have been proposed. For example, a similarity metric for static textures known as local radius index (LRI)[132, 133], which incorporates LBP along with other pixel to neighbors relationship. Besides, there is another method that utilizes the Weber law of sensation, that is known as Weber Local Descriptor (WLD) [14].

Rather than restricting the neighborhood relationship to binary descriptors, other studies have introduced also trinary number [6, 46, 47] in what is known as texture spectrum.

It is worth also mentioning that some studies consider the textons as the results of frequency analysis of texture patches. The study of Liu et al. [61] considered the marginal distribution of the filter bank response as the "quantitative definition" of texton. In contrast, textons are defined [120] as the representation that results from codebook generation of a frequency histogram.

4.4 Motion Based Modeling

The motion based analysis and modeling of dynamic textures has been in large body of studies. This is because motion can be considered as a very important visual cue, and also because the dynamic texture signal is mostly governed by motion statistics. To elaborate on motion analysis, let's start with basic assumption that we have an image patch $I(x, y, t)$ in a spatial position (x, y) and at time (t), and this patch would appear in the next frame, shifted by $(\Delta x, \Delta y)$. Mathematically:

$$I(x, y, t) = I(x + \Delta x, y + \Delta y, t + 1) \tag{3}$$

This equation is known as *Brightness Constancy Equation*, as it states that the brightness doesn't change from one frame to another. The equation can be simplified by employing the Taylor expansion as follows (removing the spatial and temporal indexes for simplicity):

$$I = \sum_{n=0}^{\infty} \left(\frac{I_{xn}}{n!} \times \Delta x + \frac{I_{yn}}{n!} \times \Delta y + \frac{I_{tn}}{n!} \times \Delta t \right) \tag{4}$$

where I_{xn}, I_{yn} and I_{tn} are the nth order partial derivatives with respect to x, y and t. The equation can be further simplified by neglecting the terms of order higher than one, then it becomes:

$$I_x \times V_x + I_y \times V_y = -I_t \tag{5}$$

where V_x, V_y are the velocities in x and y directions ($V_x = \Delta x / \Delta t$ and so on). The solution of Eq. (5) is known as *optical flow*. However, further constraints are needed to solve the equation because of the high number of unknowns. One of the constraints is the smoothness, in which a patch is assumed to move with the same direction and speed between two frames. This is not usually the case for dynamic texture, in which the content could possibly change a lot in a short time instant. Accordingly, there exists also another formulation of the brightness constancy assumption, that doesn't require the analytical solution. This is known as the *normal flow*. It is a vector of flow, that is normal to the spatial contours (parallel to the spatial gradient), and its amplitude is proportional to the temporal derivative. Mathematically, it is expressed as:

$$\mathbf{NF} = \frac{-I_t}{\sqrt{I_x^2 + I_y^2}} \mathbf{N} \tag{6}$$

where $\mathbf{N}$ is a unit vector in the direction of the gradient.

The normal flow, as compared to the optical flow, is easy to compute. It needs only the image derivatives in the three dimensions (x, y, t), and no computation of the flow speed is needed. One drawback of normal flow is that it can be very noisy (especially for low detailed region) when the spatial derivatives are low. For this reason, a threshold is usually set before evaluating any statistical property of the normal flow.

The motion based modeling of dynamic textures was pioneered by Nelson and Palonan in [82], where they used normal flow statistics for dynamic textures classification. This model has been extended in [89] to include both the normal flow and some static texture features (coarseness, directionality and contrast). Other than that, Peteri et al. [92] have augmented the normal flow with a regularity measure, computed from correlation function.

The optical flow has been also used in dynamic texture analysis. In [33], the authors compared different optical flow approaches to normal flow, and showed that the recognition rate can be significantly enhanced by optical flow.

Similar to the concept of co-occurrence matrix, Rahman et al. have developed the concept of *motion co-occurrence* [96], in which they compute the statistics of occurrence of a motion field with another one for a given length.

It is worth also mentioning here there are other approaches beyond the concept of brightness constancy. Since dynamic textures can change their appearance over time, it is more logical to move towards *brightness conservation assumption*. It can be mathematically expressed as [3, 34]:

$$I(x, y, t)(1 - \Delta x_x - \Delta y_y) = I(x + \Delta x, y + \Delta y, t + 1) \tag{7}$$

Where Δx_x and Δy_y are the partial derivatives of the shifts in x and y. Comparing this equation to Eq. (3), the model allows the brightness I to change over time to better cover the dynamic change inherited in the dynamic textures. The model has been used for detecting dynamic textures [3], in which regions satisfying this assumption are considered as dynamic textures. However, further extensions of this ideas were not found.

4.5 Others

Along with other aforementioned models, there exist other approaches that cannot be straightforwardly put in one category. This is because the research on texture similarity is quite matured, but still very active.

One major approach for modeling texture and expressing similarity is by using the fractal analysis. It can be simply understood as an analysis of measurements at different scales, which in turn reveals the relationship between them. For images, this can be implemented by measuring the energies of a gaussian filter at different scales. The relationship is expressed in terms of the fractional dimension. Recent approaches of fractal analysis can be found in [126–128].

Another notable way is to use the self avoiding walks. In this, a traveler walks through the video pixels using a specified rule and memory to store the last steps. A histogram of walks is then computed and considered as features for characterizing the texture (cf. [37, 38]).

Beside these, there exist also other models that are based on the physical behavior of textures (especially dynamic textures). This includes models for fire [24], smoke [7] and water [70].

Although these models suit very well specific textural phenomenon, they cannot be considered as perceptual ones. This is because they are not meant to mimic the visual processing, but rather the physical source. For this reason, these are out of scope of this book chapter.

5 Benchmarking and Comparison

After viewing several approaches for assessing the texture similarity (Sect. 4), the fundamental question here is how to compare these approaches, and to establish a benchmark platform in order to differentiate the behavior of each approach. This is of course not a straightforward method, and a reasonable construction of ground truth data is required.

Broadly speaking, comparison can either be performed *subjectively* or *objectively*. In other words, either by involving observers in a kind of psycho-physical test, or by testing the similarity approaches performance on a pre-labeled dataset. Both have advantages and disadvantages, which are explained here.

The subjective comparison is generally considered as the most reliable one. This is because it directly deals with human judgment on similarity. However, there are several problems that can be encountered in such a methodology. First, the selection and accuracy of the psycho-physical test. For example, a binary test can be the simplest for the subjects, and would result in very accurate results. In contrast, this test can be very slow to cover all the test conditions, and possibly such a test would not be suitable. Second, the budget-time limitation behind the subjective tests would result in a limited testing material. Thus, it is practically unfeasible to perform a large scale comparison with subjective testing.

Accordingly, there exist few studies on the subjective evaluation of texture similarity models. For example, the subjective quality of the synthesized textures were assessed and predicted in [42, 109], and adaptive selection among the synthesis algorithms was provided in [121]. The similarity metrics correlation with subjective evaluation was also assessed in [5, 139].

As explained earlier, subjective evaluation suffers from test accuracy and budget time-limitation. One can also add the problem of irreproducibility, in which the subjective test results cannot be retained after repeating the subjective test. There is also a certain amount of uncertainty with the results, which is usually reported in terms of confidence levels. To encounter this, research in computer vision is usually leaded by objective evaluations.

One commonly used benchmarking procedure is to test the performance on recognition task. For static textures, two large datasets of 425 and 61 homogeneous texture images are cropped into 128x128 images with substantial point-wise differences [140]. The common test is to perform a retrieval test, in which for a test image if the retrieved image is from the correct image source then it is considered as correct retrieval. This is performed for all of the images in the dataset, and the retrieval rate is considered as the criteria to compare different similarity measure approaches. For example, Table 1 provides the information about the performance of different metrics. In this table, one can easily observe that simple point-wise comparison metric like the Peak Signal to Noise Ratio (PSNR) provides the worst performance.

For dynamic textures, similar task is defined. Commonly, the task consists of classification of three datasets. These are the UCLA [100], DynTex [93] and DynTex++ [36] datasets. For each dataset, the same test conditions are commonly used. For example, DynTex++ contains 36 classes, each of 100 exemplar sequences. The test condition is to randomly assign 50% of the data for training and the rest for

Table 1 Retrieval rate as a benchmark tool for different texture similarity metrics

Metric	Retrieval rate (%)
PSNR	4
LBP	90
Wavelet features [25]	84
Gabor features [67]	92
STSIM	96
LRI	99

Results obtained from [133, 140]

Table 2 Recognition rate on the DynTex++ as a benchmark tool for different texture similarity metrics

Metric	Recognition rate (%)
VLBP	94.98
LBP-TOP	94.05
WLBPC [115]	95.01
CVLBP [113]	96.28
MEWLSP [114]	98.48

Results obtained from [113, 114]

testing. The train data are used for training the models, and the recognition rate is reported for the test data. The procedure is repeated 20 times and the average value is retained. This is shown in Table 2.

6 Texture Similarity for Perceptual Image and Video Compression

Image/Video compression is the key technology that enables several applications related to storage and transmission. For video, the amount of data is increasingly huge, and research on better compression is always growing.

In the context of compression, texture is usually referred to homogeneous regions of high spatial and/or temporal activities with mostly irrelevant details. According to this, textures would usually consume high amount of bitrate for unnecessary details. Thus, a proper compression of texture signal is needed. In the following subsections, an overview of different approaches for texture similarity in video compression is provided.

6.1 Bottom-Up Approaches

As mention in Sect. 3.3, bottom up approaches try to perform the same neural processing of the human visual system. We have seen many transform based models (Sect. 4.1) that showed good performance for measuring the texture similarity. These models can be also used in image/video compression scenario, such that the compression algorithm is tuned to provide the best rate-similarity trade-off instead of rate-distortion. By doing so, the compression is relying more on a perceptual similarity measure, rather than a computational distortion metric. Consequently, this could perceptually enhance the compression performance.

In our previous studies [71, 73, 74], we have used the perceptual distortion metrics inside the state of the art video compression standard, known as High Efficiency Video Coding (HEVC [106]), and evaluated their performance. We used the two metrics of STSIM and LRI (Sects. 4.1 and 4.3) inside as distortion measure

Fig. 9 Examples of decoded textures using the same QP. *From left to right*: Original texture, compressed using HEVC with default metrics, with STSIM and with LRI

(dissimilarity) inside the rate-distortion function of HEVC reference software (HM software [50]). The measured distortion is used to select the prediction mode and the block splitting. Examples of the results are shown in Fig. 9.

The visual comparison between the compression artifacts of the default HEVC versus texture similarity metrics based optimization shows that structural information are better preserved. We can also clearly see the point-wise differences, when using texture metrics, but the overall visual similarity is much higher. We have also performed objective evaluation for comparing the rate-similarity performance at different compression levels. For this, we used another metric [67] that is based on comparing the standard deviations of the Gabor subbands. The results shown in Fig. 10 indicate that both LRI and STSIM outperform HEVC default metrics, especially for the case of high compression (low bitrate).

Beside this, Jin et al. presented another method for using STSIM in image compression. They developed an algorithm for structurally lossless compression known as *Matched-Texture Coding* [49]. In this algorithm, a texture patch is copied from another patch of the image, if the similarity score, measured by STSIM, is above a certain threshold. By doing this, higher compression is achieved as it is

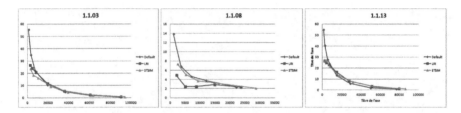

Fig. 10 Rate Distortion (using Gabor distance metric [67]) of the textures shown in Fig. 9. *x*-axes: Bytes used to encode the texture, *y*-axes: distance to the original texture

not necessary to encode the patch but rather its copy index. The visual comparison showed some point-wise difference, but high overall similarity.

6.2 Top-Down Approaches

In contrast to Bottom-Up approaches, Top-Down approaches do not try to model the neural processing of the human visual system, but rather to formulate a hypothesis about human vision properties, and validate it with some examples (Sect. 3.3). In the context of image/video compression, the common hypothesis is that original and synthesized textures would look similar, if a good synthesis algorithm is used. By synthesizing the textures, there is no need to encode them, but rather to encode the synthesis parameters, which needs to be significantly easier to encode in order to provide an improved compression ratio.

One of the first approaches for synthesis based coding was introduced by Ndjiki-Nya et al. in [78, 79]. The proposed algorithm consists of two main functions: texture analyzer (TA) and texture synthesizer (TS). The TA is responsible of detecting regions of details irrelevant textures, via spatial segmentation and temporal grouping of segmented textures. The TS, on the other hand, is responsible of reproducing the removed parts in the decoder side. TS contains two types of synthesizers, one employs image warping, which is used to warp texture with simple motion (camera motion mostly), the other one is based on Markov Random Fields and is responsible for synthesizing textures containing internal motion. This algorithm was implemented in the video coding standard, in which irrelevant texture signals are skipped by the encoder, and only the synthesis parameters is sent to the decoder as side information.

Ndjiki-Nya et al. produced several extensions of the above mentioned approach. In [80], a rate distortion optimization was also used for the synthesis part. The rate is the number of bits required to encode the synthesis parameters and the distortion accounts for the similarity between the original and synthesized texture, in which they used an edge histogram as well as color descriptor for computing the quality. A review of their work, as well as others, is given in [81].

Similar to these approaches, many other researchers have developed texture removal algorithms varying in their compression capability, complexity, synthesis algorithm and distortion measure. Interested reader may refer to [9] and [134]. For HEVC, there exist also initial investigations about the pyramid based synthesis [111] and motion based synthesis for dynamic textures [17].

Recently, as a part of study on texture synthesis for video compression, a new approach for texture synthesis has been proposed by Thakur et al. in [112]. In this approach, half of the frames is encoded, and the rest is synthesized based on subband linear phase interpolation. This is shown in Fig. 11, where each intermediate frame is skipped at the encoder side, and synthesized at the decoder side after reconstructing the previous and next frames. With this approach, the half of the frames are encoded, and the rest is synthesized.

Visually, the synthesized frames as compared to the compressed frames, at a similar bitrate, are in much better quality (Fig. 12). There is significant reduction of the blocking artifacts. The results have been verified with a subjective testing, and it was shown that observers tend to prefer the synthesis based model against the default compression, for the same bitrate.

One issue of the synthesis based approaches is the necessity of altering the existing standard by modifying the decoder side. This is certainly undesired as it required changing the users' software and/or hardware, and thus could negatively impact the user experience. To encounter this issue, Dumitras et al. in [31] proposed

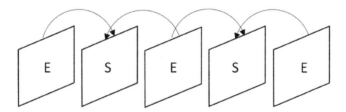

Fig. 11 Dynamic texture synthesis approach for alternative frames [112]. E is a decoded picture and S is synthesized one

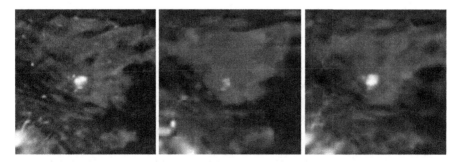

Fig. 12 An example of visual comparison between default compression and proposed method in [112]. *Left*: original frame, *middle*: is compressed frame with HEVC and *right*: synthesized frame at the decoder side

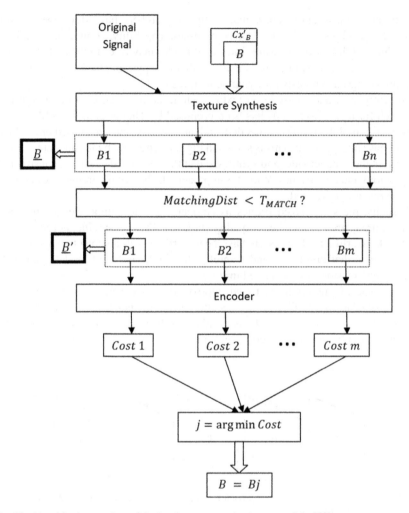

Fig. 13 Algorithmic overview of the local texture synthesis approach in [72]

a "texture replacement" method at the encoder, in which the encoder synthesizes some texture areas in a way that it is simpler to encode. By doing this, the encoded image/video would be the simplified synthetic signal, which would have a similar look to the original one. Accordingly, it is only a pre-processing step, that doesn't require any further modification of the encoder and decoder. However, the approach was only limited to background texture with simple camera motion.

In one of our studies, we presented a new *online* synthesis algorithm that is fully compatible with HEVC. It is named as Local Texture Synthesis (LTS [72]). The algorithm, as described in Fig. 13, generates for each block to be encoded B a set of synthetic blocks $\underline{B}$ containing n blocks ($B1$, $B2$, ..., Bn) that are visually similar to B. A subset $\underline{B}'$ out of $\underline{B}$ that has a good match with the given context is only maintained. Then, the encoder tries encoding block by replacing its content by the

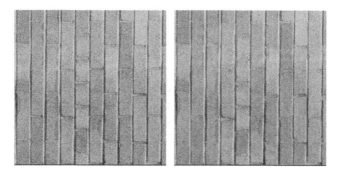

Fig. 14 Compressed texture with QP=27. *Left*: default encoder, *right*: LTS. Bitrate saving=9.756%

contents in $\underline{B'}$, and will then select the block Bj such that Bj has the minimum rate and distortion. Thus, the algorithm tries to replace the contents while encoding, by visually similar ones, such that the contents will be easier to encode.

An example for comparing the behavior of LTS against HEVC is shown in Fig. 14. Due to the simplification procedure of the contents in LTS, one can achieve about 10% bitrate saving. On the other hand, there is also some visual artifacts due to this simplification. By carefully examining the differences in Fig. 14, we can see that some of the wall boundaries are eliminated by LTS. This is because encoding an edge costs more than a flat area, and thus LTS would choose to replace this edge by another possible synthesis that is easier to encode.

6.3 Indirect Approaches

Instead of relying on the existing metrics of texture similarity for improving the compression quality (Sect. 6.1), we have also conducted a psycho-physical experiment to evaluate the perceived differences (or dis-similarity) due to HEVC compression on dynamic textures [77]. The maximum likelihood difference scaling (MLDS [66]) was used for this task. The results of this test are shown in Fig. 15, in which perceived differences for two sequences are plotted against the HEVC compression distortions measured in terms of mean squared error (MSE-YUV). The figure presents two interesting scenarios. First, on the left, the computed distortion (MSE-YUV) highly deviates from the perceived difference, whereas in the second (right), the computed distortion is mostly linearly proportional to the perceived difference.

In the same manner as for STSIM and LRI, a dissimilarity metric is defined as a mapping function from the computed distortion (MSE) to perceived difference. It was used inside the HEVC reference software. A subjective test was used to verify the performance of the proposed metric, and it was shown to achieve significant bitrate saving. An extension of this work is given in [75], in which a

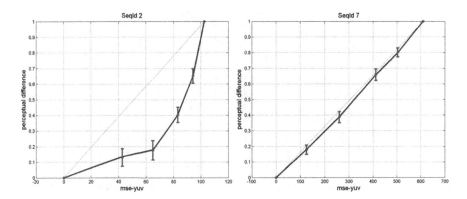

Fig. 15 Subjective test results of MLDS for two sequences

machine learning based estimation of the curve is performed, and used to provide an improved compression result.

The other indirect use of texture similarity measure is to exploit the analysis tools and features from that domain in image and video compression. For example, in [76], the visual redundancies of dynamic textures can be easily predicted by a set of features, such as normal flow and gray level co-occurrence matrix. Similarity, the optimal rate-distortion parameter (Lagrangian multiplier) can be predicted similarly [63].

Beside texture synthesis based coding, there also exist several studies on perceptually optimizing the encoder based on texture properties. These studies fall generally into the category of noise shaping, where the coding noise (compression artifact) is distributed to minimize the perceived distortions. Examples can be found in [60, 107, 125, 129, 130]. Besides, textures are considered as non-salient areas, and less bitrate is consumed there [43, 44].

7   Conclusion

Understanding texture perception is of particular interest in many fields of computer vision applications. The key concept in texture perception is texture similarity. A large body of research has been put to understand how textures look similar despite the individual point-by-point differences.

The objective of this chapter is to give an overview of the perceptual mechanisms on textures, and summarize different approaches for texture similarity. Common benchmarking tests are also provided, with a highlight on the difference between objective and subjective evaluation. The chapter also includes a review about the use of texture similarity in the special context of image and video compression, showing its promising results and outcome.

As it is shown, static textures, or texture images, have been extensively studied in different disciplines. There exists large scale knowledge about their perception and analysis. In contrast, studies on dynamic textures (or video textures) are relatively newer. The literature covered in this chapter showed that there is no clear definition for them. More importantly, there are many computational models for measuring similarity, but they don't follow a perceptual/neural model. They mostly formulate a high level hypothesis about the visual similarity and design the model accordingly (Top-down approach).

The existing models can be classified into different categories (Sect. 4). They have proved excellent performance in different applications, such as multimedia retrieval, classification and recognition. They have also shown a successful synthesis results. However, large scale visual comparison, in terms of subjective testing, for differentiating the performance of different models is unfeasible to be performed. Thus, it is still unclear which one provides the best outcome.

Due to the success of the texture similarity models, different studies have employed these models in the context of image and video compression. The chapter provided an overview of two main approaches: Bottom-up (similarity-based) and Top-down (synthesis-based). Both have shown an improved rate-quality performance over the existing coding standards. However, the compatibility issue could be the main factor preventing the deployment of such approaches.

Acknowledgements This work was supported by the Marie Sklodowska-Curie under the PROVISION (PeRceptually Optimized VIdeo CompresSION) project bearing Grant Number 608231 and Call Identifier: FP7-PEOPLE-2013-ITN.

References

1. Abraham, B., Camps, O.I., Sznaier, M.: Dynamic texture with fourier descriptors. In: Proceedings of the 4th International Workshop on Texture Analysis and Synthesis, pp. 53–58 (2005)
2. Amadasun, M., King, R.: Textural features corresponding to textural properties. IEEE Trans. Syst. Man Cybern. **19**(5), 1264–1274 (1989)
3. Amiaz, T., Fazekas, S., Chetverikov, D., Kiryati, N.: Detecting regions of dynamic texture. In: Scale Space and Variational Methods in Computer Vision, pp. 848–859. Springer, Berlin (2007)
4. Bao, Z., Xu, C., Wang, C.: Perceptual auto-regressive texture synthesis for video coding. Multimedia Tools Appl. **64**(3), 535–547 (2013)
5. Ballé, J.: Subjective evaluation of texture similarity metrics for compression applications. In: Picture Coding Symposium (PCS), 2012, pp. 241–244. IEEE, New York (2012)
6. Barcelo, A., Montseny, E., Sobrevilla, P.: Fuzzy texture unit and fuzzy texture spectrum for texture characterization. Fuzzy Sets Syst. **158**(3), 239–252 (2007)
7. Barmpoutis, P., Dimitropoulos, K., Grammalidis, N.: Smoke detection using spatio-temporal analysis, motion modeling and dynamic texture recognition. In: 2013 Proceedings of the 22nd European Signal Processing Conference (EUSIPCO), pp. 1078–1082. IEEE, New York (2014)
8. Beck, J.: Textural segmentation, second-order statistics, and textural elements. Biol. Cybern. **48**(2), 125–130 (1983)

9. Bosch, M., Zhu, F., Delp, E.J.: An overview of texture and motion based video coding at Purdue University. In: Picture Coding Symposium, 2009. PCS 2009, pp. 1–4. IEEE, New York (2009)

10. Bradley, D.C., Goyal, M.S.: Velocity computation in the primate visual system. Nature Rev. Neurosci. **9**(9), 686–695 (2008)

11. Caenen, G., Van Gool, L.: Maximum response filters for texture analysis. In: Conference on Computer Vision and Pattern Recognition Workshop, 2004. CVPRW'04, pp. 58–58. IEEE, New York (2004)

12. Campbell, N., Dalton, C., Gibson, D., Oziem, D., Thomas, B.: Practical generation of video textures using the auto-regressive process. Image Vis. Comput. **22**(10), 819–827 (2004)

13. Chang, W.-H., Yang, N.-C., Kuo, C.-M., Chen, Y.-J., et al.: An efficient temporal texture descriptor for video retrieval. In: Proceedings of the 6th WSEAS International Conference on Signal Processing, Computational Geometry & Artificial Vision, pp. 107–112. World Scientific and Engineering Academy and Society (WSEAS), Athens (2006)

14. Chen, J., Shan, S., He, C., Zhao, G., Pietikainen, M., Chen, X., Gao, W., Wld: a robust local image descriptor. IEEE Trans. Pattern Anal. Mach. Intell. **32**(9), 1705–1720 (2010)

15. Chessa, M., Sabatini, S.P., Solari, F.: A systematic analysis of a v1–mt neural model for motion estimation. Neurocomputing **173**, 1811–1823 (2016)

16. Chetverikov, D., Péteri, R.: A brief survey of dynamic texture description and recognition. In: Computer Recognition Systems, pp. 17–26. Springer, Berlin (2005)

17. Chubach, O., Garus, P., Wien, M.: Motion-based analysis and synthesis of dynamic textures. In: Proceedings of International Picture Coding Symposium PCS '16, Nuremberg. IEEE, Piscataway (2016)

18. Costantini, R., Sbaiz, L., Süsstrunk, S.: Higher order SVD analysis for dynamic texture synthesis. IEEE Trans. Image Process. **17**(1), 42–52 (2008)

19. Crivelli, T., Cernuschi-Frias, B., Bouthemy, P., Yao, J.-F.: Motion textures: modeling, classification, and segmentation using mixed-state Markov random fields. SIAM J. Image. Sci. **6**(4), 2484–2520 (2013)

20. David, S.V., Vinje, W.E., Gallant, J.L.: Natural stimulus statistics alter the receptive field structure of v1 neurons. J. Neurosci. **24**(31), 6991–7006 (2004)

21. Derpanis, K.G., Wildes, R.P.: Dynamic texture recognition based on distributions of spacetime oriented structure. In: 2010 IEEE Conference on Computer Vision and Pattern Recognition (CVPR), pp. 191–198. IEEE, New York (2010)

22. Derpanis, K.G., Wildes, R.P.: Spacetime texture representation and recognition based on a spatiotemporal orientation analysis. IEEE Trans. Pattern Anal. Mach. Intell. **34**(6), 1193–1205 (2012)

23. Derpanis, K.G., Sizintsev, M., Cannons, K.J., Wildes, R.P.: Action spotting and recognition based on a spatiotemporal orientation analysis. IEEE Trans. Pattern Anal. Mach. Intell. **35**(3), 527–540 (2013)

24. Dimitropoulos, K., Barmpoutis, P., Grammalidis, N.: Spatio-temporal flame modeling and dynamic texture analysis for automatic video-based fire detection. IEEE Trans. Circ. Syst. Video Technol. **25**(2), 339–351 (2015). doi:10.1109/TCSVT.2014.2339592

25. Do, M.N., Vetterli, M.: Texture similarity measurement using Kullback-Leibler distance on wavelet subbands. In: 2000 International Conference on Image Processing, 2000. Proceedings, vol. 3, pp. 730–733. IEEE, New York (2000)

26. Do, M.N., Vetterli, M.: Wavelet-based texture retrieval using generalized gaussian density and Kullback-Leibler distance. IEEE Trans. Image Process. **11**(2), 146–158 (2002)

27. Doretto, G., Soatto, S.: Editable dynamic textures. In: 2003 IEEE Computer Society Conference on Computer Vision and Pattern Recognition, 2003. Proceedings, pp. II–137, vol. 2. IEEE, New York (2003)

28. Doretto, G., Soatto, S.: Modeling dynamic scenes: an overview of dynamic textures. In: Handbook of Mathematical Models in Computer Vision, pp. 341–355. Springer, Berlin (2006)

29. Doretto, G., Chiuso, A., Wu, Y.N., Soatto, S.: Dynamic textures. Int. J. Comput. Vis. **51**(2), 91–109 (2003)
30. Dubois, S., Péteri, R., Ménard, M.: A comparison of wavelet based spatio-temporal decomposition methods for dynamic texture recognition. In: Pattern Recognition and Image Analysis, pp. 314–321. Springer, Berlin (2009)
31. Dumitras, A., Haskell, B.G.: A texture replacement method at the encoder for bit-rate reduction of compressed video. IEEE Trans. Circuits Syst. Video Technol. **13**(2), 163–175 (2003)
32. Fan, G., Xia, X.-G.: Wavelet-based texture analysis and synthesis using hidden Markov models. IEEE Trans. Circuits Syst. I, Fundam. Theory Appl. **50**(1), 106–120 (2003)
33. Fazekas, S., Chetverikov, D.: Dynamic texture recognition using optical flow features and temporal periodicity. In: International Workshop on Content-Based Multimedia Indexing, 2007. CBMI'07, pp. 25–32. IEEE, New York (2007)
34. Fazekas, S., Amiaz, T., Chetverikov, D., Kiryati, N.: Dynamic texture detection based on motion analysis. Int. J. Comput. Vis. **82**(1), 48–63 (2009)
35. Ghadekar, P., Chopade, N.: Nonlinear dynamic texture analysis and synthesis model. Int. J. Recent Trends Eng. Technol. **11**(2), 475–484 (2014)
36. Ghanem, B., Ahuja, N.: Maximum margin distance learning for dynamic texture recognition. In: European Conference on Computer Vision, pp. 223–236. Springer, Berlin (2010)
37. Goncalves, W.N., Bruno, O.M.: Dynamic texture analysis and segmentation using deterministic partially self-avoiding walks. Expert Syst. Appl. **40**(11), 4283–4300 (2013)
38. Goncalves, W.N., Bruno, O.M.: Dynamic texture segmentation based on deterministic partially self-avoiding walks. Comput. Vis. Image Underst. **117**(9), 1163–1174 (2013)
39. Gonçalves, W.N., Machado, B.B., Bruno, O.M.: Spatiotemporal Gabor filters: a new method for dynamic texture recognition (2012). arXiv preprint arXiv:1201.3612
40. Grill-Spector, K., Malach, R.: The human visual cortex. Annu. Rev. Neurosci. **27**, 649–677 (2004)
41. Grossberg, S., Mingolla, E., Pack, C.: A neural model of motion processing and visual navigation by cortical area MST. Cereb. Cortex **9**(8), 878–895 (1999)
42. Guo, Y., Zhao, G., Zhou, Z., Pietikainen, M.: Video texture synthesis with multi-frame LBP-TOP and diffeomorphic growth model. IEEE Trans. Image Process. **22**(10), 3879–3891 (2013)
43. Hadizadeh, H.: Visual saliency in video compression and transmission. Ph.D. Dissertation, Applied Sciences: School of Engineering Science (2013)
44. Hadizadeh, H., Bajic, I.V.: Saliency-aware video compression. IEEE Trans. Image Process. **23**(1), 19–33 (2014)
45. Haindl, M., Filip, J.: Visual Texture: Accurate Material Appearance Measurement, Representation and Modeling. Springer Science & Business Media, London (2013)
46. He, D.-C., Wang, L.: Texture unit, texture spectrum, and texture analysis. IEEE Trans. Geosci. Remote Sens. **28**(4), 509–512 (1990)
47. He, D.-C., Wang, L.: Simplified texture spectrum for texture analysis. J. Commun. Comput. **7**(8), 44–53 (2010)
48. Hubel, D.H., Wiesel, T.N.: Receptive fields and functional architecture of monkey striate cortex. J. Physiol. **195**(1), 215–243 (1968)
49. Jin, G., Zhai, Y., Pappas, T.N., Neuhoff, D.L.: Matched-texture coding for structurally lossless compression. In: 2012 19th IEEE International Conference on Image Processing (ICIP), pp. 1065–1068. IEEE, New York (2012)
50. Joint Collaborative Team on Video Coding (JCT-VC) of ITU-T SG 16 WP 3 and ISO/IEC JTC 1/SC 29/WG: High Efficiency Video Coding (HEVC) Test Model 16 (HM 16) Encoder Description. Technical Report (2014)
51. Julesz, B.: Visual pattern discrimination. IRE Trans. Inf. Theory **8**(2), 84–92 (1962)
52. Julesz, B.: Textons, the elements of texture perception, and their interactions. Nature **290**(5802), 91–97 (1981)
53. Julész, B., Gilbert, E., Shepp, L., Frisch, H.: Inability of humans to discriminate between visual textures that agree in second-order statistics-revisited. Perception **2**(4), 391–405 (1973)

54. Julesz, B., Gilbert, E., Victor, J.D.: Visual discrimination of textures with identical third-order statistics. Biol. Cybern. **31**(3), 137–140 (1978)
55. Khandelia, A., Gorecha, S., Lall, B., Chaudhury, S., Mathur, M.: Parametric video compression scheme using ar based texture synthesis. In: Sixth Indian Conference on Computer Vision, Graphics & Image Processing, 2008. ICVGIP'08. IEEE, New York (2008), pp. 219–225
56. Kwatra, V., Essa, I., Bobick, A., Kwatra, N.: Texture optimization for example-based synthesis. In: ACM Transactions on Graphics (TOG), vol. 24(3), pp. 795–802. ACM, New York (2005)
57. Landy, M.S.: Texture Analysis and Perception. The New Visual Neurosciences, pp. 639–652. MIT, Cambridge (2013)
58. Landy, M.S., Graham, N.: Visual perception of texture. Vis. Neurosci. **2**, 1106–1118 (2004)
59. Li, Y., Wang, T., Shum, H.-Y.: Motion texture: a two-level statistical model for character motion synthesis. In: ACM Transactions on Graphics (ToG), vol. 21(3), pp. 465–472. ACM, New York (2002)
60. Liu, M., Lu, L.: An improved rate control algorithm of h. 264/avc based on human visual system. In: Computer, Informatics, Cybernetics and Applications, pp. 1145–1151. Springer, Berlin (2012)
61. Liu, X., Wang, D.: A spectral histogram model for texton modeling and texture discrimination. Vis. Res. **42**(23), 2617–2634 (2002)
62. Liu, L., Fieguth, P., Guo, Y., Wang, X., Pietikäinen, M.: Local binary features for texture classification: taxonomy and experimental study. Pattern Recogn. **62**, 135–160 (2017)
63. Ma, C., Naser, K., Ricordel, V., Le Callet, P., Qing, C.: An adaptive lagrange multiplier determination method for dynamic texture in HEVC. In: IEEE International Conference on Consumer Electronics China. IEEE, New York (2016)
64. Maggioni, M., Jin, G., Foi, A., Pappas, T.N.: Structural texture similarity metric based on intra-class variances. In: 2014 IEEE International Conference on Image Processing (ICIP), pp. 1992–1996. IEEE, New York (2014)
65. Malik, J., Perona, P.: Preattentive texture discrimination with early vision mechanisms. JOSA A **7**(5), 923–932 (1990)
66. Maloney, L.T., Yang, J.N.: Maximum likelihood difference scaling. J. Vis. **3**(8), 5 (2003)
67. Manjunath, B.S., Ma, W.-Y.: Texture features for browsing and retrieval of image data. IEEE Trans. Pattern Anal. Mach. Intell. **18**(8), 837–842 (1996)
68. Medathati, N.K., Chessa, M., Masson, G., Kornprobst, P., Solari, F.: Decoding mt motion response for optical flow estimation: an experimental evaluation. Ph.D. Dissertation, INRIA Sophia-Antipolis, France; University of Genoa, Genoa, Italy; INT la Timone, Marseille, France; INRIA (2015)
69. Montoya-Zegarra, J.A., Leite, N.J., da S Torres, R.: Rotation-invariant and scale-invariant steerable pyramid decomposition for texture image retrieval. In: SIBGRAPI 2007. XX Brazilian Symposium on Computer Graphics and Image Processing, 2007, pp. 121–128. IEEE, New York (2007)
70. Narain, R., Kwatra, V., Lee, H.-P., Kim, T., Carlson, M., Lin, M.C.: Feature-guided dynamic texture synthesis on continuous flows,. In: Proceedings of the 18th Eurographics conference on Rendering Techniques, pp. 361–370. Eurographics Association, Geneva (2007)
71. Naser, K., Ricordel, V., Le Callet, P.: Experimenting texture similarity metric STSIM for intra prediction mode selection and block partitioning in HEVC. In: 2014 19th International Conference on Digital Signal Processing (DSP), pp. 882–887. IEEE, New York (2014)
72. Naser, K., Ricordel, V., Le Callet, P.: Local texture synthesis: a static texture coding algorithm fully compatible with HEVC. In: 2015 International Conference on Systems, Signals and Image Processing (IWSSIP), pp. 37–40. IEEE, New York (2015)
73. Naser, K., Ricordel, V., Le Callet, P.: Performance analysis of texture similarity metrics in HEVC intra prediction. In: Video Processing and Quality Metrics for Consumer Electronics (VPQM) (2015)

74. Naser, K., Ricordel, V., Le Callet, P.: Texture similarity metrics applied to HEVC intra prediction. In: The Third Sino-French Workshop on Information and Communication Technologies, SIFWICT 2015 (2015)

75. Naser, K., Ricordel, V., Le Callet, P.: A foveated short term distortion model for perceptually optimized dynamic textures compression in HEVC. In: 32nd Picture Coding Symposium (PCS). IEEE, New York (2016)

76. Naser, K., Ricordel, V., Le Callet, P.: Estimation of perceptual redundancies of HEVC encoded dynamic textures. In: 2016 Eighth International Conference on Quality of Multimedia Experience (QoMEX), pp. 1–5. IEEE, New York (2016)

77. Naser, K., Ricordel, V., Le Callet, P.: Modeling the perceptual distortion of dynamic textures and its application in HEVC. In: 2016 IEEE International Conference on Image Processing (ICIP), pp. 3787–3791. IEEE, New York (2016)

78. Ndjiki-Nya, P., Wiegand, T.: Video coding using texture analysis and synthesis. In: Proceedings of Picture Coding Symposium, Saint-Malo (2003)

79. Ndjiki-Nya, P., Makai, B., Blattermann, G., Smolic, A., Schwarz, H., Wiegand, T.: Improved h. 264/avc coding using texture analysis and synthesis. In: 2003 International Conference on Image Processing, 2003. ICIP 2003. Proceedings, vol. 3, pp. III–849. IEEE, New York (2003)

80. Ndjiki-Nya, P., Hinz, T., Smolic, A., Wiegand, T.: A generic and automatic content-based approach for improved h. 264/mpeg4-avc video coding. In: IEEE International Conference on Image Processing, 2005. ICIP 2005, vol. 2, pp. II–874. IEEE, New York (2005)

81. Ndjiki-Nya, P., Bull, D., Wiegand, T.: Perception-oriented video coding based on texture analysis and synthesis. In: 2009 16th IEEE International Conference on Image Processing (ICIP), pp. 2273–2276. IEEE, New York (2009)

82. Nelson, R.C., Polana, R.: Qualitative recognition of motion using temporal texture. CVGIP: Image Underst. 56(1), 78–89 (1992)

83. Nishimoto, S., Gallant, J.L.: A three-dimensional spatiotemporal receptive field model explains responses of area mt neurons to naturalistic movies. J. Neurosci. 31(41), 14551–14564 (2011)

84. Ojala, T., Pietikainen, M., Maenpaa, T.: Multiresolution gray-scale and rotation invariant texture classification with local binary patterns. IEEE Trans. Pattern Anal. Mach. Intell. 24(7), 971–987 (2002)

85. Ontrup, J., Wersing, H., Ritter, H.: A computational feature binding model of human texture perception. Cogn. Process. 5(1), 31–44 (2004)

86. Oxford Dictionaries. [Online]. Available: http://www.oxforddictionaries.com

87. Pack, C., Grossberg, S., Mingolla, E.: A neural model of smooth pursuit control and motion perception by cortical area MST. J. Cogn. Neurosci. 13(1), 102–120 (2001)

88. Pappas, T.N., Neuhoff, D.L., de Ridder, H., Zujovic, J.: Image analysis: focus on texture similarity. Proc. IEEE 101(9), 2044–2057 (2013)

89. Peh, C.-H., Cheong, L.-F.: Synergizing spatial and temporal texture. IEEE Trans. Image Process. 11(10), 1179–1191 (2002)

90. Perrone, J.A.: A visual motion sensor based on the properties of v1 and mt neurons. Vision Res. 44(15), 1733–1755 (2004)

91. Perry, C.J., Fallah, M.: Feature integration and object representations along the dorsal stream visual hierarchy. Front. Comput. Neurosci. 8, 84 (2014)

92. Péteri, R., Chetverikov, D.: Dynamic texture recognition using normal flow and texture regularity. In: Pattern Recognition and Image Analysis, pp. 223–230. Springer, Berlin (2005)

93. Péteri, R., Fazekas, S., Huiskes, M.J.: Dyntex: a comprehensive database of dynamic textures. Pattern Recogn. Lett. 31(12), 1627–1632 (2010)

94. Pollen, D.A., Ronner, S.F.: Visual cortical neurons as localized spatial frequency filters. IEEE Trans. Syst. Man Cybern. SMC-13(5), 907–916 (1983)

95. Portilla, J., Simoncelli, E.P.: A parametric texture model based on joint statistics of complex wavelet coefficients. Int. J. Comput. Vis. 40(1), 49–70 (2000)

96. Rahman, A., Murshed, M.: Real-time temporal texture characterisation using block-based motion co-occurrence statistics. In: International Conference on Image Processing (2004)

97. Rahman, A., Murshed, M.: A motion-based approach for temporal texture synthesis. In: TENCON 2005 IEEE Region 10, pp. 1–4. IEEE, New York (2005)
98. Rosenholtz, R.: Texture perception. Oxford Handbooks Online (2014)
99. Rust, N.C., Mante, V., Simoncelli, E.P., Movshon, J.A.: How mt cells analyze the motion of visual patterns. Nature Neurosci. **9**(11), 1421–1431 (2006)
100. Saisan, P., Doretto, G., Wu, Y.N., Soatto, S.: Dynamic texture recognition. In: CVPR 2001. Proceedings of the 2001 IEEE Computer Society Conference on Computer Vision and Pattern Recognition, 2001, vol. 2, pp. II–58. IEEE, New York (2001)
101. Simoncelli, E.P., Freeman, W.T., Adelson, E.H., Heeger, D.J.: Shiftable multiscale transforms. IEEE Trans. Inf. Theory **38**(2), 587–607 (1992)
102. Simoncelli, E.P., Heeger, D.J.: A model of neuronal responses in visual area mt. Vis. Res. **38**(5), 743–761 (1998)
103. Smith, J.R., Lin, C.-Y., Naphade, M., Video texture indexing using spatio-temporal wavelets. In: 2002 International Conference on Image Processing. 2002. Proceedings, vol. 2, pp. II–437. IEEE, New York (2002)
104. Soatto, S., Doretto, G., and Wu, Y.N., Dynamic textures. In: Eighth IEEE International Conference on Computer Vision, 2001. ICCV 2001. Proceedings, vol. 2, pp. 439–446. IEEE, New York (2001)
105. Solari, F., Chessa, M., Medathati, N.K., Kornprobst, P.: What can we expect from a v1-mt feedforward architecture for optical flow estimation? Signal Process. Image Commun. **39**, 342–354 (2015)
106. Sullivan, G.J., Ohm, J., Han, W.-J., Wiegand, T.: Overview of the high efficiency video coding (HEVC) standard. IEEE Trans. Circuits Syst. Video Technol. **22**(12), 1649–1668 (2012)
107. Sun, C., Wang, H.-J., Li, H., Kim, T.-H.: Perceptually adaptive Lagrange multiplier for rate-distortion optimization in h. 264. In: Future Generation Communication and Networking (FGCN 2007), vol. 1, pp. 459–463. IEEE, New York (2007)
108. Sun, X., Yin, B., Shi, Y.: A low cost video coding scheme using texture synthesis. In: 2nd International Congress on Image and Signal Processing, 2009. CISP'09, pp. 1–5. IEEE, New York (2009)
109. Swamy, D.S., Butler, K.J., Chandler, D.M., Hemami, S.S.: Parametric quality assessment of synthesized textures. In: Proceedings of Human Vision and Electronic Imaging (2011)
110. Tamura, H., Mori, S., Yamawaki, T.: Textural features corresponding to visual perception. IEEE Trans. Syst. Man Cybern. **8**(6), 460–473 (1978)
111. Thakur, U.S., Ray, B.: Image coding using parametric texture synthesis. In: 2016 IEEE 18th International Workshop on Multimedia Signal Processing (MMSP), pp. 1–6 (2016)
112. Thakur, U., Naser, K., Wien, M.: Dynamic texture synthesis using linear phase shift interpolation. In: Proceedings of International Picture Coding Symposium PCS '16, Nuremberg. IEEE, Piscataway (2016)
113. Tiwari, D., Tyagi, V.: Dynamic texture recognition based on completed volume local binary pattern. Multidim. Syst. Sign. Process. **27**(2), 563–575 (2016)
114. Tiwari, D., Tyagi, V.: Dynamic texture recognition using multiresolution edge-weighted local structure pattern. Comput. Electr. Eng. **11**, 475–484 (2016)
115. Tiwari, D., Tyagi, V.: Improved weber's law based local binary pattern for dynamic texture recognition. Multimedia Tools Appl. **76**, 1–18 (2016)
116. Tlapale, E., Kornprobst, P., Masson, G.S., Faugeras, O.: A neural field model for motion estimation. In: Mathematical image processing, pp. 159–179. Springer, Berlin (2011)
117. Tuceryan, M., Jain, A.K.: Texture Analysis. The Handbook of Pattern Recognition and Computer Vision, vol. 2, pp. 207–248 (1998)
118. Turner, M.R.: Texture discrimination by Gabor functions. Biol. Cybern. **55**(2–3), 71–82 (1986)
119. Valaeys, S., Menegaz, G., Ziliani, F., Reichel, J.: Modeling of 2d+ 1 texture movies for video coding. Image Vis. Comput. **21**(1), 49–59 (2003)
120. van der Maaten, L., Postma, E.: Texton-based texture classification. In: Proceedings of Belgium-Netherlands Artificial Intelligence Conference (2007)

121. Varadarajan, S., Karam, L.J.: Adaptive texture synthesis based on perceived texture regularity. In: 2014 Sixth International Workshop on Quality of Multimedia Experience (QoMEX), pp. 76–80. IEEE, New York (2014)
122. Wang, Y., Zhu, S.-C.: Modeling textured motion: particle, wave and sketch. In: Ninth IEEE International Conference on Computer Vision, 2003. Proceedings, pp. 213–220. IEEE, New York (2003)
123. Wang, L., Liu, H., Sun, F.: Dynamic texture classification using local fuzzy coding. In: 2014 IEEE International Conference on Fuzzy Systems (FUZZ-IEEE), pp. 1559–1565. IEEE, New York (2014)
124. Wei, L.-Y., Lefebvre, S., Kwatra, V., Turk, G.: State of the art in example-based texture synthesis. In: Eurographics 2009, State of the Art Report, EG-STAR, pp. 93–117. Eurographics Association, Geneva (2009)
125. Wong, C.-W., Au, O.C., Meng, B., Lam, K.: Perceptual rate control for low-delay video communications. In: 2003 International Conference on Multimedia and Expo, 2003. ICME'03. Proceedings, vol. 3, pp. III–361. IEEE, New York (2003)
126. Xu, Y., Quan, Y., Ling, H., Ji, H.: Dynamic texture classification using dynamic fractal analysis. In: 2011 International Conference on Computer Vision, pp. 1219–1226. IEEE, New York (2011)
127. Xu, Y., Huang, S., Ji, H., Fermüller, C.: Scale-space texture description on sift-like textons. Comput. Vis. Image Underst. **116**(9), 999–1013 (2012)
128. Xu, Y., Quan, Y., Zhang, Z., Ling, H., Ji, H.: Classifying dynamic textures via spatiotemporal fractal analysis. Pattern Recogn. **48**(10), 3239–3248 (2015)
129. Xu, L., et al.: Free-energy principle inspired video quality metric and its use in video coding. IEEE Trans. Multimedia **18**(4), 590–602 (2016)
130. Yu, H., Pan, F., Lin, Z., Sun, Y.: A perceptual bit allocation scheme for h. 264. In: IEEE International Conference on Multimedia and Expo, 2005. ICME 2005, p. 4. IEEE, New York (2005)
131. Yuan, L., Wen, F., Liu, C., Shum, H.-Y.: Synthesizing dynamic texture with closed-loop linear dynamic system. In: Computer Vision-ECCV 2004, pp. 603–616. Springer, Berlin (2004)
132. Zhai, Y., Neuhoff, D.L.: Rotation-invariant local radius index: a compact texture similarity feature for classification. In: 2014 IEEE International Conference on Image Processing (ICIP), pp. 5711–5715. IEEE, New York (2014)
133. Zhai, Y., Neuhoff, D.L., Pappas, T.N.: Local radius index-a new texture similarity feature. In: 2013 IEEE International Conference on Acoustics, Speech and Signal Processing (ICASSP), pp. 1434–1438. IEEE, New York (2013)
134. Zhang, F., Bull, D.R.: A parametric framework for video compression using region-based texture models. IEEE J. Sel. Top. Sign. Proces. **5**(7), 1378–1392 (2011)
135. Zhang, J., Tan, T.: Brief review of invariant texture analysis methods. Pattern Recogn. **35**(3), 735–747 (2002)
136. Zhao, G., Pietikainen, M.: Dynamic texture recognition using local binary patterns with an application to facial expressions. IEEE Trans. Pattern Anal. Mach. Intell. **29**(6), 915–928 (2007)
137. Zhao, X., Reyes, M.G., Pappas, T.N., Neuhoff, D.L.: Structural texture similarity metrics for retrieval applications. In: 15th IEEE International Conference on Image Processing, 2008. ICIP 2008, pp. 1196–1199. IEEE, New York (2008)
138. Zujovic, J., Pappas, T.N., Neuhoff, D.L.: Structural similarity metrics for texture analysis and retrieval. In: 2009 16th IEEE International Conference on Image Processing (ICIP). IEEE, New York (2009)
139. Zujovic, J., Pappas, T.N., Neuhoff, D.L., van Egmond, R., de Ridder, H.: Subjective and objective texture similarity for image compression. In: 2012 IEEE International Conference on Acoustics, Speech and Signal Processing (ICASSP), pp. 1369–1372. IEEE, New York (2012)
140. Zujovic, J., Pappas, T.N., Neuhoff, D.L.: Structural texture similarity metrics for image analysis and retrieval. IEEE Trans. Image Process. **22**(7), 2545–2558 (2013)

Deep Saliency: Prediction of Interestingness in Video with CNN

Souad Chaabouni, Jenny Benois-Pineau, Akka Zemmari,
and Chokri Ben Amar

Abstract Deep Neural Networks have become winners in indexing of visual information. They have allowed achievement of better performances in the fundamental tasks of visual information indexing and retrieval such as image classification and object recognition. In fine-grain indexing tasks, namely object recognition in visual scenes, the CNNs classifiers have to evaluate multiple "object proposals", that is windows in the image plane of different size and location. Hence the problem of recognition is coupled with the problem of localization. In this chapter a model of prediction of Areas-if-Interest in video on the basis of Deep CNNs is proposed. A Deep CNN architecture is designed to classify windows in salient and non-salient. Then dense saliency maps are built upon classification score results. Using the known sensitivity of human visual system (HVS) to residual motion, the usual primary features such as pixel colour values are completed with residual motion features. The experiments show that the choice of the input features for the Deep CNN depends on visual task: for the interest in dynamic content, the proposed model with residual motion is more efficient.

1 Introduction and Related Work

Computational analysis and prediction of digital interestingness is a challenging task, according to the nature of interestingness. Several researches were conducted to construct a reliable measure and obtain a better understanding of interestingness based on various psychological study results that define interestingness as it occupies the mind with no connotation of pleasure or displeasure. Several studies

S. Chaabouni (✉) • J. Benois-Pineau • A. Zemmari
LaBRI UMR 5800, Univ. Bordeaux, CNRS, Bordeaux INP, Univ. Bordeaux, 351, crs de la Liberation, F33405 Talence Cedex, France
e-mail: souad.chaabouni@u-bordeaux.fr; jenny.benois-pineau@u-bordeaux.fr; akka.zemmari@u-bordeaux.fr

C. Ben Amar
REGIM-Lab LR11ES48, National Engineering School of Sfax, BP1173, 3038 Sfax, Tunisia
e-mail: chokri.benamar@ieee.org

© Springer International Publishing AG 2017
J. Benois-Pineau, P. Le Callet (eds.), *Visual Content Indexing and Retrieval with Psycho-Visual Models*, Multimedia Systems and Applications,
DOI 10.1007/978-3-319-57687-9_3

were conducted to quantify the interestingness of video content. Hence, an in-depth study on the interestingness of animated GIFs [11] was conducted to investigate the sources of interest. GIFs were labeled on five point scale in order to describe the degree of interestingness, aesthetics, arousal, valence and curiosity. Using this range of visual features, a support vector regression (SVR) with an RBF kernel predicted the interestingness of GIFs. To understand the video interestingness by human perception, Jiang [17] proposes a simple computational method. Color histograms, Scale invariant feature transform (SIFT) descriptors, histograms of gradient (HOG), self-similarities, global visual features, mel-frequency cepstral coefficients, spectrogram SIFT, audio features, object bank and style attributes present the features used to train an SVM classifier. In the authors [51] proposed a mid-level representation of sentiment sequence to predict interestingness of videos. Using equal weights for all kernels, the ranking SVM was employed to predict the interestingness score. Using mouse activity while watching video, presents the key idea of Zen [54]. And [50] focuses on the problem of egocentric video summarization on the basis of measured gaze fixations. All these works are devoted to the detection of interestingness of video segments or frames, while since the early 90s, the notions of Region-of-Interest (ROI) or Area-of-Interest (AOI) have penetrated the domain of visual information coding and understanding. In this case, interestingness relates to the attraction of HVS by specific areas in images or video frames. Such a "local" interestingness is otherwise called "saliency" of regions and pixels in image plane. Prediction of it on the basis of visual attention modeling has received an ever growing interest in fine-grain visual indexing tasks, such as recognition of objects[10] or actions [47] in image and video content. In various applications, it is not necessary to predict saliency for each pixel in an image, but only to predict the "window" where the content could attract human attention. This is for instance the case for new approaches of object recognition in images and videos, where classifiers evaluate multiple "object proposals", that is windows of different sizes and scales to maximize the response to a trained object model. The necessity to classify multiple windows makes the process of recognition heavy. The authors of [9] proposed a so called Region-based convolutional network (R-CNN). They restrict number of windows using "selective search" approach [45] thus the classifier has to evaluate a limited number of (2K) "object proposals". Prediction of the interestingness or saliency of windows is another way to bound the search space [35].

Prediction of visual saliency in image plane is a rather old and well explored research topic. Following the psychophysics of human cognitive process when observing visual content two kinds of models are known from literature. Bottom-up models based on low-level features such as luminance, color, orientation and motion, are inspired by the popular "feature integration theory" [44]. Top-down models express a task-driven visual observation when humans search for specific objects, concepts and activities in visual scenes. Intuitively, when humans are observing a continuous video scene [41], the "top-down" attention [36] becomes prevalent with the time, as the observer understands the unknown content and performs smooth pursuit of objects which are of interest for him. To learn more about the history of the taxonomy of visual attention studies, we refer the reader to the paper by Borgi [1]. What is clear today, that any model trying to predict human visual attention attractors in visual scenes, needs to combine both: bottom-up and top-down components. Therefore, it is believable that supervised machine learning methods, which combine stimuli driven features measures and capability of prediction on the basis of seen data, will bring a satisfactory solution to this complex problem. With the explosion of research with deep networks and their proven efficiency, different models of visual attention have been proposed using this supervised learning approach. Shen [42] proposed a deep learning model to extract salient areas in images, which allows firstly to learn the relevant characteristics of the saliency of natural images, and secondly to predict the eye fixations on objects with semantic content. Simonyan [43] defined a multi-class classification problem using "task-dependent" visual experiment to predict the saliency of image pixels. Vig [47] tackles prediction of saliency of pixels using feature maps extracted from different architectures of a deep network. In [25], a multi-resolution convolutional neural network model has been proposed using three different scales of the raw images and the eye fixations as targets. In [22], three CNN models are designed to predict saliency using a segmented input image. The authors of [23, 34] propose to adopt the end-to-end solution as a regression problem to predict the saliency. In [24] global saliency map is computed by summing all intermediate saliency maps that are obtained by convolving the images with learned filters and pooling their Gaussian-weighted responses at multiple scales. In [55], a class activation maps using average pooling in order to produce the desired class was proposed. Deep Neural Networks classifiers have become winners in indexing of visual information, they show ever increasing performances in prediction. This is why they have also become a methodological framework for prediction of saliency or interestingness of visual content. In summary, this chapter makes the following contributions:

- construct from four benchmark datasets with ground-truth labels the support to study of interestingness of areas in video frames.
- To incorporate the top-down "semantic" cues in the prediction of interestingness in video, a Deep CNNs architecture is proposed with a novel residual motion feature.

2 Deep CNN as a Tool for Prediction of Interestingness in Video

Machine Learning is a set of techniques used to achieve, automatically, a task by learning from a training data set. There is a plethora of methods based on different mathematical fundamentals. Neural networks were intended to model learning and pattern recognition done by physiological neurons. This was first introduced by Hebb [57] who modeled synapses by weighted links from the outputs of nodes to the inputs of other nodes. Rosenblatt [58] continued the Hebb model and investigated how the links between neurons could be developed, in particular, he defined the basic mathematical model for neural networks (NN for short). His basic unit was called the perceptron, which when it receives a signal, would either respond or not, depending on whether a function exceeded a threshold. Figure 1 presents a formal neurone. It receives input signals $(x_1, x_2, \cdots , x_p)$, and applies an activation function f to a linear combination of the signals. This combination is determined by a vector of weights $w_1, w_2, \cdots , w_p$ and a bias w_0. More formally, the output neurone value y defined as follows:

$$y = f\left(w_0 + \sum_{i=1}^{p} w_i x_i\right).$$

A neural network is then a network whose nodes are formal neurones, and to define a neural network, one needs to design its architecture (the number of hidden layers and the number of nodes per layer, etc.) as well as estimation of parameters once the network is fixed. Figure 2 gives an example of such a network.

Fig. 1 A formal neurone

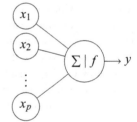

Fig. 2 An example of a NN. Data X is fed into the first (and here only) hidden layer. Each node in the hidden layer is the composition of a sigmoid function with an affine function of X. The outputs from hidden layer are combined linearly to give the output y

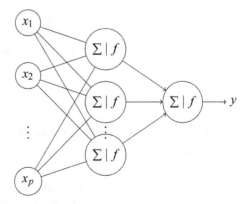

2.1 Deep Neural Networks

Deep learning is a branch of machine learning introduced in 1980s. Nevertheless, its emergence started really by the computational power of the 2000s. It is a machine learning process structured on a so-called convolutional neural network (CNN). A CNN is composed of several stacked layers of different types: convolutional layers (CONV), non-linearity layers , such as ReLu layers, pool layers and (generally the last layer) fully connected layers (FC). Figure 3 gives an example of an architecture of a CNN.

2.1.1 Convolutional Layers (CONV)

In order to extract the most important information for further analysis or exploitation of image patches, the convolution with a fixed number of filters is needed. It is necessary to determine the size of the convolution kernel to be applied to the input image in order to highlight its areas. Two stages are conceptually necessary to create a convolutional layer. The first refers to the convolution of the input image with linear filters. The second consists in adding a bias term. Generally, the equation of convolution can be written as (1):

$$X_j^l = f\left(\sum_{i \in M_j} X_i^{l-1} * \omega_{ij}^l + B_j^l\right) \tag{1}$$

with X_j^l: the activity of the unit j according to the layer l,

   X_i represents a selection of the input feature maps,

   B_j^l is the additive bias of the unit j in the features maps of the layer l,

   ω_{ij}^l: presents the synaptic weights between unit j of the layer l and $l - 1$.

2.1.2 Pooling Layers (POOL)

Pooling reduces the computational complexity for the upper layers and summarizes the outputs of neighboring groups of neurons from the same kernel map. It reduces

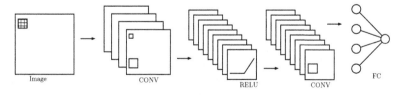

Fig. 3 An example of a CNN

the size of each input feature map by the acquisition of a value for each receptive field of neurons of the next layer. We use max-pooling, see Eq. (2):

$$h_j^n(x, y) = \max_{\bar{x}, \bar{y} \in \mathcal{N}} h_j^{n-1}(\bar{x}, \bar{y}) \qquad (2)$$

Here $\mathcal{N}$ denotes the neighborhood of (x,y).

2.1.3 ReLu Layers

The Rectified Linear Unit (ReLu for short) has become very popular in the last few years. It computes the function $f(x) = \max(0, x)$. Thus, the activation is thresholded at zero. It was found to accelerate the convergence of a very popular parameter optimization method, stochastic gradient descent, compared to the sigmoid function.

2.1.4 Local Response Normalization Layers (LRN and ReLu)

A local Response Normalization (LRN) layer normalizes values of feature maps which are calculated through the neurons having unbounded (due to ReLu) activations to detect the high-frequency characteristics with a high response of the neuron, and to scale down answers that are uniformly greater in a local area. The output computation is presented in Eq. (3):

$$f(U_f^{x,y}) = \frac{U_f^{x,y}}{(1 + \frac{\alpha}{N^2} \sum_{x'=\max(0,x-[N/2])}^{\min(S,x-[N/2]+N)} \sum_{y'=\max(0,y-[N/2])}^{\min(S,y-[N/2]+N)} (U_f^{x',y'})^2)^\beta} \qquad (3)$$

Here $U_f^{x,y}$ represents the value of the feature map at (x, y) coordinates and the sums are taken in the neighborhood of (x, y) of size $N \times N$, α and β regulate normalization strength.

Once the architecture of the network is fixed, the next step is to estimate its parameters. In next section, we explain how this can be done.

2.2 Loss Functions and Optimization Methods

A neural network be it a fully connected NN or a CNN is a supervised machine learning model. It learns a prediction function from a training set [46]. Each sample from this set can be modeled by a vector which describes the observation and its corresponding response. The learning model aims to construct a function which can be used to predict the responses for new observations while committing a prediction error as lowest as possible.

More formally, a sample i from the training set is denoted $(x_1^i, x_2^i, \cdots, x_n^i, y^i)$ and the response of the model is denoted $\hat{y}^i$.

There are many functions used to measure prediction errors. They are called *loss functions*. A loss function somehow quantifies the deviation of the output of the model from the correct response. We are speaking here about "empirical loss" functions [46], that is the error computed on all available ground truth training data. Here we will shortly present one of them.

2.2.1 One-Hot Encoding

Back to the training set, the known response of each observation is encoded in a one-hot labels vector. More formally, given an observation $(x_1^i, x_2^i, \cdots, x_n^i, y^i)$, we introduce a binary vector $L^i = (L_1^i, L_2^i, \cdots, L_k^i)$ such that if $y^i = c_j$ then $L_j^i = 1$ and $\forall m \neq j, L_m^i = 0$. This is the function which ensures a "hard" coding of class labels.

2.2.2 Softmax

Given a vector $Y = (y_1, y_2, \cdots, y_k)$ with positive real-valued coordinates, the softmax function aims to transform the values of Y to a vector $S = (p_1, p_2, \cdots, p_k)$ of real values in the range $(0, 1)$ that sums to 1. More precisely, it is defined for each $i \in \{1, 2, \cdots, k\}$ by:

$$p_i = \frac{e^{y_i}}{\sum_{j=1}^{k} e^{y_j}}. \tag{4}$$

The softmax function is used in the last layer of multi-layer neural networks which are trained under a cross-entropy (we will define this function in next paragraphs) regime. When used for image recognition, the softmax computes the estimated probabilities, for each input data, of being in a class from a given taxonomy.

2.2.3 Cross-Entropy

The cross-entropy loss function is expressed in terms of the result of the softmax and the one-hot encoding. It is defined as follows:

$$D(S, L) = -\sum_{i=1}^{k} L_i \log(p_i). \tag{5}$$

The definition of one-hot encoding and Eq. (5) means that only the output of the classifier corresponding to the correct class label is included in the cost.

2.2.4 Average Cross Entropy

To deal with the cross-entropy of all the training set, we introduce the average cross-entropy. This is simply the average value, over all the set, of the cross-entropy introduced in Eq. (5):

$$\mathscr{L} = \frac{1}{N} \sum_{i=1}^{N} D(S^i, L^i). \tag{6}$$

The loss function corresponds then to the average cross-entropy.

As claimed before, the machine learning models aim to construct a prediction function which minimizes the loss function. There are many algorithms which aim to minimize the loss function. Most of them are iterative and operate by decreasing the loss function following a descent direction. These methods solve the problem when the loss function is supposed to be convex. The main idea can be expressed simply as follows: starting from initial arbitrary (or randomly) chosen point in the parameter space, they allow the "descent" to the minimum of the loss function accordingly to the chosen set of directions [38]. Here we discuss some of the most known and used optimization algorithms in this field.

2.2.5 The Gradient Descent Algorithm

The gradient descent algorithm is the most simple and most used algorithm to find parameters for the learning model under the assumption of convexity of function to minimize. There are mainly two versions of this algorithm, the first one acts in a batch mode and the other in on-line mode. The batch mode: when we aim to minimize globally the loss function (this is why it is named batch), we first initialize randomly the parameters and we iteratively minimize the loss function by updating the parameters. This updating is done following the opposite direction of the gradient of the loss function which, locally, shows the highest slope of this function. Hence, at iteration t, the new values of the weights $w^{(t+1)}$ are estimated using the values of the weights at step t and the gradient of the loss function estimated at weight $w^{(t)}$:

$$\forall t \in \mathbb{N}, \ w^{(t+1)} = w^{(t)} - \eta \nabla \mathscr{L} \left(w^{(t)} \right), \tag{7}$$

where $\eta \in \mathbb{R}_+^*$ is a positive real called learning rate. One fundamental issue is how to choose the learning rate. If this rate is too large, than we may obtain oscillations around the minimum. If it is two small, then the convergence toward the minimum will be too slow and in same cases it may never happen.

The on-line mode: when we are dealing with large set of data, batch algorithms are not useful anymore since they are not scalable. Many works have been done to overcome this issue and to design on-line algorithms. These algorithms consider a single example at each iteration and are shown to be more efficient both in time and space complexities.

Among all the on-line algorithms, the *stochastic gradient Descent* (SGD for short) is considered as the most popular and the most used one. Many works have proved its efficiency and its scalability.

The SGD algorithm is an iterative process which acts as follows: at each iteration t, a training example $(x_1^t, x_2^t, \cdots, x_n^t, y^t)$ is chosen uniformly at random and is used to update the weights of the loss function following the opposite of the gradient of this function. The SGD algorithm belongs to first-order methods, i.e., those that form the parameter update on the basis of only first order gradient information. First-order methods, when used to solve convex optimization problems, have been shown to have a convergence speed, when used with large dimension problems, which can not be better than sub-linear in means of $t^{-1/2}$, [37], where t is the number of iterations. This theoretical result implies that first-order methods can not be used to solve, scalable problems in an acceptable time and with high accuracy.

Momentum is a method that helps accelerate SGD in the relevant direction. It achieves this by adding a fraction of the update vector of the past time step to the current update vector. The most popular is the method of Nesterov Momentum [32]:

$$\forall t \in \mathbb{N}, \quad y^{(t)} = w^{(t)} + \frac{t}{t+1}\left(w^{(t)} - w^{(t-1)}\right)$$
$$w^{(t+1)} = y^{(t)} - \eta \nabla \mathscr{L}\left(y^{(t)}\right), \tag{8}$$

2.3 Problem of Noise in Training Data

In data mining, noise has two different main sources [56]. Different types of measurement tools induce implicit errors that yield noisy labels in training data. Besides, random errors introduced by experts or batch processes when the data are gathered can produce the noise as well. Noise of data could adversely disturb the classification accuracy of classifiers trained on this data. In the study [33], four supervised learners (naive Bayesian probabilistic classifier, the C4.5 decision tree, the IBk instance-based learner and the SMO support vector machine) were selected to compare the sensitivity with regard to different degrees of noise. A systematic evaluation and analysis of the impact of class noise and attribute noise on the system performance in machine learning was presented in [56].

The Deep CNNs use the stacking of different kinds of layers (convolution, pooling, normalization, ...) that ensures the extraction of features which lead to the learning of the model. The training of deep CNN parameters is frequently done with the stochastic gradient descent 'SGD' technique [16], see Sect. 2.2.5. For a simple supervised learning the SGD method still remains the best learning algorithm when the training set is large. With the wide propagation of convolutional neural networks, and the massive labeled data needed to train the CNNs networks, studies of the impact of noisy data was needed. A general framework to train CNNs with only a limited number of clean labels and millions of noisy labels was introduced in [49] in order to model the relationships between images, class labels and label noises with a probabilistic graphical model and further integrate it into an end-to-end deep learning system. In [39], substantial robustness to label noise of deep CNNs was proposed using a generic way to handle noisy and incomplete labeling. This is realized by augmenting the prediction objective with a notion of consistency.

The research focused on noise produced by random errors was published in [5]. Here it typically addresses a two-class classification problem: for each region in an image/video plane it is necessary to give the confidence to be salient or not for a human observer. One main contribution of this chapter is to identify how noise of data impacts performance of deep networks in the problem of visual saliency prediction. Here, to study the impact of the noise in ground truth labels, two experiments on the large data set were conducted. In the first experiment non-salient windows were randomly selected in an image plane in a standard way, just excluding already selected salient windows. Nevertheless, in video, dynamic switching of attention to distractors or to smooth pursuit of moving objects, makes such a method fail. This policy of selection of non-salient areas yields random errors. In the second experiment, cinematographic production rule of 3/3 for non-salient patches selection was used, excluding the patches already defined as salient area in all the videos frames and excluding the area where the content producers—photographers or cameramen place important scene details. The results in [5] show the increase in accuracy in the most efficient model up to 8%, all other settings being equal: the network architecture, optimization method, input data configuration.

2.4   Transfer Learning

Transfer learning presents a technique used in the field of machine learning that increases the accuracy of learning either by using it in different tasks, or in the same task [52]. Training CNNs from scratch is relatively hard due to the insufficient size of available training dataset in real-world classification problems. Pre-training a deep CNNs by using an initialization or a fixed feature extractor presents the heart of the transfer method. Two famous scenarios of transfer learning with CNNs were followed: (1) using a fixed feature extractor with removing the last fully-connected layer. Here the training is fulfilled just for the linear classifier on the new dataset. (2) Fine-tuning the weights of the pre-trained deep CNN by continuing the back-propagation [52].

In the research of Bengio et al. [52] addressing object recognition problem, the authors show that the first layers of a Deep CNN learn characteristics similar to the responses of Gabor's filters regardless of the data set or task. Hence in their transfer learning scheme just the three first convolutional layers already trained on one training set are used for the initialization for parameter training on another training set. The coefficients on deeper layers are left free for optimization, that is initialized randomly. Several studies have proven the power of this technique [31, 53]. Transfer learning with deep CNN shows its efficiency in different application domain such as saliency prediction [4], person re-identification [8].

3   ChaboNet: A Deep CNN for Prediction of Interestingness in Natural Video

Now our question is how to predict the areas in natural video content which are of interest to a human observer, when he/she executes a free viewing task of unknown video content. Our task is to predict the interestingnees "at a glance", a precise shape of the salient area in the image is not important. We still believe that the "Rough Indexing Paradigm" [27], which means fast mining of visual information with nearly pre-attentive vision is of much interest in our era of "big" visual data. Furthermore, such a AOI can be further used by object recognition methods. Hence we consider a squared windows in the image plane as the area-of-interest for human observer.

3.1   ROI Definition and Selection: Salient and Non-salient Windows

In order to train the model able to predict saliency of a given region in the image plane, the training set has to be built to comprise salient and non-salient regions. Salient regions-patches are selected on the basis of gaze fixation density maps which are obtained during a psycho-visual experiment with cohorts of subjects. In this work, the creation of data set from available video database in order to train the model with Deep CNN, is realized under a specific policy that minimizes the noise in the training data. The approach previously presented in [5] was followed.

Figure 4 below presents the group of salient and non-salient patches selected under the proposed approach. The rows contain some examples taken from frames of a set of video sequences "actioncliptrain" from the HOLLYWOOD[1] data set. The first line presents the map built on gaze fixations by the method of Wooding [48]. The second line describes the position of the selected patches: the yellow square is the salient patch and the black one is labeled as non-salient patch. The third line presents the group of salient patches on the left and non-salient patches on the right for each frame.

---

[1] Available at http://www.di.ens.fr/~laptev/actions/hollywood2/.

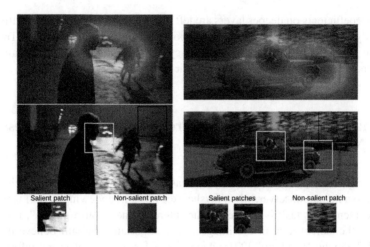

Fig. 4 Training data from HOLLYWOOD data set: (*left*) *#frame*176 of the 'actioncliptrain299', (*right*) *#frame*210 of the 'actioncliptrain254'

3.2 Salient Patches Extraction

We define a squared patch P of size $s \times s$ (in this work $s = 100$ adapted to the spatial resolution of standard definition (SD) video data) in a video frame as a vector in $R^{s \times s \times n}$. Here n stands for the quantity of primary feature maps serving as an input to the deep CNN. If $n = 3$ just color RGB planes are used as primary features in each pixel. In case when $n = 4$ the L_2 squared norm of a motion vector for each pixel, normalised on the dataset is added to RGB planes as a new feature map. We define patch "saliency" on the basis of its interest for subjects. The interest is measured by the magnitude of a visual attention map built upon gaze fixations which are recorded during a psycho-visual experiment using an eye-tracker. The fixation density maps (FDM) are built by the method of Wooding [48]. Such a map $S(x, y)$ represents a multi-Gaussian surface normalized by its global maximum.

A binary label is associated with pixels X of each patch P_i using Eq. (9).

$$l(X) = \begin{cases} 1 & if \quad S(x_{0,i}, y_{0,i}) \geq \tau_J \\ 0 & otherwise \end{cases} \tag{9}$$

with $(x_{0,i}, y_{0,i})$ the coordinates of the patch center. A set of thresholds is selected starting by the global maximum value of the normalized FDM and then relaxing threshold values as in Eq. (10):

$$\begin{cases} \tau_0 = \max(S(x, y), 0) \\ \tau_{(j+1)} = \tau_j - \epsilon \tau_j \end{cases} \tag{10}$$

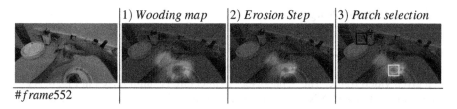

Fig. 5 Policy of patch selection: an example and processing steps from GTEA data set

Here $0 < \epsilon < 1$ is a relaxation parameter, $j = 0, \cdots, J$, and J limits the relaxation of saliency. It was chosen experimentally as $J = 5$, while $\epsilon = 0.04$.

In complex scenes several details or objects can attract human attention. Thus the map $S(x, y)$ can contain several local maxima. In order to highlight them, we apply morphological erosion to $S(x, y)$. Figure 5 above summarizes different steps needed to select salient patches. Firstly, we compute the fixation density maps, then we apply operation of erosion. Patches centered on local maxima with saliency values satisfying Eqs. (9), (10) are selected as "salient". Retained "salient" patches should be distanced at least by ($\frac{1}{2} \times s$). "Non-salient" patches extraction is described in the next section.

3.3 Non-salient Patches Extraction

By definition, a non-salient patch should not be situated in the area-of-interest in a video frame, and must not be already selected as salient. According to the rule of thirds in produced and post-produced content, the most interesting details of the image or of a video frame have to cover the frame center and the intersections of the three horizontal and vertical lines that divide the image into nine equal parts [26].

Let $(x_{0,i}, y_{0,i})$ be the coordinates of the center of the patch P_i, *width* is the width size of the video frame and *height* is its height size. The set $\{Salient\}$ presents the set of salient positions which have been already chosen. To exclude them and the area-of-interest we chose the one-fifth band of the frame starting from its border and randomly generate patch centers in this area. Hence the generated coordinates satisfy the following conditions:

$$x_{0,i} \in BorderX | x_{0,i} \notin \{Salient\}; \quad and \quad y_{0,i} \in BorderY | y_{0,i} \notin \{Salient\}$$

$$with \begin{cases} BorderX = [0, \frac{width}{5}[\cup]width - \frac{width}{5}, width] \wedge BorderY = [0, height] \\ or \\ BorderX = [\frac{width}{5}, width - \frac{width}{5}] \wedge BorderY = [0, \frac{height}{5}[\cup]height - \frac{height}{5}, height] \end{cases}$$

(11)

3.4   Chabonet Design

In this section the architecture of a deep CNN, 'ChaboNet', is presented. It was designed for the two class classification problem: prediction of a saliency of a patch in a given video frame. The 'ChaboNet' architecture is summarized in Fig. 6. As in the majority of Deep CNN architectures designed for image classification tasks [16], the 'ChaboNet' architecture is composed of a hierarchy of patterns. Each pattern consists of a cascade of operations, followed by a normalization operation if it is required. The cascading of linear and nonlinear operations successively produces high-level features that contribute to the construction of the saliency map. The softmax classifier, see Eq. (4), is the deepest layer giving the confidence for each patch to be salient or not. Taking into account the size of input patches we propose three patterns in our architecture. The diagram detailing the flow of operations is presented on the left of the Fig. 6. The cascade of operations are depicted in the upper right corner of the figure. The whole network can be detailed as follows, while the normalization operation is added after the patterns P^1 and P^2:

Pattern P^1 :
$$Input \xrightarrow{convolution} Conv^1 \xrightarrow{pooling} Pool^1 \xrightarrow{ReLu} R^1$$
Pattern P^p :   with $p \in \{2, 3\}$
$$N^{p-1} \xrightarrow{convolution} Conv^p \xrightarrow{ReLu} R^p \xrightarrow{convolution} Conv^{pp} \xrightarrow{ReLu} R^{pp} \xrightarrow{pooling}$$
$Pool^p$

The rectified linear unit operation (ReLu) is expressed as (12)

$$f(x) = max(0, x) \tag{12}$$

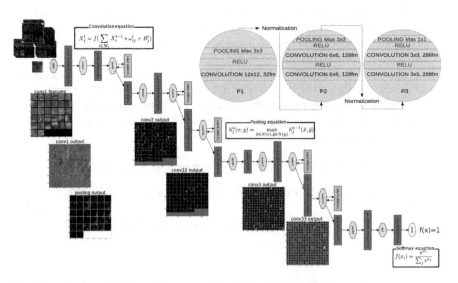

Fig. 6   Architecture of video saliency convolution network 'ChaboNet'

The ReLu operation is used due to its better performances in image classification tasks compared to sigmoid function, as it does not suppress high frequency features. The first pattern P^1 is designed in the manner that the 'ReLu' operation is introduced after the 'pooling' one. In this research, the max-pooling operator was used. As the operation of 'pooling' and 'ReLu' compute the maximum, they are commutative. Cascading 'pooling' before 'ReLu' can reduce the execution time as 'pooling' step reduces the number of neurons or nodes ('pooling' operation is more detailed in the following section). In the two last patterns, stacking two convolutional layers before the destructive pooling layer ensures the computation of more complex features that will be more "expressive".

In 'ChaboNet' network, we used 32 kernels with the size of 12×12 for the convolution layer of the first pattern $P1$. In the second pattern $P2$, 128 kernels for each convolutional layer were used. In $P2$ the size of the kernels for the first convolutional layer was chosen as 6×6 and for the second convolution layer, a kernel of 3×3 was used. Finally, 288 kernels with the size of 3×3 were used for each convolution layer of the last pattern $P3$. Here we were inspired by the literature [19, 42] where the size of convolution kernels is either maintained constant or is decreasing with the depth of layers. This allows a progressive reduction of highly dimensional data before conveying them to the fully connected layers. The number of convolution filters is growing, on the contrary, to explore the richness of the original data and highlight structural patterns. For the filter size, we made several tests with the same values as in AlexNet [19], Shen's network [42], LeNet [21], Cifar [18] and finally, we retained a stronger value of 12×12 in the first layer of the pattern $P1$ as it yielded the best accuracy of prediction in our saliency classification problem.

The kernel size of the pooling operation for the both patterns $P1$ and $P2$ is set to 3×3. However, the pooling of the third pattern $P3$ is done with a size of 1×1.

3.5 Real-World "Small" Data: Transfer Learning

The generalization power of Deep CNN classifiers strongly depends on the quantity of the data and on the coverage of data space in the training data set. In real-life applications, e.g. prediction of benchmark models for studies of visual attention of specific populations [6] or saliency prediction for visual quality assessment [2], the database volumes are small. Hence, in order to predict saliency in these small collections of videos, we use the transfer learning approach.

Our preliminary study on transfer learning performed in the task of learning areas that attract visual attention in natural video [4] showed the efficiency of weights already learned on a large database, for the training on small databases. In the present work, we benchmark our transfer learning scheme designed for saliency prediction with regard to the popular approach proposed in [52]. Saliency prediction task is different from object recognition task. Thus our proposal is to initialize all parameters in all layers of the network to train on a small data set by the best trained model on a large data set. The following Eq. (13) expresses the transfer of the classification knowledge obtained from the larger database to the new smaller database. Here the Stochastic Gradient descent with momentum is used as in [16].

$$
\begin{cases}
V_{i+1} = m \cdot V_i - weightDecay \cdot \epsilon \cdot W_i - \epsilon \cdot \langle \frac{\partial L}{\partial W} | W_i \rangle_{D_i} \\
W_{i+1} = W_i + V_{i+1} \quad | \quad W_0 = W'_n
\end{cases}
\tag{13}
$$

With $m = 0.9$; $weightDecay = 0.00004$ and W'_n presents the best learned model parameters pre-trained on the large data set. We set the initial value of the velocity V_0 to zero. These parameter values are inspired by the values used in [16] and show the best performances on a large training data set.

3.6 POI or Pixel-Wise Saliency Map

If we have predicted for each selected window in a given video frame its "saliency" or interest for a human observer, the natural question rises how can we assess the quality of this prediction. The quality of trained model is evaluated on the validation dataset when training the network. The accuracy gives the classification power of the network for a given training iteration. But we cannot compare the classified windows with a "manually" selected ground truth on a test set. First of all, it would require a tedious annotation process, and secondly human annotation is not free of errors: how to trace an "interesting window" of a given size? We are not focused on any specific objects, hence this question will be difficult to answer for a human annotator. His visual system instead gives the ground truth: humans are fixating areas which are of interest for them. Hence we come now back to image pixels in order to be able to asses the quality of our prediction comparing the saliency maps we can predict by the trained network with Wooding maps built on gaze fixations. Hence we will speak about Pixels of Interest (POI) or pixel-wise saliency maps. The pixel-wise saliency map of each frame F of the video is constructed using the output value of the trained deep CNN model. The soft-max classifier, Eq. (4) which takes the output of the third pattern P^3 as input, see Fig. 6, gives the probability for a patch of belonging to the salient class.

Hence, from each frame F we select local region having the same size as training patches (here $s = 100$). The output value of the soft-max classifier on each local region defines the degree of saliency of this area. In the center of each local region, a Gaussian is applied with a pick value of $\frac{10f(i)}{2\pi\sigma^2}$ with the spread parameter σ chosen as a half-size of the patch. In this way, a sparse saliency map is predicted. If we slide the patch on the input frame, with a step of one pixel, then a dense saliency map will be produced for the whole frame by the trained CNN. To avoid computational overload, sampling of windows to classify can be more sparse, e.g. with a stride of 5 pixels. Then score values assigned to the centers are interpolated with Gaussian filters. Hence from Regions-of-interest (ROI) we come to Pixels-of-Interest (POI) and can compare the quality of our prediction using classical saliency-comparison approaches with regard to gaze fixation maps of Wooding.

3.7 Results and Conclusion

3.7.1 Data Sets

To learn the model for prediction of visually interesting areas in image plane, four data sets were used, HOLLYWOOD [29, 30], GTEA corpus [7], CRCNS [14] and IRCCYN [3].

The HOLLYWOOD database contains 823 training videos and 884 videos for the validation step. The number of subjects with recorded gaze fixations varies according to each video with up to 19 subjects. The spatial resolution of videos varies as well. In others terms the HOLLYWOOD data set contains 229,825 frames for training and 257,733 frames for validation. From the frames of the training set we have extracted 222,863 salient patches and 221,868 non-salient patches. During the validation phase, we have used 251,294 salient patches and 250,169 non-salient patches respectively (Tables 1, 2, 3, and 4).

Table 1 Preview of action in Hollywood dataset

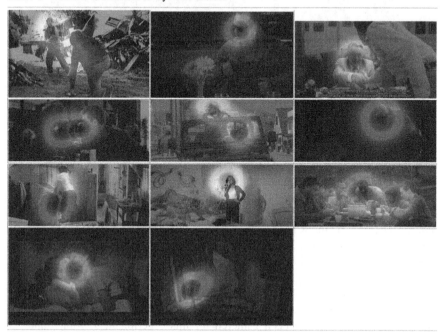

Table 2 Preview of GTEA dataset

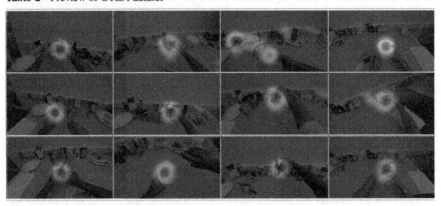

Table 3 Preview of CRCNS dataset

Publicly available GTEA corpus [7] contains 17 egocentric videos with a total duration of 19 min. GTEA dataset consists of videos with 15 fps rate and a 640 × 480 pixel resolution. The subjects who recorded the video were preparing meal and manipulating different every day life objects. On this dataset, we have conducted a psycho-visual experiment with the task of observation of manipulated objects. The gaze fixations have been recorded with a HS-VET 250 Hz eye-tracker from Cambridge Research Systems Ltd at a rate of 250 Hz/s. The experiment conditions and the experiment room were compliant with the recommendation ITU-R BT.500-11 [28]. Videos were displayed on a 23 in. LCD monitor with a native resolution of 1920 × 1080 pixels. To avoid image distortions, videos were not re-sized to screen resolution. A mid-gray frame was inserted around the displayed video. 31 participants have been gathered for this experiment, 9 women and 22

Table 4   Preview of IRCCyN dataset

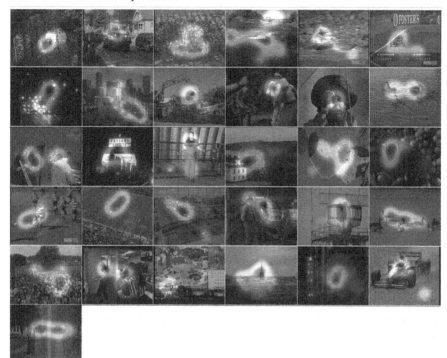

men. For three participants some problems occurred in the eye-tracking recording process. These three records were thus excluded. From the 17 available videos of GTEA dataset, ten were selected for the training step with a total number of frames of 10,149. And seven videos with 7840 frames were selected for the validation step. The split of salient and non-salient patches for the total of 19,910 at the training step and 15,204 at the validation step is presented in Table 5.

In the CRCNS[2] data set [14], 50 videos of 640×480 resolution are available with gaze recordings of up to eight different subjects. The database was split equally: training and validation sets contain 25 videos each. From the training set, we have extracted 30,374 salient- and 28,185 non-salient patches. From the validation set, 19,945 salient and 17,802 non-salient patches were extracted.

IRCCYN [3] database is composed of 31 SD videos and gaze fixations of 37 subjects. These videos contain certain categories of attention attractors such as high contrast, faces. However, videos with objects in motion are not frequent. Our purpose of saliency prediction modeling the "smooth pursuit" cannot be evaluated by using all available videos of IRCCyN data set. Videos that do not contain a real object motion were eliminated. Therefore, only SRC02, SRC03, SRC04, SRC05, SRC06, SRC07, SRC10, SRC13, SRC17, SRC19, SRC23, SRC24 and SRC27

---

[2] Available at https://crcns.org/data-sets/eye/eye-1.

Table 5 Distribution of learning data: total number of salient and NonSalient patches selected from each database

Datasets		Training step	Validation step
HOLLYWOOD	SalientPatch	222,863	251,294
	NonSalientPatch	221,868	250,169
	Total	444,731	501,463
GTEA	SalientPatch	9961	7604
	NonSalientPatch	9949	7600
	Total	19,910	15,204
CRCNS	SalientPatch	30,374	19,945
	Non-SalientPatch	28,185	17,802
	Total	58,559	37,747
IRCCyN-MVT	SalientPatch	2013	511
	Non-SalientPatch	1985	506
	Total	3998	1017

were used in experiments, this data set is referenced as IRCCyN-MVT in the following. For each chosen video of this database, one frame is taken for the testing step, one frame for the validation step and four frames for the training step. The distribution of the data between "salient" and "non-salient" classes is presented in Table 5.

3.7.2 Evaluation of Patches' Saliency Prediction with the Deep CNN

The network was implemented using a powerful graphic card Tesla K40m and processor (2×14 cores). Therefore a sufficiently large amount of patches, 256, was used per iteration. After a fixed number of training iterations, a model validation step was implemented: here the accuracy of the model at the current iteration was computed on the validation data set.

To evaluate our deep network and to prove the importance of the addition of the residual motion map, two models were created with the same parameter settings and architecture of the network: the first one contains R, G and B primary pixel values in patches, denoted as *ChaboNet3k*. The *ChaboNet4k* is the model using RGB values and the normalized energy of residual motion as input data, see Sect. 3.2. The following Fig. 7 illustrates the variations of the accuracy along iterations of all the models tested for the database "HOLLYWOOD". The results of learning experiments on HOLLYWOOD data set yield the following conclusions: (1) when adding residual motion as an input feature to RGB plane values, the accuracy is improved by almost 2%. (2) The accuracy curve (Fig. 7a) show that the best trained model reached 80% of accuracy at the iteration #8690. The model obtained after 8690 iterations is used to predict saliency on the validation set of this database, and to initialize the parameters when learning with transfer on other used data sets.

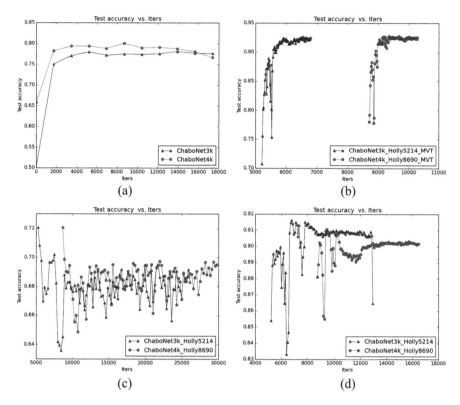

Fig. 7 Training the network—accuracy vs iterations of *ChaboNet3k* and *ChaboNet4k* for all tested databases. (**a**) Accuracy vs iterations Hollywood dataset. (**b**) Accuracy vs iterations IRCCyN-MVT dataset. (**c**) Accuracy vs iterations CRCNS dataset. (**d**) Accuracy vs iterations GTEA dataset

3.7.3 Validation of Our Proposed Method of Transfer Learning

Two experiments were conducted with the same small data set IRCCyN-MVT and CRCNS, and the same definition of network "ChaboNet":

(1) Our method: start training of all ChaboNet layers from the best model already trained on the large HOLLYWOOD data set (see Sect. 3.5).
(2) Bengio's method [52]: the three first convolutional layers are trained on the HOLLYWOOD data set and then fine-tuned on the target data set, other layers are trained on target data set with random initialization.

The following Fig. 8 illustrates the variations of the accuracy along iterations of the two experiments performed with the data sets "CRCNS" , "IRCCyN-MVT" and GTEA.

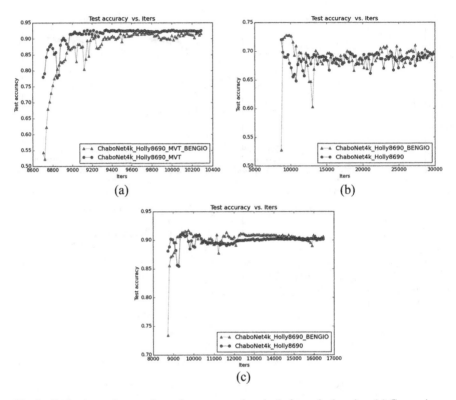

Fig. 8 Evaluation and comparison of our proposed method of transfer learning. (**a**) Comparison on IRCCyN-MVT data set. (**b**) Comparison on CRCNS data set. (**c**) Comparison on GTEA data set

Our method of transfer learning outperformed the Bengio's method by almost 2.85% in IRCCyN-MVT data set and by around 0.5% in CRCNS data set. For the GTEA dataset the maximum accuracy is the same for the two methods. The gain on stability of training in our method for the three small datasets is about 50%, see Tables 6 and 7.

3.7.4 Evaluation Metrics for Predicted Visual Saliency Maps

After training and validation of the model on HOLLYWOOD data set, we choose the model obtained at the iteration #8690 having the maximum value of accuracy 80.05%. This model will be used to predict the probability of a local region to be salient. Hence, the final saliency map will be built. For the CRCNS data set, the model obtained at the iteration #21984 with the accuracy of 69.73% is

Table 6 Accuracy results on HOLLYWOOD, IRCCyN-MVT, CRCNS and GTEA data sets

	HOLLYWOOD		IRCCyN-MVT		CRCNS		GTEA	
	ChaboNet3k	ChaboNet4k	ChaboNet3k	ChaboNet4k	ChaboNet3k	ChaboNet4k	ChaboNet3k	ChaboNet4k
Interval-stabilization	—	—	$[5584\dots6800]$	$[8976\dots10288]$	$[8702\dots26106]$	$[11908\dots29770]$	$[6630\dots12948]$	$[12090\dots16458]$
$min_{(\#iter)}$	$50.11\%_{(\#0)}$	$65.73\%_{(\#0)}$	$89.94\%_{(\#5632)}$	$90.72\%_{(\#9264)}$	$64.51\%_{(\#8702)}$	$65.73\%_{(\#11908)}$	$86.46\%_{(\#7566)}$	$89.80\%_{(\#9750)}$
$max_{(\#iter)}$	$77.98\%_{(\#5214)}$	$80.05\%_{(\#8690)}$	$92.67\%_{(\#6544)}$	$92.77\%_{(\#9664)}$	$69.48\%_{(\#19923)}$	$69.73\%_{(\#21984)}$	$91.61\%_{(\#6786)}$	$90.30\%_{(\#15678)}$
$avg \pm std$	$77.30\% \pm 0.864$	$78.73\% \pm 0.930$	$91.84\% \pm 0.592$	$92.24\% \pm 0.417$	$67.89\% \pm 0.907$	$68.61\% \pm 0.805$	$90.78\% \pm 0.647$	$90.13\% \pm 0.106$

Table 7 Accuracy results on IRCCyN-MVT, CRCNS and GTEA dataset

	Our transfer method			Bengio's Transfer method [52]		
	IRCCyN-MVT	CRCNS	GTEA	IRCCyN-MVT	CRCNS	GTEA
$max_{(\#iter)}$	92.77%$_{(\#9664)}$	72.034%$_{(\#8702)}$	0.91%$_{(\#9438)}$	92.08%$_{(\#9680)}$	72.83%$_{(\#9389)}$	0.91%$_{(\#9750)}$
avg_{pmstd}	91.08%$_{\pm 3.107}$	68.52%$_{\pm 1.049}$	0.89%$_{\pm 0.008}$	87.48%$_{\pm 7.243}$	69.017%$_{\pm 2.417}$	0.90%$_{\pm 0.019}$

Comparison with [52]

used to predict saliency. In the same manner, the model with the accuracy of 92.77% obtained at the iteration #9664 is used for the IRCCyN-MVT data set. To evaluate our method of saliency prediction, performances were compared with the most popular saliency models from the literature. Two spatial saliency models were chosen: Itti and Koch spatial model [15], Signature Sal [13] (the algorithm introduces a simple image descriptor referred to as the image signature, performing better than Itti model), GBVS (regularized spatial saliency model of Harel [12]) and the spatio-temporal model of Seo [40] built upon optical flow.

In Tables 8 and 9 below, we show the comparison of Deep CNN prediction of pixel-wise saliency maps with the gaze fixations and compare performances with the most popular saliency prediction models (Signature Sal, GBVS, Seo). Hence, in Table 10, we compare our *ChaboNet4k* model with the model of Itti, GBVS and Seo. In Tables 8, 9, 10 and 11 the best performance figures are underlined.

The comparison is given in terms of the widely used AUC metric [20]. Mean value of the metric is given together with standard deviation for some videos. In general it can be stated that spatial models (Signature Sal, GBVS or Itti) performed better in half of the tested videos. This is due to the fact that these videos contain very contrasted areas in the video frames, which attract human gaze. They do not contain areas having an interesting residual motion. Nevertheless, the *ChaboNet4K* model outperforms the Seo model which uses motion features such as optical flow. This shows definitively that the use of a Deep CNN is a way for prediction of visual saliency in video scenes. However, for IRCCyN-MVT data set, see Table 9, despite videos without any motion were set aside, the gain in the proposed model is not very clear due to the complexity of these visual scenes, such as presence of strong contrasts and faces.

In Table 11 below we show the comparison of Deep CNN prediction of pixel-wise saliency maps with the saliency maps built by Wooding's method on gaze fixations and also compare performances with the most popular saliency prediction models form the literature. In general we can state that spatial models perform better (Signature Sal, GBVS). Nevertheless, our 4K model outperforms that one of Seo in four cases on this seven examples. This shows that definitely the use of a Deep CNN is a way for prediction of top-down visual saliency in video scenes.

Table 8 The comparison of AUC metric of gaze fixations 'Gaze-fix' vs predicted saliency 'GBVS', 'SignatureSal' and 'Seo') and our ChaboNet4k for the videos from HOLLYWOOD data set

VideoName	TotFrame=2248	Gaze-fix vs GBVS	Gaze-fix vs SignatureSal	Gaze-fix vs Seo	Gaze-fix vs ChaboNet4k
clipTest56	137	0.76 ± 0.115	0.75 ± 0.086	0.64 ± 0.116	0.77 ± 0.118
clipTest105	154	0.63 ± 0.169	0.57 ± 0.139	0.54 ± 0.123	0.69 ± 0.186
clipTest147	154	0.86 ± 0.093	0.90 ± 0.065	0.70 ± 0.103	0.81 ± 0.146
clipTest250	160	0.74 ± 0.099	0.69 ± 0.110	0.47 ± 0.101	0.71 ± 0.180
clipTest350	66	0.65 ± 0.166	0.68 ± 0.249	0.57 ± 0.124	0.72 ± 0.177
clipTest400	200	0.75 ± 0.127	0.67 ± 0.110	0.60 ± 0.106	0.71 ± 0.146
clipTest451	132	0.70 ± 0.104	0.59 ± 0.074	0.57 ± 0.068	0.63 ± 0.151
clipTest500	166	0.82 ± 0.138	0.84 ± 0.150	0.75 ± 0.152	0.84 ± 0.156
clipTest600	200	0.75 ± 0.131	0.678 ± 0.149	0.53 ± 0.108	0.71 ± 0.180
clipTest650	201	0.72 ± 0.106	0.74 ± 0.087	0.61 ± 0.092	0.70 ± 0.078
ClipTest700	262	0.74 ± 0.128	0.76 ± 0.099	0.50 ± 0.059	0.78 ± 0.092
clipTest800	200	0.70 ± 0.096	0.75 ± 0.071	0.53 ± 0.097	0.66 ± 0.141
ClipTest803	102	0.86 ± 0.106	0.87 ± 0.068	0.73 ± 0.148	0.88 ± 0.078
ClipTest849	114	0.75 ± 0.155	0.91 ± 0.070	0.55 ± 0.122	0.74 ± 0.132

Table 9 The comparison of AUC metric of gaze fixations 'Gaze-fix' vs predicted saliency 'GBVS', 'SignatureSal' and 'Seo') and our ChaboNet4k for the videos from IRCCyN-MVT data set

VideoName	TotFramesNbr	Gaze-fix vs GBVS	Gaze-fix vs SignatureSal	Gaze-fix vs Seo	Gaze-fix vs ChaboNet4k
src02	37	0.68 ± 0.076	0.49 ± 0.083	0.44 ± 0.017	0.48 ± 0.073
src03	28	0.82 ± 0.088	0.87 ± 0.057	0.76 ± 0.091	0.70 ± 0.149
src04	35	0.79 ± 0.058	0.81 ± 0.029	0.59 ± 0.057	0.57 ± 0.135
src05	35	0.73 ± 0.101	0.67 ± 0.122	0.48 ± 0.071	0.53 ± 0.128
src06	36	0.85 ± 0.080	0.71 ± 0.151	0.73 ± 0.148	0.60 ± 0.180
src07	36	0.72 ± 0.070	0.73 ± 0.060	0.57 ± 0.060	0.55 ± 0.135
src10	33	0.87 ± 0.048	0.92 ± 0.043	0.82 ± 0.101	0.60 ± 0.173
src13	35	0.79 ± 0.103	0.75 ± 0.111	0.64 ± 0.144	0.52 ± 0.138
src17	42	0.55 ± 0.092	0.33 ± 0.099	0.45 ± 0.033	0.51 ± 0.098
src19	33	0.76 ± 0.094	0.68 ± 0.086	0.59 ± 0.117	0.75 ± 0.123
src23	40	0.76 ± 0.050	0.69 ± 0.070	0.58 ± 0.067	0.66 ± 0.105
src24	33	0.63 ± 0.071	0.58 ± 0.054	0.55 ± 0.059	0.50 ± 0.052
src27	33	0.59 ± 0.117	0.64 ± 0.091	0.52 ± 0.057	0.54 ± 0.106

Table 10 The comparison of AUC metric of gaze fixations 'Gaze-fix' vs predicted saliency 'GBVS', 'IttiKoch' and 'Seo') and our ChaboNet4k for 5330 frames of CRCNS videos

VideoName	TotFrame=5298	Gaze-fix vs GBVS	Gaze-fix vs IttiKoch	Gaze-fix vs Seo	Gaze-fix vs ChaboNet4k
beverly03	479	0.78 ± 0.151	0.77 ± 0.124	0.66 ± 0.172	0.75 ± 0.153
gamecube02	1819	0.73 ± 0.165	0.74 ± 0.180	0.61 ± 0.179	0.78 ± 0.160
monica05	611	0.75 ± 0.183	0.73 ± 0.158	0.54 ± 0.156	0.80 ± 0.144
standard02	515	0.78 ± 0.132	0.72 ± 0.141	0.61 ± 0.169	0.70 ± 0.156
tv-announce01	418	0.60 ± 0.217	0.64 ± 0.203	0.52 ± 0.206	0.65 ± 0.225
tv-news04	486	0.78 ± 0.169	0.79 ± 0.154	0.61 ± 0.162	0.71 ± 0.158
tv-sports04	970	0.68 ± 0.182	0.69 ± 0.162	0.56 ± 0.193	0.75 ± 0.173

Table 11 The comparison of AUC metric gaze fixations 'Gaze-fix' vs predicted saliency 'GBVS', 'SignatureSal' and 'Seo') and our 4*k_model* for the videos from GTEA dataset

VideoName	TotFrame=7693	Gaze-fix vs GBVS	Gaze-fix vs SignatureSal	Gaze-fix vs Seo	Gaze-fix vs 4k_model
S1_CofHoney_C1_undist	1099	0.811 ± 0.109	0.800 ± 0.091	0.578 ± 0.120	0.732 ± 0.157
S1_Pealate_C1_undist	1199	0.824 ± 0.099	0.846 ± 0.080	0.594 ± 0.139	0.568 ± 0.185
S1_Teac1_undist	1799	0.770 ± 0.127	0.816 ± 0.074	0.567 ± 0.135	0.745 ± 0.211
S2_Cheese_C1_undist	499	0.813 ± 0.116	0.766 ± 0.0138	0.552 ± 0.127	0.643 ± 0.218
S2_Coffee_C1_undist	1599	0.802 ± 0.098	0.720 ± 0.094	0.594 ± 0.116	0.636 ± 0.193
S3_Hotdog_C1_undist	699	0.768 ± 0.103	0.851 ± 0.088	0.585 ± 0.114	0.415 ± 0.145
S3_Peanut_C1_undist	799	0.757 ± 0.115	0.758 ± 0.135	0.519 ± 0.100	0.570 ± 0.162

3.7.5 Conclusion

This study addressed the problem of prediction of visual attention in video content with Deep CNNs. We hypothesized, that adding residual motion maps to primary colour pixel values could model smooth pursuit oculomotor behavior. The performances of prediction with Deep CNNs when different kinds of features are ingested by the network—color pixel values only, color values with residual motion—were compared. As a dynamic content is concerned, the saliency is better predicted with spatio-temporal features (RGB and residual motion) when scenes do not contain distracting contrasts. A new selection process of non-salient patches, based on composition rules of produced content, was proposed. The transfer learning scheme introduced in our previous work and applied to the prediction of saliency on small data sets by fine-tuning parameters pre-trained on a large data set (Hollywood) successfully outperforms the state-of-the-art, i.e. Bengio's method. Finally, a method for building pixel-wise saliency maps, using the probability of patches to be salient, was proposed. The method has to be further improved, as despite the high accuracy obtained by the network-based classification, the pixel-wise model does not always outperform spatial reference models from the literature due to low-level distractors. Further study is needed in order to tackle the distractors problem and address the use of temporal continuity of visual scenes.

Acknowledgements This research has been supported by University of Bordeaux, University of Sfax and the grant UNetBA.

References

1. Borji, A., Itti, L.: State-of-the-art in visual attention modeling. IEEE Trans. Pattern Anal. Mach. Intell. **35**(1), 185–207 (2013)
2. Boulos, F., Chen, W., Parrein, B., Le Callet, P.: Region-of-interest intra prediction for H.264/AVC error resilience. In: IEEE International Conference on Image Processing, Cairo, pp. 3109–3112 (2009)
3. Boulos, F., Chen, W., Parrein, B., Le Callet, P.: Region-of-interest intra prediction for H.264/AVC error resilience. In: IEEE International Conference on Image Processing, Cairo, pp. 3109–3112 (2009). https://hal.archives-ouvertes.fr/hal-00458957
4. Chaabouni, S., Benois-Pineau, J., Ben Amar, C.: Transfer learning with deep networks for saliency prediction in natural video. In: 2016 IEEE International Conference on Image Processing, ICIP 2016, vol. 91 (2016)
5. Chaabouni, S., Benois-Pineau, J., Hadar, O.: Prediction of visual saliency in video with deep CNNs. Proceedings of the SPIE Optical Engineering + Applications, pp. 9711Q-99711Q-14 (2016)
6. Chaabouni, S., Benois-Pineau, J., Tison, F., Ben Amar, C.: Prediction of visual attention with Deep CNN for studies of neurodegenerative diseases. In: 14th International Workshop on Content-Based Multimedia Indexing CBMI 2016, Bucharest, 15–17 June 2016
7. Fathi, A., Ren, X., Rehg, J.M.: Learning to recognize objects in egocentric activities. In: 2011 IEEE Conference on Computer Vision and Pattern Recognition (CVPR), pp. 3281–3288 (2011)
8. Geng, M., Wang, Y., Xiang, T., Tian, Y.: Deep Transfer Learning for Person Re-identification. CoRR abs/1611.05244 (2016). http://arxiv.org/abs/1611.05244

9. Girshick, R.B., Donahue, J., Darrell, T., Malik, J.: Region-based convolutional networks for accurate object detection and segmentation. IEEE Trans. Pattern Anal. Mach. Intell. **38**(1), 142–158 (2016)
10. González-Díaz, I., Buso, V., Benois-Pineau, J.: Perceptual modeling in the problem of active object recognition in visual scenes. Pattern Recogn. **56**, 129–141 (2016)
11. Gygli, M., Soleymani, M.: Analyzing and predicting GIF interestingness. In: Proceedings of the 2016 ACM on Multimedia Conference, MM '16, pp. 122–126. ACM, New York (2016). doi:10.1145/2964284.2967195. http://doi.acm.org/10.1145/2964284.2967195
12. Harel, J., Koch, C., Perona, P.: Graph-based visual saliency. In: Advances in Neural Information Processing Systems, vol. 19, pp. 545–552. MIT Press, Cambridge (2007)
13. Hou, X., Harel, J., Koch, C.: Image signature: highlighting sparse salient regions. IEEE Trans. Pattern Anal. Mach. Intell. **34**(1), 194–201 (2012)
14. Itti, L.: CRCNS data sharing: eye movements during free-viewing of natural videos. In: Collaborative Research in Computational Neuroscience Annual Meeting, Los Angeles, CA (2008)
15. Itti, L., Koch, C., Niebur, E.: A model of saliency-based visual attention for rapid scene analysis. IEEE Trans. Pattern Anal. Mach. Intell. **20**(11), 1254–1259 (1998)
16. Jia, Y., Shelhamer, E., Donahue, J., Karayev, S., Long, J., Girshick, R., Guadarrama, S., Darrell, T.: Caffe: convolutional architecture for fast feature embedding. In: Proceedings of the ACM International Conference on Multimedia, MM '14, Orlando, FL, 03–07 November, 2014, pp. 675–678 (2014)
17. Jiang, Y., Wang, Y., Feng, R., Xue, X., Zheng, Y., Yang, H.: Understanding and predicting interestingness of videos. In: Proceedings of the Twenty-Seventh AAAI Conference on Artificial Intelligence, AAAI'13, pp. 1113–1119. AAAI Press, Palo Alto (2013). http://dl. acm.org/citation.cfm?id=2891460.2891615
18. Krizhevsky, A.: Learning multiple layers of features from tiny images. Ph.D. thesis, University of Toronto (2009)
19. Krizhevsky, A., Sutskever, I., Hinton, G.E.: ImageNet classification with deep convolutional neural networks. In: Pereira, F., Burges, C., Bottou, L., Weinberger, K. (eds.) Advances in Neural Information Processing Systems, vol. 25, pp. 1097–1105. Curran Associates, Inc., Red Hook (2012)
20. Le Meur, O., Baccino, T.: Methods for comparing scanpaths and saliency maps: strengths and weaknesses. Behav. Res. Methods **45**(1), 251–266 (2010)
21. LeCun, Y., Bottou, L., Bengio, Y., Haffner, P.: Gradient-based learning applied to document recognition. Proc. IEEE **86**(11), 2278–2324 (1998)
22. Li, G.Y.Y.: Visual saliency based on multiscale deep features. In: IEEE Conference on Computer Vision and Pattern Recognition, pp. 5455–5463 (2015)
23. Li, G.Y.Y.: Deep contrast learning for salient object detection. In: IEEE Conference on Computer Vision and Pattern Recognition. 1603.01976 (2016)
24. Lin, Y., Kong, S., Wang, D., Zhuang, Y.: Saliency detection within a deep convolutional architecture. In: Cognitive Computing for Augmented Human Intelligence: Papers from the AAAI-14 Workshop, pp. 31–37 (2014)
25. Liu, N.H.J.Z.D.W.S., Liu, T.: Predicting eye fixations using convolutional neural networks. In: IEEE Conference on Computer Vision and Pattern Recognition, pp. 362–370 (2015)
26. Mai, L., Le, H., Niu, Y., Liu, F.: Rule of thirds detection from photograph. In: 2011 IEEE International Symposium on Multimedia (ISM), pp. 91–96 (2011)
27. Manerba, F., Benois-Pineau, J., Leonardi, R.: Extraction of foreground objects from MPEG2 video stream in rough indexing framework. In: Proceedings of the EI2004, Storage and Retrieval Methods and Applications for Multimedia 2004, pp. 50–60 (2004). https://hal. archives-ouvertes.fr/hal-00308051
28. Marat, S., Ho Phuoc, T., Granjon, L., Guyader, N., Pellerin, D., Guérin-Dugué, A.: Modelling spatio-temporal saliency to predict gaze direction for short videos. Int. J. Comput. Vis. **82**(3), 231–243 (2009)

29. Marszałek, M., Laptev, I., Schmid, C.: Actions in context. In: IEEE Conference on Computer Vision & Pattern Recognition (2009)
30. Mathe, S., Sminchisescu, C.: Actions in the eye: dynamic gaze datasets and learnt saliency models for visual recognition. IEEE Trans. Pattern Anal. Mach. Intell. **37**(7), 1408–1424 (2015)
31. Mesnil, G., Dauphin, Y., Glorot, X., Rifai, S., Bengio, Y., Goodfellow, I.J., Lavoie, E., Muller, X., Desjardins, G., Warde-Farley, D., Vincent, P., Courville, A., Bergstra, J.: Unsupervised and transfer learning challenge: a deep learning approach. In: JMLR W& CP: Proceedings of the Unsupervised and Transfer Learning Challenge and Workshop, vol. 27, pp. 97–110 (2012)
32. Nesterov, Y.: A method of solving a convex programming problem with convergence rate $O\left(1/k^2\right)$. Sov. Math. Doklady **27**, 372–376 (1983)
33. Nettleton, D.F., Orriols-Puig, A., Fornells, A.: A study of the effect of different types of noise on the precision of supervised learning techniques. Artif. Intell. Rev. **33**(4), 275–306 (2010). http://dx.doi.org/10.1007/s10462--010-9156-z
34. Pan, J.G.: End-to-end convolutional network for saliency prediction. In: IEEE Conference on Computer Vision and Pattern Recognition 1507.01422 (2015)
35. Pérez de San Roman, P., Benois-Pineau, J., Domenger, J.P., Paclet, F., Cataert, D., De Rugy, A.: Saliency Driven Object recognition in egocentric videos with deep CNN. CoRR abs/1606.07256 (2016). http://arxiv.org/abs/1606.07256
36. Pinto, Y., van der Leij, A.R., Sligte, I.G., Lamme, V.F., Scholte, H.S.: Bottom-up and top-down attention are independent. J. Vis. **13**(3), 16 (2013)
37. Polyak, B.: Introduction to Optimization (Translations Series in Mathematics and Engineering). Optimization Software, New York (1987)
38. Press, W.H., Teukolsky, S.A., Vetterling, W.T., Flannery, B.P.: Numerical Recipes in C: The Art of Scientific Computing, 2nd edn. Cambridge University Press, New York (1992)
39. Reed, S., Lee, H., Anguelov, D., Szegedy, C., Erhan, D., Rabinovich, A.: Training deep neural networks on noisy labels with bootstrapping. CoRR abs/1412.6596 (2014). http://arxiv.org/abs/1412.6596
40. Seo, H.J., Milanfar, P.: Static and space-time visual saliency detection by self-resemblance. J. Vis. **9**(12), 15, 1–27 (2009)
41. Shen, J., Itti, L.: Top-down influences on visual attention during listening are modulated by observer sex. Vis. Res. **65**, 62–76 (2012)
42. Shen, C., Zhao, Q.: Learning to predict eye fixations for semantic contents using multi-layer sparse network. Neurocomputing **138**, 61–68 (2014)
43. Simonyan, K., Vedaldi, A., Zisserman, A.: Deep inside convolutional networks: visualising image classification models and saliency maps. CoRR abs/1312.6034 (2013)
44. Treisman, A.M., Gelade, G.: A feature-integration theory of attention. Cogn. Psychol. **12**(1), 97–136 (1980)
45. Uijlings, J., de Sande, K.V., Gevers, T., Smeulders, A.: Selective search for object recognition. Int. J. Comput. Vis. **104**(2), 154–171 (2013)
46. Vapnik, V.: Principles of risk minimization for learning theory. In: Moody, J.E., Hanson, S.J., Lippmann, R. (eds.) NIPS, pp. 831–838. Morgan Kaufmann, Burlington (1991)
47. Vig, E., Dorr, M., Cox, D.: Large-scale optimization of hierarchical features for saliency prediction in natural images. In: Proceedings of the 2014 IEEE Conference on Computer Vision and Pattern Recognition, CVPR '14, pp. 2798–2805 (2014)
48. Wooding, D.S.: Eye movements of large populations: II. Deriving regions of interest, coverage, and similarity using fixation maps. Behav. Res. Methods Instrum. Comput. **34**(4), 518–528 (2002)
49. Xiao, T., Xia, T., Yang, Y., Huang, C., Wang, X.: Learning from massive noisy labeled data for image classification. In: The IEEE Conference on Computer Vision and Pattern Recognition (CVPR) (2015)
50. Xu, J., Mukherjee, L., Li, Y., Warner, J., Rehg, J.M., Singh, V.: Gaze-enabled egocentric video summarization via constrained submodular maximization. In: Proceedings of the CVPR (2015)

51. Yoon, S., Pavlovic, V.: Sentiment flow for video interestingness prediction. In: Proceedings of the 1st ACM International Workshop on Human Centered Event Understanding from Multimedia, HuEvent 14, pp. 29–34. ACM, New York (2014). doi:10.1145/2660505.2660513
52. Yosinski, J., Clune, J., Bengio, Y., Lipson, H.: How transferable are features in deep neural networks? In: Ghahramani, Z., Welling, M., Cortes, C., Lawrence, N., Weinberger, K. (eds.) Advances in Neural Information Processing Systems, vol. 27, pp. 3320–3328. Curran Associates, Inc., Red Hook (2014)
53. Zeiler, M.D., Fergus, R.: Visualizing and Understanding Convolutional Networks. CoRR abs/1311.2901 (2013)
54. Zen, G., de Juan, P., Song, Y., Jaimes, A.: Mouse activity as an indicator of interestingness in video. In: Proceedings of the 2016 ACM on International Conference on Multimedia Retrieval, ICMR '16, pp. 47–54. ACM, New York (2016). doi:10.1145/2911996.2912005. http://doi.acm. org/10.1145/2911996.2912005
55. Zhou, Z., Khosla, A., Lapedriza, A., Oliva, A., Torralba, A.: Learning deep features for discriminative localization. In: IEEE Conference on Computer Vision and Pattern Recognition 1512.04150 (2015)
56. Zhu, X., Wu, X.: Class noise vs. attribute noise: a quantitative study. Artif. Intell. Rev. **22**(3), 177–210 (2004). doi:10.1007/s10462-004-0751-8
57. Hebb, D.O.: The Organisation of Behaviour: A Neurophysiological Theory, p. 379. Laurence Erlbaum Associates, Inc. Mahwah (2002). ISBN:1-4106-1240-6. Originaly published Willey, New York (1949)
58. Rosenblatt, F., The perception: a probabilistic model for information storage and organization in the brain. Psychol. Rev. **65**(6), 386-408 (1958)

Introducing Image Saliency Information into Content Based Indexing and Emotional Impact Analysis

Syntyche Gbehounou, Thierry Urruty, François Lecellier, and Christine Fernandez-Maloigne

Abstract We propose in this chapter to highlight the impact of visual saliency information in Content Based Image Retrieval (CBIR) systems. We firstly present results of subjective evaluations for emotion analysis with and without use of saliency to reduce the image size and conclude that image reduction to more salient regions implies a better evaluation of emotional impact. We also test eye-tracking methods to validate our results and conclusions. Those experiments lead us to study saliency to improve the image description for indexing purpose. We first show the influence of selecting salient features for relevant image indexing and retrieval. Then, we propose a novel approach that makes use of saliency in an information gain criterion to improve the selection of a visual dictionary in the well-known Bags of Visual Words approach. Our experiments will underline the effectiveness of the proposal. Finally, we present some results on emotional impact recognition using CBIR descriptors and Bags of Visual Words approach with image saliency information.

1 Introduction

Local feature detectors are widely used in the literature as the first step of many systems in image processing domain and its various applications: retrieval, recognition, ... Due to this large usage, lots of state-of-the-art papers are dedicated to local feature evaluation [35, 49]. Their principal aim is to define some criteria to compare existing local features. They often considered using among others the repeatability

S. Gbehounou
Jules SAS, Blagnac, France
e-mail: syntycheg@authentifier.com

T. Urruty • F. Lecellier (✉) • C. Fernandez-Maloigne
Xlim, University of Poitiers, CNRS, Poitiers, France
e-mail: thierry.urruty@univ-poitiers.fr; francois.lecellier@univ-poitiers.fr;
christine.fernandez-maloigne@univ-poitiers.fr

© Springer International Publishing AG 2017
J. Benois-Pineau, P. Le Callet (eds.), *Visual Content Indexing and Retrieval with Psycho-Visual Models*, Multimedia Systems and Applications,
DOI 10.1007/978-3-319-57687-9_4

achieved by the invariance or the robustness, the distinctiveness/informativeness, the locality, the localization accuracy and the efficiency. The importance of these properties mostly depends on the desired application.

One can select a large number of frameworks to extract local features [49, 54]. Tuytelaars et al. [54] have divided the different local feature detectors into three groups:

- **Corner detectors** which define a corner as a point in a 2D image with high curvature.
- **Blob detectors** producing coherent sets of pixels having constant properties. All pixels of a blob can be considered similar to each other in a sense.
- **Region detectors** which are directly or indirectly concerned with image region extraction.

Traditionally after the local feature detection step, feature descriptions are extracted. There is a lot of local descriptors; from different SIFT algorithms [56] to generalized color moments and color moment invariants [36]. Some of these descriptors are high dimensional: 128 dimensions for greyscale SIFT, 384 for color based SIFT. This aspect can be time consuming for applications with a matching step. Thus, different and computationally less expensive solutions were introduced [2, 22]. They often focus on reducing the dimensionality of the feature descriptors.

One of the most well known is SURF (Speeded Up Robust Features) introduced by Bay et al. [2]. It is a detector-descriptor scheme based on Hessian matrix and applied to integral images to make it more efficient than SIFT. According to Ke et al. [22], the average precision of object recognition for art in a museum was better using SURF (64 dimensions) than SIFT or PCA-SIFT. Conclusions were different for others applications, however SURF is still a good trade-off between accuracy and efficiency compared to most descriptors.

Besides descriptor dimensionality reduction approaches, another solution to improve the effectiveness is to filter the most relevant local features. In order to perform such a task, some authors propose to take advantage of saliency maps to select the more relevant features and so to decrease the amount of information to be processed [10, 27, 60]. These methods usually take the information given by the visual attention model at an early stage. Image information will be either discarded or picked as input for next stages based on the saliency values. For example Gao et al. [10] have proposed to rank all the local features according to their saliency values and only the distinctive points are reserved for the matching stage. Zdziarski et al. [60] have also selected their local features according to their saliency value. They have used SURF descriptors which are only computed for pixels with a saliency value above a fixed threshold. Their experiments have shown that the number of features can be reduced without affecting the performance of the classifier. Recently González-Díaz et al. [14] propose to use saliency for object recognition in visual scenes, they obtain state of the art results but manage to reduce computation time.

Research on filtering keypoints based on visual saliency was the starting point of our thinking. We would like to extend the use of visual saliency for local feature selection to more detectors and datasets. Then, at first, we propose in this chapter to evaluate keypoint detectors with respect to the visual saliency of their outputs. Our goal is to quantify the saliency of different local features detected using four of usual local feature detectors: Harris, Harris-Laplace, DOG and FAST. To do this we used four visual attention models [16, 18, 26, 38]. Secondly, we study the impact of selecting local feature values according to their saliency on image retrieval.

The considered features are principally used for image indexing or classification based on their semantic content. However, there is also the possibility to measure other parameters such as the emotional impact. This latter has several applications: film classification, road safety education, advertising or e-commerce by selecting the appropriate image information of the situation. The extraction of emotional impact is an ambitious task since the emotions are not only content related (textures, colours, shapes, objects, ...) but also depend on cultural and personal experiences.

Before giving more details about the emotion classification in the literature, one may need to define what an emotion is and how to classify them. There are two different approaches[28] to perform such a classification:

1. **Discrete approach**: emotional process can be explained with a set of basic or fundamental emotions, innate and common to all human (sadness, anger, happiness, disgust, fear, ...). There is no consensus about the nature and the number of these fundamental emotions.
2. **Dimensional approach**: on the contrary to the previous one, the emotions are considered as the result of fixed number of concepts represented in a dimensional space. The dimensions can be pleasure, arousal or power and vary depending to the needs of the model. The advantage of these models is to define a large number of emotions. But there are some drawbacks because some emotions may be confused or unrepresented in this kind of models.

In the literature, lots of research works are based on the discrete modeling of the emotions; for example those of Paleari and Huet [43], Kaya and Epps [21], Wei et al. [58] or Ou et al. [40–42]. In this chapter, we choose an approach close to the dimensional one in order to obtain a classification into three different classes "Unpleasant", "Neutral" and "Pleasant". Our goal is to summarize the emotions of low semantic images and since the number and nature of emotions in the discrete approach remain uncertain, the selection of specific ones may lead to an incorrect classification.

The emotion analysis is based on many factors. One of the first factors to consider consists in the link between colors and emotions [3, 5, 6, 31, 40–42, 58]. Several of those works have considered emotions associated with particular colors through culture, age, gender or social status influences. Most of the authors agreed to conclude that there is a strong link between emotions and colors. As stated by Ou et al. [40], colors play an important role in decision-making, evoking different emotional feelings. The research on color emotion or color pair emotion is now a well-established area of research. Indeed, in a series of publications, Ou et al. [40–42] studied the relationship between emotions, preferences and colors. They have established a model of emotions associated with colors from psycho-physical experiments.

Another part of the emotional impact analysis of images depends on the facial expression interpretation [43]. Emotions are then associated with facial features (such as eyebrows, lips). This seems to be the easiest way to predict emotions, since facial expressions are common to human and that the basic emotions are relatively easy to evaluate for the human (happy, fear, sad, surprise, . . .). However in this case, the system detects emotions carried by the images and not really the emotions felt by someone looking at these pictures which can depend on its empathy or on the global content of the image (for example, a baby crying in the background of an image does not necessarily implies that the image is sad).

More recently some authors considered the emotion recognition as a CBIR task [32, 53, 59]. They want to use the traditional techniques of image retrieval to extract their emotional impact. To perform such a task, they need to choose some images features such as color, texture or shape descriptors and combine them with a classification system. Those two steps, after a learning step, allow the authors to predict the emotional impact of the images. For example, Wang and Yu [57] used the semantic description of colours to associate an emotional semantic to an image. Liu et al. [28] concludes on texture for emotion classification. They stated that oblique lines could be associated with dynamism and action; horizontal and vertical ones with calm and relaxation.

In the last part of this chapter, we evaluate some low level features well adapted for object recognition and image retrieval [1, 20, 22, 29, 30, 39, 56] and experiment our study on two databases:

- A set of natural images that was assessed during subjective evaluations: Study of Emotion on Natural image databaSE (SENSE) [8];
- A database considered as a reference on psychological studies of emotions: International Affective Picture System (IAPS) [24].

The remainder of this chapter is structured as follows: we provide a brief description of the chosen detectors in Sect. 2. The visual attention model is described in Sect. 3. Then, we present the database and the local features detectors setting in Sect. 4 and the findings on our study of local feature saliency in Sect. 5. The study conducted on the importance of salient pixels for image retrieval is explained in Sect. 6, followed by a discussion on results in Sect. 7. Then in Sect. 8 we extend our results to emotion classification. Finally we conclude and present some future works in Sect. 9.

2 Local Features Detectors

This section presents the four corner and blob detectors we chose for our study. These detectors are widely used in many image processing frameworks [29, 30, 33, 47, 48, 56]. Note that evaluation of region detectors such as MSER is not in the scope of this chapter, mostly due to the detected area complexity. As these areas are not regularly shaped it is difficult to define the saliency value linked to the detected regions.

In the following, we explain briefly the four corner and blob detectors selected for our study.

1. **Harris detector** is a corner detector proposed by Harris and Stephen in 1988 [17]. It is based on the auto-correlation matrix used by Moravec in 1977 [37] and measures the intensity differences between a main window and windows shifted in different directions for each pixel. Harris and Stephen in their improved version proposed to use the matrix M defined by Eq. (1).

$$M(x, y) = \begin{bmatrix} \sum_W I_x(x_k, y_k)^2 & \sum_W I_x(x_k, y_k)I_y(x_k, y_k) \\ \sum_W I_x(x_k, y_k)I_y(x_k, y_k) & \sum_W I_y(x_k, y_k)^2 \end{bmatrix}, \quad (1)$$

where I_x and I_y are the partial derivatives.

Corners are the points with a high value C defined by Eq. (2).

$$C = det(M_{Harris}) - k * trace(M_{Harris})^2. \quad (2)$$

Harris detector is robust to the rotation but suffers from scale changes [49].

2. **Harris-Laplace detector** was proposed by Mikolajczyk and Schmid [33] and resolves the scale invariance problem of the Harris detector. Indeed, the points are firstly detected with a Harris function on multiple scales and then filtered according to a local measure. They use the Laplacian and only points with a maximal response are considered in the scale-space.

3. **Difference of Gaussians (DOG)** was used by Lowe in the SIFT (Scale-Invariant Feature Transform) algorithm [29] to approximate the Laplacian of Gaussian whose kernel is particularly stable in scale-space [34]. The local maxima allow to detect blob structures. This detector is robust to rotation and scale changes.

4. **Features from Accelerated Segment Test (FAST)** was introduced by Rosten and Drummond [47, 48] for the real-time frame-rate applications. It is a high speed feature detector based on the SUSAN (Smallest Univalue Segment Assimilating Nucleus) detector introduced by Smith and Brady [51]. For each pixel, a circular neighborhood with a fixed radius is defined. Only the 16 neighbors as shown on Fig. 1 defined on the circle are handled. p is a local feature if at least 12 contiguous neighbors have an intensity inferior to its value and some threshold.

3 Visual Attention Models

In the last decades, many visual saliency frameworks have been published [10, 18, 25, 62]. Although Borji et al. [4] have proposed an interesting comparative study of 35 different models of the literature. They also mentioned the ambiguity around saliency and attention. Visual attention is a broad concept covering many topics (e.g., bottom-up/top-down, overt/covert, spatial/spatio-temporal). On the other hand it has been mainly referring to bottom-up processes that render certain image regions

Fig. 1 Neighbour definition
for FAST detector

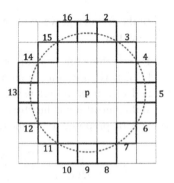

more conspicuous; for instance, image regions with different features from their surroundings (e.g., a single red dot among several blue dots).

Many visual saliency frameworks are inspired from psycho-visual features [18, 25] while others make use of several low-level features in different ways [10, 62].

The works of Itti et al. [18] can be considered as a noticeable example of the bio-inspired models. An input image is processed by the extraction of three conspicuous maps based on low level characteristic computation. These maps are representative of the three main human perceptual channels: color, intensity and orientation before combining them to generate the final saliency map as described on Fig. 2.

Moreover we used the bio-inspired model proposed by Itti et al. to assess the saliency of our local features in our first study.[1]

Figure 3b is the saliency map for Fig. 3a. The lighter pixels are the most salient ones.

4   Experimental Setup

4.1   Databases

For the evaluation of the visual saliency of local features obtained with the four detectors mentioned in the Sect. 2, we use the following image sets:

1. **University of Kentucky Benchmark** proposed by Nistér and Stewénius [39]. In the remainder, we will refer to this dataset as "UKB" to simplify the reading of this chapter. UKB is really interesting because it is a large benchmark composed of 10,200 images grouped in sets of 4 images showing the same object. They present interesting properties for image retrieval: changes of point of view, illumination, rotation, etc.

---

[1]Our saliency values are computed using the Graph-Based Visual Saliency (GBVS) software http://www.klab.caltech.edu/~harel/share/gbvs.php which implements also Itti et al.'s algorithm.

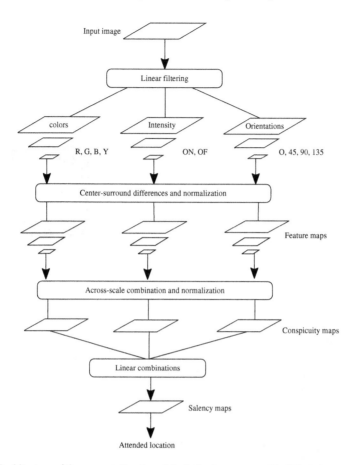

Fig. 2 Architecture of the computational model of attention proposed by Itti et al.

2. **PASCAL Visual Object Classes challenge 2012** [9] called PASCAL VOC2012. This benchmark is composed of 17,125 images. They represent realistic scenes and they are categorized in 20 object classes, e.g. person, bird, airplane, bottle, chair and dining table.
3. **The dataset proposed by Le Meur and Baccino** [25] for saliency study which contains 27 images. We will refer to this dataset as "LeMeur".
4. **The database introduced by Kootstra et al.** [23] composed of 101 images refereed as "Kootstra" in this chapter. It is also used for saliency model evaluation.

We decided to consider two image databases traditionally used for the study of visual saliency in order to quantify a potential link between the ratio of local features detected and the nature of the dataset.

Fig. 3 Example of saliency
map. (**a**) Original image. (**b**)
Saliency map

(a)

(b)

For our second study concerning the filtering of local features detected based on their visual saliency we use two databases:

1. **UKB** already described in this section;
2. **Holidays** provided by Jegou et al. [19]. This dataset is composed of 1491 images with a large variety of scene types. There are 500 groups each representing a distinct object or scene.

4.2 Local Feature Detector Settings

The different parameters chosen for the local feature detectors are the default ones. The idea of this chapter is not to have the best parameters but to use those proposed by the authors that can be considered as a average optimum. We use Opencv implementation of Harris, FAST and DOG detectors. For the last one we considered the keypoints described by SIFT algorithm. For Harris-Laplace detector, we use color descriptor software developed by van de Sande et al. [56].

In our experiments, we use $k = 0.4$ for Harris detector. The Harris threshold was defined equal to 0.05 multiplied by the best corner quality C computed using Eq. (2). The neighborhood size is 3×3 and we use $k = 0.64$. The Harris threshold is set to 10^{-9} and the Laplacian threshold to 0.03. DOG detector settings are the original values proposed by Lowe[29]. The threshold needful in the FAST algorithm to compare the intensity value of the nucleus and its neighbors is set to 30 in our experiments.

5   Local Feature Saliency Study

This section introduces our first evaluation study for the local feature saliency. Our aim is to compare the local feature detectors with respect to the ratio of visual salient features they produce. To do so, we need to find a threshold t in order to classify a local feature as salient.

The different visual saliency values that we obtained are normalized between 0 and 1. Then, an instinctive threshold might be 0.5. However we preferred to define a threshold that conserves an easy recognition for human of the scenes/different objects with the minimal number of pixels. We made a small user study to evaluate different values of thresholds. The different images of Fig. 4 show the results with three values of threshold: 0.3, 0.4 and 0.5. We chose the threshold equal to 0.4 as it is the minimal value where most users in our study recognized the objects in most of the images. Thus we consider that a local feature is salient if the saliency on its position is greater than or equal to 0.4.

Before studying the local feature saliency, we have tested if there is a significant difference between the studied databases related to the ratio of salient pixels they contain. Detailed results of our experiments are not presented here, however we summarize them in the Table 1. For this study we consider the median (the second

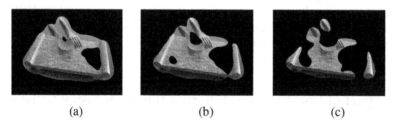

| | (a) | (b) | (c) |

Fig. 4   Figure 3a quantised with different saliency thresholds. (**a**) $t = 0.3$, (**b**) $t = 0.4$, (**c**) $t = 0.5$

Table 1   Distribution of the salient features for each detector and dataset. Bold values correspond to best scores

		LeMeur	Kootstra	UKB	PascalVOC12	Average
Harris	Median	**48.72**	**42.91**	**56.71**	50	**49.59**
	Inter-quartile	37.41	28.34	40.18	30.87	34.2
FAST	Median	34.76	33.29	43.38	37.70	**37.28**
	Inter-quartile	21.66	21.89	37.98	25.75	26.82
DOG	Median	30.71	31.84	41.13	36.42	**35.03**
	Inter-quartile	12.53	21.01	33.50	22.45	22.37
H-L*	Median	**26.80**	**29.38**	**34.95**	**32.46**	**30.90**
	Inter-quartile	14.25	21.04	30.55	20.05	21.47

H-L* detector corresponds to Harris-Laplace detector. The median and inter-quartile values are percentages

quartile) and the inter-quartile intervals (the difference between the third and the first quartiles). We notice that LeMeur and Kootstra databases [23, 25] specially proposed for saliency studies have in average more salient pixels. However the four databases contain a lot of non-salient information. The highest median values are observed for the interval $[0, 0.1]$: >30% for LeMeur, >20% for Kootstra, >40% for UKB and ~30% for Pascal VOC2012.

If we consider the average of different medians, Harris detector with 49.59% appears as the one that extracts the most salient features despite the nature of the images of these bases. It could be explained by the fact that it measures intensity differences in the image space that can be interpreted as a measure of contrast useful for visual saliency. The difference between the three other detectors is minimal. The results of Harris-Laplace and DoG could be explained by the scale changes they incorporate. Despite its good results for image retrieval and object categorization [61], Harris-Laplace detector selects less salient local features.

Our study of local feature detector saliency confirms that they do not detect the most salient information.[2] These observations are comprehensible since the local detectors used and the visual saliency models are not based on the same concept. The fact that the Harris detector produces more salient corners is interesting. It may advise to use Harris detector if any scale change invariant is needed for local feature filtering.

In the following, we focus on Harris-Laplace, and assess the importance of the local features according to their visual attention for image retrieval on UKB. We no longer consider the previous threshold $t = 0.4$. The local features are ranked according to their saliency value.

6   Impact of Local Feature Filtering Based on Visual Saliency

In this section, we study the impact of filtering the local features according to their saliency value before the image signature computation. To do so, we consider two local descriptors:

1. **Colour Moment Invariants (CMI)** descriptor [36] that describes local features obtained with one of the following detectors:

   - Harris-Laplace detector;
   - a dense detection scheme.

   We choose to use the Bag of Visual Words representation [7, 50] which is widely used to create image signatures and to index images from UKB dataset. The visual codebook we have computed has been introduced in our previous work [55]. In this work, we proposed a random iterative visual word selection

---

[2]Those from the chosen detectors.

algorithm and their results are interesting for this descriptor using only 300 visual words. The visual codebook is computed with Pascal VOC2012 [9].

2. **SIFT** [29] and the local features are detected with:

- a grid-dense detection scheme for UKB dataset images;
- Hessian-Affine detector for INRIA Holidays images.[3]

For this descriptor, we also use the Bag of words model as visual signature with:

- 10,000 visual words computed with *K-means* algorithm for UKB. The visual codebook is computed with Pascal VOC2012 [9].
- 10,000 and 200,000 visual words used by Jegou et al. [19].

For the UKB retrieval results, a score of 4 means that the system returns all correct neighbors for the 10,200 images. In fact, the database contains a set of four identical images with different transformations. In this case the query is included in the score calculation. Concerning Holidays, we compute the mean Average Precision (mAP) as detailed in [46].

As we previously mentioned we rank the local features according to their saliency values. For our study, we filtered local features with two different configurations:

- "More salient": the more salient features are removed;
- "Less salient": the less salient features are removed.

The image signature is then built with the residual local features after filtering. The full algorithm is presented on Fig. 5.

The results for UKB are presented in Fig. 6a for CMI and Fig. 6b for SIFT.

The results clearly highlight the importance of salient local features for the retrieval. For example, removing 50% of the most salient features with SIFT induces a loss of retrieval accuracy of 8.25% against 2.75% for the 50% of the least salient ones. The results are similar for CMI: -20% when filtering 50% of the most salient features and -3.55% otherwise.

Whatever the descriptor, our findings go in the same direction as the previous for UKB: local features can be filtered according to their saliency without affecting significantly the retrieval results. The most salient local features are very discriminative to have an accurate retrieval. These conclusions are valid for Harris-Laplace detector. We have tested these assumptions with another keypoint detection scheme: grid-dense quantization. Indeed increasing research works consider this feature selection approach [15, 45] which poses a problem: the large number of keypoints affecting the efficiency of the retrieval. If the previous results are confirmed then the visual attention can be used to filter local keypoints regardless the descriptor and the feature detector.

---

[3]We used the descriptors provided by Jegou et al. available at http://lear.inrialpes.fr/people/jegou/data.php.

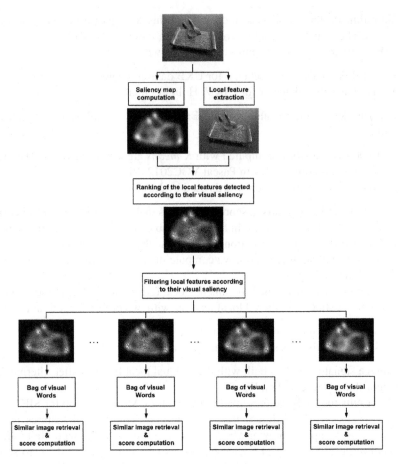

Fig. 5 The used algorithm to perform local feature filtering based on visual saliency. On the last step of the algorithm the four images correspond to different percentages of removed features with the lowest saliency values

For our grid-dense scheme we selected a pixel on a grid of 15*15 every 5 pixels producing ~11,000 local features per image of size 800*600.

The results for example, for UKB are presented in Fig. 7a for CMI and Fig. 7b for SIFT.

Filtering dense local features with respect to their visual saliency values has the same impact as previous filtering (Fig. 6). We can conclude that using CMI on UKB, saliency filtering does not impact in a negative way the retrieval results respecting an adequate threshold. Moreover, our results show that the precision score increases while deleting up to 50% of least salient local features: +1.25 to +2.5%. This highlights that using too many non salient keypoints has the same effect as introducing noise leading to a small decrease in the retrieval precision. With a grid-dense selection and filtering by visual saliency value, CMI shows that

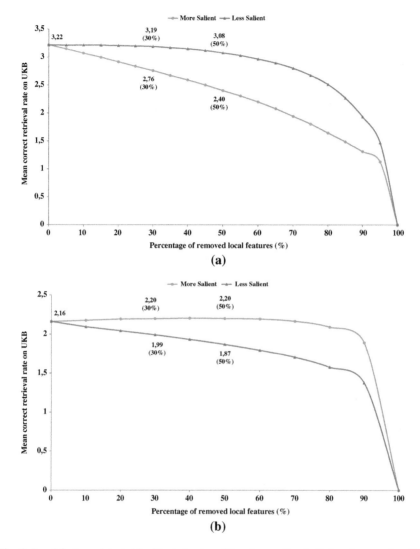

Fig. 6 Local features detected by Harris-Laplace filtered according to their saliency value. K is the size of the visual codebook. (**a**) CMI: K= 300. (**b**) SIFT: K= 10,000

salient local features are particularly important as so far as the difference between the two curves on Fig. 7a is 19.25% for 30% and 31% for 50%.

Our different results highlight the importance of salient local features for a correct retrieval on UKB both with Harris-Laplace detection and dense selection.

To validate the independence to the database we conducted the same evaluations on Holidays. The impact on the retrieval is measured with the mean Average Precision (mAP) scores represented in Fig. 8. The observations are similar: the salient local features lead to better retrieval. The difference between deleting less salient and more salient on Holidays (∼5%) is less important than those observed

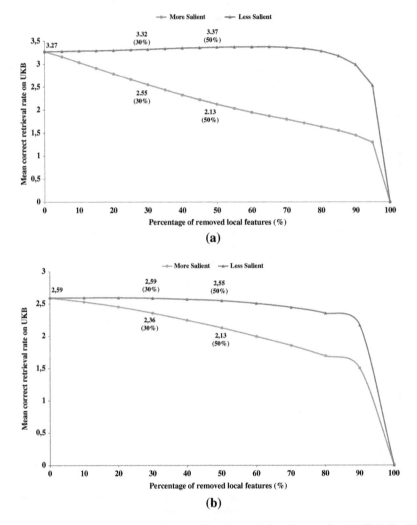

Fig. 7 Filtering dense selected local features according to their saliency value. (**a**) CMI: K= 300, (**b**) SIFT: K= 10,000

on UKB. It supposes that the local salient feature importance for retrieval depends on the database and the descriptor.

These first results obtained with Itti et al.'s model [18] are also confirmed with the three following models:

1. Graph Based Visual Saliency (GBVS) which is a bottom-up visual saliency model proposed by Harel et al. [16];
2. Prediction of INterest point Saliency (PINS) proposed by Nauge et al. [38] and based on the correlation between interest points and gaze points;

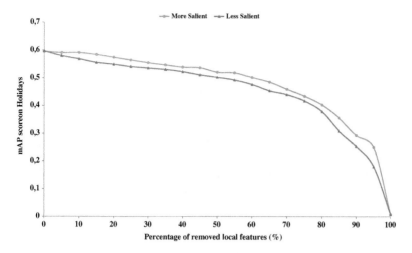

Fig. 8 mAP scores after filtering local features according to their saliency values on Holidays

Table 2 Computation of the area between the curves of deleting most salient and less salient local features. Bold values correspond to best scores

Databases	Descriptors	Saliency model	Area value
UKB	CMI	Itti et al.	**10.06**
	K=300	GBVS	9.11
		PINS	8.95
		Yin Li	8.85
	SIFT	Itti et al.	3.61
	K=10,000	GBVS	**4.34**
		PINS	3.54
		Yin Li	3.32
Holidays	SIFT	Itti et al.	0.63
	K=10,000	GBVS	**1.65**
		PINS	0.40
		Yin Li	0.51
	SIFT	Itti et al.	0.51
	K=200,000	GBVS	**2.28**
		PINS	1.20
		Yin Li	0.62

3. The visual saliency model based on conditional entropy introduced by Li et al. [26].

We give in Table 2 the value of the area (illustrated in Fig. 7b) between the two curves of deleting local features according to their visual saliency; most salient ones on the one hand, and in the other the less salient.

Let $\mathscr{C}_1$ and $\mathscr{C}_2$, two curves, the area value, $\mathscr{A}$ is obtained with Eq. (3).

$$\mathscr{A} = \sum_I |\, \mathscr{C}_1(i) - \mathscr{C}_2(i) \,|, \tag{3}$$

$|\, x \,|$ is the absolute value of x, i is the different value of the percentage of local features deleted according to their visual saliency.

The evaluations are conducted on UKB and Holidays.

We can see that the area between the two curves has not the same size according to the used saliency model and the local feature descriptor considered. We do not compare the area value according to the descriptors and the databases but its size behavior. If the area value is high, it indicates a significant difference between the two curves. It means that deleting the more salient features induces an important decrease of the results.

Except for CMI descriptors on UKB, the area values of GBVS model are the highest for the two datasets. It means that the visually salient local features defined with this model have an important weight in the retrieval process using BoVW signature.

Figure 9 presents the results of comparison of the results obtained according to the features and the saliency models when deleting the less salient local features. There is no significant difference before 50%. The four models that we chose offer equivalent accuracy. Then, the choice of the suitable saliency model can be based on the filtering threshold. Anyway GBVS seems to be more adapted to our study.

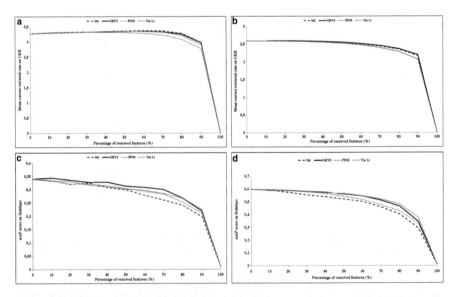

Fig. 9 The results obtained deleting less salient local features. (**a**) UKB-CMI, (**b**) UKB-SIFT, (**c**) Holidays-SIFT 10,000, (**d**) Holidays-SIFT 200,000

Even if this study shows that the results are much better with GBVS, the main conclusion of our experiments is the importance of filtering local keypoints with the saliency value.

7 Discussion

The different evaluations we have conducted about the impact of selecting local features according to their visual saliency show that:

- this filtering does not significantly affect the results;
- the salient local features are important for image retrieval.

The results presented in this chapter confirm that the visual saliency can be useful and helpful for a more accurate image retrieval. Especially, they highlight that it can easily enhance dense selection results:

- by deleting a certain proportion of less salient keypoints;
- by reducing the quantity of local features without negative impact for the retrieval score.

The different detectors studied do not extract important quantity of salient information. This observation has among others two important outcomes:

1. Visual saliency usage should be an additional process in the whole framework of image retrieval, while indexing and retrieving images; the most of available tools today do not include the saliency information.
2. Adding more salient local features could create more accurate signatures for most of usual images, improving at the same time the retrieval process.

We have just started our investigations on the second outcome by replacing the less salient local features detected by more salient ones. First results obtained with this new research investigation were conducted on UKB dataset using CMI descriptor. We add salient local features from the dense CMI to the Harris Laplace CMI. The results presented in Fig. 10 confirm our hypothesis.

Replacing less salient local features by the most salient ones from dense detection seems to be a good compromise to use visual saliency in order to improve the retrieval. Indeed the score increases by 3.75% with 20% of replaced keypoints. Of course, this improvement is small but it shows the importance to research deeper this way as all results were improved.

8 Emotion Classification

In this section we applied the previous image feature detectors to emotion classification. In order to perform such a classification, one needs to use a specific database constructed for this application. There are many datasets proposed in

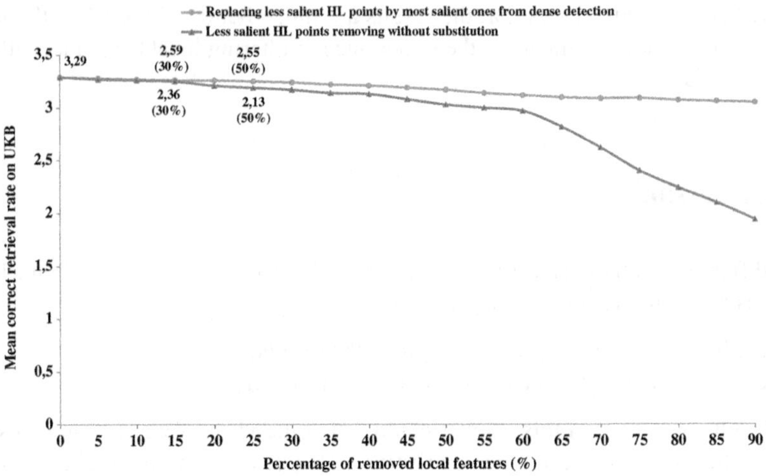

Fig. 10 Replacing the less salient points detected buy Harris-Laplace by the most salient selected with dense quantization

the literature, however one of them appears to be a reference in psychological studies, the International Affective Picture System (IAPS). It is a database composed of photographs used in emotion research. This dataset has been developed and improved since the late 1980s at NIMH Center for Emotion and Attention (CSEA) at the University of Florida [24]. Since it is a well known database, many papers consider this base to compare their results to the literature [28, 32, 59].

IAPS is a very large database with more than 1100 images and still evolving but it presents also very strong emotional content and very semantic one. So it appears that the emotional impact of those images is very straightforward and does not reflect the most frequent images in real life. We then propose another base, named SENSE (Study of Emotion on Natural image databaSE) [8, 12]. It is a low semantic, natural and diversified database containing 350 images free to use for research and publication. It is composed of animals, food and drink, landscapes, historic and tourist monuments. It contains low semantic images because they minimize the potential interactions between emotions on following images during subjective evaluations. This database has been rated by two different ways:

1. SENSE1 composed of the whole images assessed by 1741 participants;
2. SENSE2 composed of Regions of Interest (ROI) of the images obtained for each image with an hybrid saliency model proposed by Perreira Da Silva et al. [44]. It is based on the classical algorithm proposed by Itti [18] and adds a competitive approach to enhance the saliency map obtained: a preys/predators system. The authors show that despite the non deterministic behavior of preys/predators equations, the system exhibits interesting properties of stability, reproducibility and reactiveness while allowing a fast and efficient exploration of the scene.

We applied the same optimal parameters used by the authors to create the thumbnails of the images of our database. This second database has been rated by 1166 participants.

8.1   Classification Results

In this section we present our results for local and global feature evaluation for emotional impact recognition. At first we discuss about those obtained on SENSE and IAPS. To finish we compare those from IAPS to some baselines from the literature.

8.1.1   Results on SENSE1 and IAPS

In a previous work [13], we have shown that CBIR local and global descriptors can be used to define the emotional impact of an image. In Table 3, we summarize the results obtained after classification in Positive and Negative emotion class for each descriptor. In this table:

- WA4 and WA5 respectively mean Wave Atoms Scale 4 and Wave Atoms Scale 5.
- CM denotes Color Moments and CMI, Color Moment Invariants.
- OpSIFT means OpponentSIFT.

For the results, we use the notation Dataset_Visual codebook to resume the different configurations we have tested. Then in SENSE1_I configuration, the visual signatures (Bags of Visual Words) of the images of SENSE1 are computed using the visual vocabulary from IAPS. The different configurations allow us to determine whether or not the results are dependant from the image database used to create the visual dictionary.

The different features do not have the same behaviors on predicting emotions in the different configurations tested. For example, SIFT have approximately the same results for negative and positive emotions on IAPS and SENSE regardless the vocabulary changes. On the contrary, CMI and WA4, for example, seem more adequate for negative images with at least 50%.

Overall, the visual dictionary has little impact on the behavior of descriptors for classification for SENSE and IAPS. However, CM descriptors for example, are affected. The rate of recognized negative images is significantly higher with codebook from IAPS (+70% for SENSE images and +20% for IAPS images). The opposite effect is observed for positive images: −34% for SENSE images and −17% for IAPS images. This illustrates very well the impact of the variability of the database. Indeed, IAPS contains a lot of negative images: the dictionary built with this dataset allows to better recognize negative emotions. Building the visual dictionary with SENSE improves recognition of positive images since this base contains a lot. We also conclude that the negative images are much easier to recognize in the two databases that we have chosen.

Table 3 Classification rates after classification for each descriptor

Descriptors		Nature of emotions	Configuration base de test_Dictionnaire visuel				Average (%)
			SENSE1_S (%)	SENSE1_I (%)	IAPS_S (%)	IAPS_I (%)	
Global descriptors	Colours	Negative	40	70	85.25	78.69	68.49
		Positive	80.21	43.75	27.59	29.31	45.22
	WA4	Negative	50	50	77.05	68.85	61.48
		Positive	30.21	52.08	20.69	32.76	33.94
	WA5	Negative	30	60	57.38	44.26	47.91
		Positive	50	65.62	41.38	58.62	53.91
	GIST	Negative	90	40	42.62	62.3	58.73
		Positive	27.08	61.46	56.90	37.93	45.84
Local descriptors	CM	Negative	10	80	40.98	60.66	47.91
		Positive	88.54	54.17	68.97	51.72	65.85
	CMI	Negative	70	60	60.66	86.89	69.39
		Positive	57.29	58.33	55.17	27.59	49.60
	SIFT	Negative	70	70	52.46	60.66	63.28
		Positive	56.25	52.08	51.72	53.45	53.38
	CSIFT	Negative	80	90	73.77	67.21	77.75
		Positive	50	54.17	53.45	50	51.91
	OpSIFT	Negative	60	60	65.57	60.66	61.56
		Positive	47.92	52.08	48.28	63.79	53.02
	Average	Negative	55.55	64.44	61.75	65.58	61.83
		Positive	54.16	54.86	47.13	45.02	50.29

Table 4 Comparison of correct average classification rates on SENSE and IAPS before and after fusion with Majority Voting

		Before fusion (%)	After fusion (%)
SENSE1_S	Negative	55.56	60
	Positive	54.17	57.29
	Average	54.86	57.55
SENSE1_I	Negative	64.44	90
	Positive	54.86	64.58
	Average	59.65	66.98
IAPS_S	Negative	61.75	75.41
	Positive	47.13	41.38
	Average	54.44	58.82
IAPS_I	Negative	65.58	77.05
	Positive	45.02	46.55
	Average	55.30	62.18

To study the complementarity of the chosen features, we have evaluated their result combination with Majority Voting. In Table 4 we compare the classification rates before and after fusion.

There is a significant improvement after the fusion. For example, the recognition of negative images is impacted positively by 15% on average. Besides the best classification rates are obtained after merging using the dictionary built from IAPS. This conclusion is also valid for positive images. For both configurations (SENSE1_I and IAPS_I) before the fusion, 54.86 and 45.02% positive images were recognized against 64.58 and 46.55% after. If we generally consider these results after fusion, we see that they have been improved especially on our image database, independently of visual dictionaries and emotions:

- $\sim$ +15% for negative images and $\sim$ +6% for positive ones;
- $\sim$ +17% with the codebook from IAPS and $\sim$ +3.7% with the codebook from SENSE1.

Note that for IAPS, positive image average results are lower than a simple random selection. This can be due to the database or simply because negative images are easy to recognize.

8.1.2   Comparison with Literature on IAPS

In order to validate our approach, we chose to compare our results on IAPS to three different papers on the literature:

- Wei et al. [58] are using a semantic description of the images for emotional classification of images. The authors chose a discrete modeling of emotions in eight classes: "Anger", "Despair", "Interest", "Irritation", "Joy", "Fun", "Pride" and "Sadness". The classification rates they obtained vary from 33.25% for the class "Pleasure" to 50.25% for "Joy."

- Liu et al. [28] have proposed a system based on color, texture, shape features and a set of semantic descriptors based on colors. Their results on IAPS are 54.70% in average after a fusion with the Theory of evidence and 52.05% with MV fusion.
- Machajdik et al. [32] are using color, texture, composition and content descriptors. They chose a discrete categorization in eight classes: "Amusement", "Anger", "Awe", "Contentment", "Disgust", "Excitement", "Fear" and "Sad". The average rates of classification vary from 55 to 65%. The lowest rate is obtained for the class "Contentement" and the highest for the class "Awe".

If we compare our results with those three, we clearly see that our method compete with them since we obtain classification rates from 54.44 to 62.18%. The goal of this study is then correctly achieved by proving that the use of classical features of CBIR can improve the performance of emotional impact classification.

8.1.3 Consideration of the Visual Saliency: SENSE2 Image Classification

The results from the subjective evaluations SENSE2 show that the regions of interest evaluation is equivalent to the full image evaluation [11]. So we decided to substitute the SENSE1 images by those used during SENSE2. The results presented here are with respect to the local descriptors. Because of the variable sizes of the ROI images (from 3 to 100% of the size of the original images) we chose a grid-dense selection. For effective comparison, we also consider a grid-dense selection for SENSE1. The average classification rates are shown in Fig. 11. We notice that for a majority of descriptors, limiting the informative area to the salient region improves the results. The results by local keypoints descriptor are summarized in Fig. 12.

An improvement is made for negative and positive classes when using SENSE2. The usage of the regions of interest obtained with visual saliency model improves the results for positive and negative images especially for SIFT and OpponentSIFT: +10%. The previous conclusions about SIFT based descriptors remain valid.

9 Conclusion and Future Works

In this chapter we have evaluated the saliency for four local features detectors: Harris, Harris-Laplace, DOG and FAST. The threshold to decide that a point is salient has been fixed after conducting a user study. In fact, this threshold allows to easily recognize the different objects in the image. We choose to study the behavior of local feature saliency on two databases used for image retrieval and categorization and two others for saliency studies. The observations are globally similar:

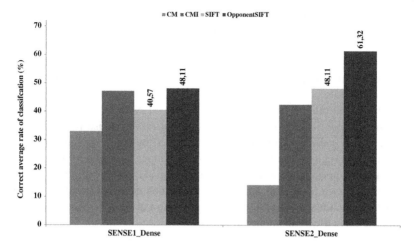

Fig. 11 Average classification rates obtained for SENSE2 and SENSE1 with a dense selection of local features

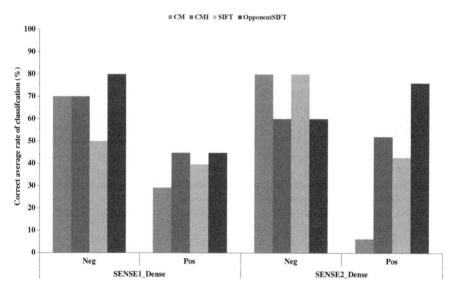

Fig. 12 Classification rates obtained for SENSE2 and SENSE1 for 2 class classification by feature

- the larger part of the pixel saliency values are ≤ 0.1;
- Harris detector produces the most salient local features according to the median values and in contrast Harris-Laplace features are globally the less salient.

The results of local feature filtering according to the saliency value highlight the importance of salient keypoints for retrieval on UKB and Holidays datasets regardless the detection method (Harris-Laplace, Hessian-Affine and dense selection) and the saliency model used among the four we tested. These conclusions are consistent with previous studies from the literature and allow to consider different perspectives which include finding the good proportion for the filtering of the less salient local features without affecting the retrieval results. Another perspective of our study is to consider top-down visual saliency model as the four tested are bottom-up and to compare the results.

Concerning emotional impact recognition, for SENSE2, we used a bounding box of the different salient areas, we think that a more precise region definition must be studied: defining different regions of interest by image and determining the emotion of each region. The final emotion of the image could be a combination of the negative and positive areas thereby resuming the idea of the harmony of a multi-colored image from Solli et al. [52]. The fusion method could be found based on subjective evaluations to find the correct weighting between negative and positive "patches" to form the final emotional impact.

References

1. Abdel-Hakim, A.E., Farag, A.A.: CSIFT: A SIFT Descriptor with color invariant character-istics. In: Proceedings of the IEEE Computer Society Conference on Computer Vision and Pattern Recognition (2006)
2. Bay, H., Tuytelaars, T., Van Gool, L.: Surf: speeded up robust features. Lecture Notes in Computer Science, vol. 3951, pp. 404–417. Springer, Berlin (2006)
3. Beke, L., Kutas, G., Kwak, Y., Sung, G.Y., Park, D., Bodrogi, P.: Color preference of aged observers compared to young observers. Color. Res. Appl. **33**(5), 381–394 (2008)
4. Borji, A., Sihite, D., Itti, L.: Quantitative analysis of human-model agreement in visual saliency modeling: A comparative study. IEEE Trans. Image Process. **22**(1), 55–69 (2013)
5. Boyatziz, C., Varghese, R.: Children's emotional associations with colors. J. Gen. Psychol. **155**, 77–85 (1993)
6. Bradley, M.M., Codispoti, M., Sabatinelli, D., Lang, P.J.: Emotion and motivation ii: sex differences in picture processing. Emotion **1**(3), 300–319 (2001)
7. Csurka, G., Bray, C., Dance, C., Fan, L.: Visual categorization with bags of keypoints. In: Workshop on Statistical Learning in Computer Vision, ECCV, pp. 1–22 (2004)
8. Denis, P., Courboulay, V., Revel, A., Gbehounou, S., Lecellier, F., Fernandez-Maloigne, C.: Improvement of natural image search engines results by emotional filtering. EAI Endorsed Trans. Creative Technologies **3**(6), e4 (2016). https://hal.archives-ouvertes.fr/hal-01261237
9. Everingham, M., Van Gool, L., Williams, C.K.I., Winn, J., Zisserman, A.: The pascal visual object classes (VOC) challenge. Int. J. Comput. Vis. **88**(2), 303–338 (2010)
10. Gao, K., Lin, S., Zhang, Y., Tang, S., Ren, H.: Attention model based sift keypoints filtration for image retrieval. In: Proceedings of IEEE International Conference on Computer and Information Science, pp. 191–196 (2008)
11. Gbèhounou, S., Lecellier, F., Fernandez-Maloigne, C., Courboulay, V.: Can Salient Interest Regions Resume Emotional Impact of an Image?, pp. 515–522 Springer, Berlin (2013). doi:10.1007/978-3-642-40261-6_62. http://dx.doi.org/10.1007/978-3-642-40261-6_62
12. Gbehounou, S., Lecellier, F., Fernandez-Maloigne, C.: Evaluation of local and global des-criptors for emotional impact recognition. J. Vis. Commun. Image Represent. **38**, 276–283 (2016)
13. Gbèhounou, S., Lecellier, F., Fernandez-Maloigne, C.: Evaluation of local and global des-criptors for emotional impact recognition. J. Vis. Commun. Image Represent. **38**(C), 276–283 (2016). doi:10.1016/j.jvcir.2016.03.009. http://dx.doi.org/10.1016/j.jvcir.2016.03.009

14. González-Díaz, I., Buso, V., Benois-Pineau, J.: Perceptual modeling in the problem of active object recognition in visual scenes. Pattern Recognition **56**, 129–141 (2016). doi:10.1016/j.patcog.2016.03.007. http://dx.doi.org/10.1016/j.patcog.2016.03.007

15. Gordoa, A., Rodriguez-Serrano, J.A., Perronnin, F., Valveny, E.: Leveraging category-level labels for instance-level image retrieval. In: Proceedings of the IEEE Conference on Computer Vision and Pattern Recognition, pp. 3045–3052 (2012)

16. Harel, J., Koch, C., Perona, P.: Graph-based visual saliency. In: Advances in Neural Information Processing Systems, pp. 545–552. MIT Press, Cambridge (2007)

17. Harris, C., Stephens, M.: A combined corner and edge detector. In: Proceedings of the 4th Alvey Vision Conference, pp. 147–151 (1988)

18. Itti, L., Koch, C., Niebur, E.: A model of saliency-based visual attention for rapid scene analysis. IEEE Trans. Pattern Anal. Mach. Intell. **20**(11), 1254–1259 (1998)

19. Jegou, H., Douze, M., Schmid, C.: Hamming embedding and weak geometric consistency for large scale image search. In: Proceedings of the 10th European Conference on Computer Vision: Part I, ECCV'08, pp. 304–317. Springer, Berlin (2008)

20. Jégou, H., Douze, M., Schmid, C., Pérez, P.: Aggregating local descriptors into a compact image representation. In: Proceedings of the 23rd IEEE Conference on Computer Vision & Pattern Recognition, pp. 3304–3311. IEEE Computer Society, New York (2010)

21. Kaya, N., Epps, H.H.: Color-emotion associations: Past experience and personal preference. In: AIC Colors and Paints, Interim Meeting of the International Color Association (2004)

22. Ke, Y., Sukthankar, R.: PCA-SIFT: a more distinctive representation for local image descriptors. In: Proceedings of the IEEE Computer Society Conference on Computer Vision and Pattern Recognition, vol. 2, pp. 506–513 (2004)

23. Kootstra, G., de Boer, B., Schomaker, L.: Predicting eye fixations on complex visual stimuli using local symmetry. Cogn. Comput. **3**(1), 223–240 (2011)

24. Lang, P.J., Bradley, M.M., Cuthbert, B.N.: International affective picture system (IAPS): affective ratings of pictures and instruction manual. technical report A-8. Technical Report, University of Florida (2008)

25. Le Meur, O., Le Callet, P., Barba, D., Thoreau, D.: A coherent computational approach to model bottom-up visual attention. IEEE Trans. Pattern Anal. Mach. Intell. **28**(5), 802–817 (2006)

26. Li, Y., Zhou, Y., Yan, J., Niu, Z., Yang, J.: Visual saliency based on conditional entropy. Lecture Notes in Computer Science, vol. 5994, pp. 246–257. Springer, Berlin (2010)

27. Liu, W., Xu, W., Li, L.: A tentative study of visual attention-based salient features for image retrieval. In: Proceedings of the 7th World Congress on Intelligent Control and Automation, pp. 7635–7639 (2008)

28. Liu, N., Dellandréa, E., Chen, L.: Evaluation of features and combination approaches for the classification of emotional semantics in images. In: International Conference on Computer Vision Theory and Applications (2011)

29. Lowe, D.G.: Object recognition from local scale-invariant features. In: International Conference on Computer Vision, vol. 2, pp. 1150–1157 (1999)

30. Lowe, D.G.: Distinctive image features from scale-invariant keypoints. Int. J. Comput. Vis. **60**, 91–110 (2004)

31. Lucassen, M.P., Gevers, T., Gijsenij, A.: Adding texture to color: quantitative analysis of color emotions. In: Proceedings of CGIV (2010)

32. Machajdik, J., Hanbury, A.: Affective image classification using features inspired by psychology and art theory. In: Proceedings of the international conference on Multimedia, pp. 83–92 (2010)

33. Mikolajczyk, K., Schmid, C.: Indexing based on scale invariant interest points. In: Proceedings of the 8th IEEE International Conference on Computer Vision, vol. 1, pp. 525–531 (2001)

34. Mikolajczyk, K., Schmid, C.: An affine invariant interest point detector. In: Computer Vision-ECCV. Lecture Notes in Computer Science, vol. 2350, pp. 128–142. Springer, Berlin (2002)

35. Mikolajczyk, K., Tuytelaars, T., Schmid, C., Zisserman, A., Matas, J., Schaffalitzky, F., Kadir, T., Van Gool, L.: A comparison of affine region detectors. Int. J. Comput. Vision **65**(1-2), 43–72 (2005)

36. Mindru, F., Tuytelaars, T., Van Gool, L., Moons, T.: Moment invariants for recognition under changing viewpoint and illumination. Comput. Vis. Image Underst. **94**(1–3), 3–27 (2004)
37. Moravec, H.P.: Towards automatic visual obstacle avoidance. In: Proceedings of the 5th International Joint Conference on Artificial Intelligence, vol. 2, pp. 584–584. Morgan Kaufmann, San Francisco (1977)
38. Nauge, M., Larabi, M.C., Fernandez-Maloigne, C.: A statistical study of the correlation between interest points and gaze points. In: Human Vision and Electronic Imaging, p. 12. Burlingame (2012)
39. Nistér, D., Stewénius, H.: Scalable recognition with a vocabulary tree. In: Proceedings of the IEEE Conference on Computer Vision and Pattern Recognition, vol. 2, pp. 2161–2168 (2006)
40. Ou, L.C., Luo, M.R., Woodcock, A., Wright, A.: A study of colour emotion and colour preference. part i: Colour emotions for single colours. Color. Res. Appl. **29**(3), 232–240 (2004)
41. Ou, L.C., Luo, M.R., Woodcock, A., Wright, A.: A study of colour emotion and colour preference. part ii: Colour emotions for two-colour combinations. Color. Res. Appl. **29**(4), 292–298 (2004)
42. Ou, L.C., Luo, M.R., Woodcock, A., Wright, A.: A study of colour emotion and colour preference. Part iii: colour preference modeling. Color. Res. Appl. **29**(5), 381–389 (2004)
43. Paleari, M., Huet, B.: Toward emotion indexing of multimedia excerpts. In: Proceedings on Content-Based Multimedia Indexing, International Workshop, pp. 425–432 (2008)
44. Perreira Da Silva, M., Courboulay, V., Prigent, A., Estraillier, P.: Evaluation of preys/predators systems for visual attention simulation. In: Proceedings of the International Conference on Computer Vision Theory and Applications, pp. 275–282, INSTICC (2010)
45. Perronnin, F.: Universal and adapted vocabularies for generic visual categorization. IEEE Trans. Pattern Anal. Mach. Intell. **30**(7), 1243–1256 (2008)
46. Philbin, J., Chum, O., Isard, M., Sivic, J., Zisserman, A.: Object retrieval with large vocabularies and fast spatial matching. In: IEEE Computer Society Conference on Computer Vision and Pattern Recognition (CVPR), Minneapolis, MI (2007)
47. Rosten, E., Drummond, T.: Fusing points and lines for high performance tracking. In: Proceedings of the IEEE International Conference on Computer Vision, vol. 2, pp. 1508–1511 (2005)
48. Rosten, E., Drummond, T.: Machine learning for high-speed corner detection. In: Proceedings of the European Conference on Computer Vision, vol. 1, pp. 430–443 (2006)
49. Schmid, C., Mohr, R., Bauckhage, C.: Evaluation of interest point detectors. Int. J. Comput. Vision **37**(2), 151–172 (2000)
50. Sivic, J., Zisserman, A.: Video Google: A text retrieval approach to object matching in videos. In: Proceedings of the International Conference on Computer Vision, pp. 1470–1477 (2003)
51. Smith, S.M., Brady, J.M.: Susan—a new approach to low level image processing. Int. J. Comput. Vision **23**(1), 45–78 (1997)
52. Solli, M., Lenz, R.: Color harmony for image indexing. In: Proceedings of the 12th International Conference on Computer Vision Workshops, pp. 1885–1892 (2009)
53. Solli, M., Lenz, R.: Emotion related structures in large image databases. In: Proceedings of the ACM International Conference on Image and Video Retrieval, pp. 398–405. ACM, New York (2010)
54. Tuytelaars, T., Mikolajczyk, K.: Local invariant feature detectors: a survey. Found. Trends Comput. Graph. Vis. **3**(3), 177–280 (2008)
55. Urruty, T., Gbèhounou, S., Le, T.L., Martinet, J., Fernandez-Maloigne, C.: Iterative random visual words selection. In: Proceedings of International Conference on Multimedia Retrieval, ICMR'14, pp. 249–256. ACM, New York (2014)
56. van de Sande, K.E.A., Gevers, T., Snoek, C.G.M.: Evaluating color descriptors for object and scene recognition. IEEE Trans. Pattern Anal. Mach. Intell. **32**(9), 1582–1596 (2010)
57. Wang, W., Yu, Y.: Image emotional semantic query based on color semantic description. In: Proceedings of the The 4th International Conference on Machine Leraning and Cybernectics, vol. 7, pp. 4571–4576 (2005)

58. Wei, K., He, B., Zhang, T., He, W.: Image Emotional classification based on color semantic description. Lecture Notes in Computer Science, vol. 5139, pp. 485–491. Springer, Berlin (2008)
59. Yanulevskaya, V., Van Gemert, J.C., Roth, K., Herbold, A.K., Sebe, N., Geusebroek, J.M.: Emotional valence categorization using holistic image features. In: Proceedings of the 15th IEEE International Conference on Image Processing, pp. 101–104 (2008)
60. Zdziarski, Z., Dahyot, R.: Feature selection using visual saliency for content-based image retrieval. In: Proceedings of the IET Irish Signals and Systems Conference, pp. 1–6 (2012)
61. Zhang, J., Marszalek, M., Lazebnik, S., Schmid, C.: Local features and kernels for classification of texture and object categories: a comprehensive study. Int. J. Comput. Vis. **73**(2), 213–238 (2007)
62. Zhang, L., Tong, M.H., Marks, T.K., Shan, H., Cottrell, G.W.: Sun: A Bayesian framework for saliency using natural statistics. J. Vis. **8**(7), 1–20 (2008)

Saliency Prediction for Action Recognition

Michael Dorr and Eleonora Vig

Abstract Despite all recent progress in computer vision, humans are still far superior to machines when it comes to the high-level understanding of complex dynamic scenes. The apparent ease of human perception and action cannot be explained by sheer neural computation power alone: Estimates put the transmission rate of the optic nerve at only about 10 MBit/s. One particular effective strategy to reduce the computational burden of vision in biological systems is the combination of attention with space-variant processing, where only subsets of the visual scene are processed in full detail at any one time. Here, we report on experiments that mimic eye movements and attention as a preprocessing step for state-of-the-art computer vision algorithms.

1 Introduction

The human brain is remarkably energy efficient and runs on about 10–15 W of power, less than most laptop computers. By the standards of the animal kingdom, however, the human brain is already quite big, and many species with much less neural hardware nevertheless perceive and act in complex environments seemingly without effort. In contrast to this, even supercomputers still struggle with the understanding of dynamic scenes, despite a highly active computer vision community, its rapid progress, and the recent surge of bio-inspired, "deep" neural-network architectures that have shattered many benchmarks. Computer vision performance may have reached or even surpassed human performance in more abstract, static object recognition scenarios such as handwritten character or traffic sign recognition [9]; in fully dynamic, unconstrained environments, this has not been the case yet. One particular processing strategy that biological agents employ to improve

M. Dorr (✉)
Technical University Munich, Munich, Germany
e-mail: michael.dorr@tum.de

E. Vig
German Aerospace Center, Oberpfaffenhofen, Germany
e-mail: eleonora.vig@dlr.de

© Springer International Publishing AG 2017
J. Benois-Pineau, P. Le Callet (eds.), *Visual Content Indexing and Retrieval with Psycho-Visual Models*, Multimedia Systems and Applications,
DOI 10.1007/978-3-319-57687-9_5

efficiency is selective attention: at any given time, only a fraction of the entire (visual) input is processed in full detail. In combination with efficient coding, this allows humans to process complex visual inputs despite the limited transmission bandwidth of the optic nerve that is estimated to be comparable to an Ethernet link (10 Mbit/s) [21]. In humans, attention is also closely linked to eye movements, which are executed several times per second and direct the high-resolution centre of the retina to points of interest in the visual scene.

Because of the potential to reduce bandwidth requirements, models of attention and eye movements, or saliency models, have long been and still are an active research field [4]. For static images, state-of-the-art models have come close to human performance (meaning the implicit, typically subconscious choice where to direct gaze), although there are at least two caveats: first, it is still a matter of debate how to best quantify the similarity between machine predictions and actual human eye movements [5]; second, the laboratory-based presentation of static images for prolonged inspection is not a very accurate representation of real-world viewing behaviour and thus might give rise to idiosyncratic viewing strategies [11].

The more challenging case of saliency for videos, however, has received less attention (but see Chap. 3 in this book [8]). A likely contributor to this deficit has been the lack of standardized benchmarks that make it easier to directly compare different models, and consequently improve upon them. Yet, video processing has high computational cost and therefore could particularly benefit from attention-inspired efficiency gains. One computer vision application of note is action recognition: out of a set of (human) actions, which action is depicted by a short video clip? Current approaches to this problem extract densely sampled descriptors from the whole scene. While this provides full coverage, it also comes at high computational cost, and descriptors from uninformative, non-salient image regions may even impair classification performance.

In this chapter, we shall therefore extend previous work on saliency-based descriptor pruning for action recognition [41, 42]; very similar, independently developed work was published in [25, 26]. Since these original publications, the state-of-the-art action recognition processing pipeline has been improved to incorporate an implicit foreground saliency estimation step [48], and we shall investigate whether an additional explicit pruning can further improve performance.

2   Related Work

For recent overviews of the highly active and very wide field of action recognition, we point the reader to the surveys [12, 44].

Despite the recent success of deep learning methods for video-related tasks, hand-crafted features are still indispensable when designing state-of-the-art action recognition solutions. These methods typically rely on the—by now—standard *improved Dense Trajectories (iDT)* [45, 46, 48] representation that aggregates local spatio-temporal descriptors into a global video-level representation through the Bag of Words (BoW) or the Fisher Vector encoding. Along trajectories located at high motion contrast, rich appearance and motion descriptors, such as HOG, HOF, and MBH are extracted. Several improvements have been proposed to this standard pipeline, from stacking features extracted at temporally subsampled versions of the video [22] to employing various descriptor- and representation-level fusion methods [28]. Interestingly, by paying careful attention to details (of normalization, and data- and spatio-temporal augmentations), [12] could show that the iDT pipeline is on par with the state of the art, including recent deep methods, on five standard benchmarks.

A number of more recent works explored deep architectures for action recognition. These methods aim at automatically learning discriminative representations end-to-end and must therefore rely on vast training data sets, such as Sports-1M [20] comprising of more than a million YouTube videos. Notable deep approaches include the extension of 2D convolutional neural networks (CNNs) to the time domain [20], the Two-Stream architecture [35] with two separate CNNs for appearance and motion modeling, as well as the combination of recurrent and convolutional networks to encode the temporal evolution of actions [10]. Overall, however, end-to-end deep models only achieved marginal improvements over the established hand-tuned baselines. For better performance, these methods often complement their learned representations with dense trajectory features. Alternatively, hybrid architectures leverage the representational power of deep per-frame feature maps in a Bag of Words pipeline (e.g. TDD method [47]).

2.1 Selective Feature Sampling and Reweighting Strategies for Action Recognition

Aware of the limitations of densely sampling an often prohibitive number of video descriptors, several works focused on reducing the number of local descriptors through various sampling strategies. Here we summarize the main directions.

Shi et al. [34] proposed a real-time action recognition system that combines fast random sampling with the Local Part Model to extract features, which has the benefit of including more structure and an ordering of events. Several feature sampling strategies are investigated in [50] with the best performing ones being based on object proposal techniques (such as Edge Boxes [51]). Their selective sampling based on motion object proposals reports better accuracy by using 25% less features than without sampling.

Predicting *foreground motion saliency* was also found to be an effective method for descriptor reweighting. For the challenging task of cross-data set action recognition, [38] relied on video foreground confidences for a soft-assignment (and reweighting) of features in a Bag of Words paradigm. Graph-based visual saliency [16] was used as one of their cues to predict foreground confidences. A foreground motion saliency is defined in [14] as well. Their spatio-temporal saliency is based on directional motion energy contrast (corresponding to spatio-temporal oriented filtering) and spatial variance. As is common practice, the predicted saliency measure reweights the features during pooling in a Bag of Words pipeline to enhance the contribution of local features by their saliency.

Another line of research looked at how *top-down, task-specific saliency* can simultaneously inform the tasks of action classification and localization. Sapienza et al. [31, 32], for example, learn *action-specific saliency maps*, by distilling the discriminative parts of the video for a specific action. To this end, weakly-labelled video histograms are extracted for overlapping subvolumes of the video, and a Multiple Instance Learning (MIL) framework is adopted to associate action instance models to latent class labels. The learned action models are thus not only able to classify actions, but also to localize them via the action-specific saliency map. A similar structured prediction model, aimed at both action classification and localization, is presented in [33]. To learn the top-down, action-specific saliency though, this work relies on eye movements as weak supervisory signals. In a max-margin framework, a latent smooth path through the video is identified that maximizes action classification accuracy and coincides with high gaze concentration. In addition to action classification and localization, their model is thus capable of predicting top-down video saliency conditioned on the performed action.

Saliency-based non-uniform descriptor sampling has also been adopted for other related tasks, such as object recognition in egocentric videos [3].

3   Methods

In this section, we shall describe materials and methods of the work underlying this chapter. Because several of the analyses presented here are extensions of previous work and thus have been described before, we will put particular emphasis on the novel saliency measure based on smooth pursuit eye movements.

3.1   Data Set

Even for a single human action alone, the space of possible scenes depicting that particular action is incredibly large. Thus, any finite data set for action recognition can only be a coarse approximation to real-world action recognition. Over the past few years, several benchmark data sets have been made available with varying difficulty and complexity.

For this chapter, we focus on the Hollywood2 data set of short excerpts from professionally produced Hollywood movies [24]. This data set comprises 823 training and 884 test clips with overall about half a million frames and 100 billion pixels, and using the Dense Trajectories pipeline (see below), intermediate processing steps require about half a terabyte of storage space. This makes it still possible to handle this data set without very large-scale computing facilities, and yet bandwidth gains by saliency-based descriptor pruning would be desirable. At the same time, performance has not reached ceiling on this challenging data set yet, after almost a decade of intense research.

Because of its popularity, there are two independent eye movement data sets that were recorded for the Hollywood2 data set [25, 26, 41, 42], namely by Mathe et al. and Vig et al. Both groups used different eye trackers to record gaze: the Mathe data set was collected monocularly with an SMI iView X HiSpeed 1250 at 500 Hz, while data collection for the Vig data set used an SR Research EyeLink 1000 at 1000 Hz that tracked both eyes simultaneously. Whereas at least theoretically, this should have negligible consequences for recorded gaze locations, the viewing distances (60 and 75 cm, respectively) and screen sizes (38.4 and 41.3 deg, respectively) also differed; previous work has shown an effect of stimulus size on saccade behaviour [49].

Most importantly, however, tasks also subtly differed between the data sets: in the Mathe data set, subjects either performed a free-viewing task or the same action recognition task as in the original computer vision benchmark, where they had to explicitly name the presented actions after each video clip. By comparison, the task in the Vig data set was constrained to an intermediate degree, and subjects were asked to silently identify the presented actions.

We therefore computed the Normalized Scanpath Saliency (NSS) [29] to check for systematic differences in the spatio-temporal distribution of gaze in the two data sets. For NSS, a fixation map is first created by superimposing spatio-temporal Gaussians (128×128 pixels and 5 frames support, $\sigma = 0.21$) at each gaze sample of one "reference" group (e.g. the Mathe data set). This fixation map is then normalized to zero mean and unit standard deviation, and NSS is the average of this fixation map's values for all gaze samples of the other "test" group (e.g. the Vig data set). Similar gaze patterns in both groups correspond to high NSS values, and unrelated gaze patterns (chance) correspond to zero. For a comparative evaluation, we computed NSS both within- and between data sets: if NSS between subsets of e.g. Mathe is similar to NSS between Mathe and Vig, we can assume that both data sets have little systematic difference. Because of the differing number of subjects, we used gaze data from only one subject at a time to form the initial fixation map; this was repeated for each subject and for up to 5 other subjects as "tests".

3.2 Baseline Action Recognition

We follow the standard (improved) Dense Trajectories pipeline from [45, 46, 48]. Based on optical flow fields, trajectories are computed first, and then descriptors are extracted along these trajectories from densely sampled interest points. These descriptors comprise the shape of the trajectory, HOG, HOG, and Motion Boundary Histograms (MBH). Mostly due to camera motion, many descriptors were extracted by the original pipeline that corresponded to trajectories of irrelevant background objects. By estimating a frame-to-frame homography and compensating for camera motion, these irrelevant descriptors could be suppressed and thus action recognition performance was substantially improved. A further improvement then was achieved by incorporating a human detection step using the algorithm from [30]. Regions with detected humans are excluded from the homography estimation, making the suppression more specific to the background. However, it should be noted that the automatic detection works best for frontal views, and thus many episodes where on-screen characters are shown from the side or other angles are missed by the algorithm.

For the work presented in this chapter, we used the publicly available implementation[1] with default parameters and the provided human detection bounding boxes. As already shown in [48], larger codebooks give better performance, and we thus randomly sampled 256,000 features to train a codebook of size 4096.

3.3   Central Bias of Descriptors and Human Detection

We evaluated the spatial distribution of extracted improved Dense Trajectory descriptors and human bounding boxes as a baseline for other central bias measures (see below). In order to compensate for different aspect ratios, we resampled all video clips to a size of 1024 by 1024 pixels and superimposed all pixels within the detected human bounding boxes. For better legibility, we report the marginal distribution along the horizontal and the vertical axis.

3.4   Central Bias Saliency

It is well-established that human eye movements and attention show a bias towards the centre of a visual stimulus [11, 19, 39, 40]. On the one hand, the central, resting position of the eyeball requires the least energy expenditure by the six ocular muscles. Under truly naturalistic free-viewing conditions, head movements therefore typically immediately follow eye movements to reinstate the central gaze position. On the other hand, the central position yields the best trade-off for allocating the space-variant retinal resolution to the whole scene.

In Hollywood movies, this effect is typically further exacerbated by deliberate staging of relevant persons and objects at the centre of the scene. As in previous work, we therefore computed a central bias saliency measure that simply comprised the distance to the screen centre.

---

[1]http://lear.inrialpes.fr/~wang/improved_trajectories.

3.5   Empirical Saliency

Both available gaze data sets were combined and in a first step, blinks and blink-induced artefacts immediately before or after them were removed. For each video, we then created a spatio-temporal fixation density map by superimposing 3D-Gaussians at each valid gaze sample position; these Gaussians had a support of 384 by 384 pixels and 5 temporal frames and a σ of 80 pixels in space and one frame in time. Subsequently, these gaze density maps were linearly normalized per frame to [0, 255] and stored to disk as MPEG-4 video streams.

Note that for simplicity, we did not perform explicit fixation detection, and thus included saccadic and smooth pursuit gaze samples as well. Because of the strong spatio-temporal blurring, the effect of this inclusion should be negligible.

3.6   Smooth Pursuit Empirical Saliency

Historically, most of research on eye movements in naturalistic scenes in general, and on models of saliency and attention in particular, has used static images as experimental stimuli. Given that the real world is decidedly non-static, dynamic stimuli such as image sequences are ecologically more valid, but they incur a much greater computational cost and also introduce problems of their own: how similar or different are fixations to the same spatial location at different points in time? One further consequence of the focus on static stimuli has been that gaze traces have typically been categorized as *fixations*, i.e. stationary phases of the eye when information processing takes place, and *saccades*, i.e. rapid eye movements that take the fovea from one fixation to the next. During saccades, information processing is severely limited because of the high speed of the retinal image.

In the real world and in dynamic contexts, however, another type of eye movements may occur, namely smooth pursuit eye movements. Typically, they reach speeds of a few degrees per second [1] and are used to stabilize the retinal projection of moving objects by tracking them. One hypothesis of our work here is that smooth pursuit eye movements are particularly useful for highlighting relevant image regions for the action recognition task. First, one could argue that smooth pursuit eye movements are "fixations on moving objects", which require more neural investment to maintain, and thus they ought to be reserved for especially informative image objects. Second, there is evidence that motion perception is enhanced during smooth pursuit [37], and thus it stands to reason that such eye movements are executed when detailed processing of the visual input is required. In the following, we shall therefore present a recently developed algorithm to automatically detect smooth pursuit eye movements, and analyse how a saliency measure based on these eye movements influences action recognition performance.

Hand-labelling is still considered the gold standard for the classification of eye movement recordings. Despite tremendous progress in eye movement technology, gaze traces can still be noisy and exhibit severe artefacts [18]. This is especially problematic during the detection of smooth pursuit eye movements because these have relatively low speeds and thus are harder to distinguish from fixations than high-speed saccades. However, hand-labelling on large-scale data sets such as Hollywood2, with more than 100 subject-video hours available [25, 42], is not practically feasible anymore. Recently, we thus have developed a novel algorithm for the automatic classification of smooth pursuit eye movements [1] that employs a simple trick to substantially improve classification performance compared to state-of-the-art algorithms. Because smooth pursuit can only be performed in the presence of a moving target, there typically should only be a few candidate locations (objects) for smooth pursuit per scene or video frame. As discussed above, we expect pursuit mainly on especially informative image regions, and thus it is likely that more than one observer will follow any particular pursuit target. At the same time, noise in the gaze signal should be independent across different observers. Combining these two observations, we can assume that the likelihood of a smooth pursuit is high whenever several observers exhibit similar dynamic gaze patterns in the same spatio-temporal video location; conversely, slow shifts in the gaze position of individual observers are more likely noise artefacts. This approach can be summarized in the following steps:

1. Discard all those gaze traces that are clearly fixations (fully static) or saccades (very high speed).
2. Cluster remaining gaze samples using the DBSCAN algorithm [13].
3. Discard clusters that comprise gaze data from fewer than four observers.
4. Post-process clusters; discard episodes of less than 50 ms duration.

This algorithm has been evaluated against a hand-labelled subset of the GazeCom data set of naturalistic videos and has shown dramatically improved precision at better recall than state-of-the-art algorithms [1]. However, the GazeCom data set comprises unstaged everyday outdoor scenes that lead to high eye movement variability except for some 'hot spots' [11]. By contrast, professionally cut video material such as Hollywood movies is specifically designed to focus attention on few 'objects' (typically, characters) of interest, and thus gaze patterns are highly coherent [11, 15, 17, 27]. In principle, it would thus be possible that almost all observers cluster in very few locations, and noise in the gaze traces might get misclassified as smooth pursuit. However, visual inspection of a sample of detected smooth pursuit episodes showed that this was typically not the case; nevertheless, even subtle image motion such as a character tilting their head often evoked corresponding gaze motion.

An additional complication compared to the empirical saliency based on fixations is the sparsity of smooth pursuit: whereas in the case of static images, fixations will make up about 90% of the viewing time (with the remainder mainly spent on saccades), the occurrence of smooth pursuit heavily depends on the stimulus. In the Hollywood2 video set, the smooth pursuit rate per video clip ranged from 0% to almost 50%, with a mean of about 15% when considering the recall rate of our algorithm. As a consequence of this sparsity, we used stronger spatio-temporal blurring than for the empirical saliency above ($\sigma = 105$ pixels in space and three frames in time).

3.7 Analytical Saliency

Whereas a wealth of saliency models exists for static images [2], often even with publicly available implementations, there are much fewer available models for video saliency. As in previous work, we here chose to use the geometrical invariants of the structure tensor, which indicate the locally used degrees of freedom in a signal, or its intrinsic dimensionality (inD). The invariants H, S, and K correspond to a change in the signal in one, two, and three directions, respectively. They are computed based on the structure tensor

$$J = \omega * \begin{pmatrix} f_x f_x & f_x f_y & f_x f_t \\ f_x f_y & f_y f_y & f_y f_t \\ f_x f_t & f_y f_t & f_t f_t \end{pmatrix} \tag{1}$$

with f_x, f_y, f_t partial spatio-temporal derivatives and ω a spatio-temporal smoothing operator. The rank of J then allows us to compute intrinsic dimensionality,

$$H = 1/3 \operatorname{trace}(J)$$

$$S = M_{11} + M_{22} + M_{33}$$

$$K = |J|$$

where M_{ii} are the minors of J. Since i1D regions (H) mainly comprise spatial edges and we were rather interested in spatio-temporal features, we here used i2D and i3D features (S and K). K has previously been shown to be more predictive of eye movements in dynamic natural scenes [43], but is also sparser than S. Because we are interested more in salient regions than very fine localization, we first computed the invariants on the second spatial scale of the Hollywood2 video clips as described in [43] and then additionally blurred the resulting saliency videos with a spatial Gaussian with a support of 21 and $\sigma = 4$ pixels.

3.8 Relationship of Human Detection and Saliency

Humans are social creatures, and thus depictions of humans and particularly faces are very strong attractors of attention, regardless of bottom-up saliency [7, 23]. Our analytical saliency measures S and K do not contain an explicit face or human detector, and we therefore computed the distribution of both analytical and empirical saliency values in regions where humans had been detected, relative to saliency values at randomly sampled locations.

In analogy to the central bias analysis above, we also computed the distribution of saliency values at the locations of extracted iDT descriptors.

3.9   Descriptor Pruning

Based on previous work, we hypothesized that salient regions are more informative than non-salient regions, and thus discarding descriptors extracted in less-salient regions should either improve action recognition performance, or enable us to maintain baseline performance with fewer descriptors and thus at reduced bandwidth. To prune descriptors based on saliency, we used an equation loosely based on the CDF of the Weibull function,

$$F(x; \Theta; k; \lambda) = \begin{cases} (1 - e^{-(x/\lambda)^k}, & x > 0 \\ \Theta, & \text{otherwise} \end{cases} \tag{2}$$

where x is the raw saliency value (normalized from [0, 255] to [0, 1]), and $k, \lambda > 0$ are the shape and scale parameters, respectively; we here used $k=1$ and $\lambda=0.001$. Θ is an additional parameter that allows for low-probability sampling outside salient regions in order to achieve broad coverage of the scene. Throughout this chapter, we use $\Theta = 0.01$ unless noted otherwise.

4   Results

In this section, we shall describe the results for the analyses as described above.

4.1   Central Bias in Hollywood2

The Hollywood2 data set exhibits central biases on several levels as evidenced by Figs. 1 and 2. The spatial distribution of human detection bounding boxes is shown in Fig. 1. Along the horizontal dimension, the distribution is roughly symmetrical with a clear peak in the centre, likely reflecting the cinematographer's preference to frame relevant characters in the centre of the scene. The distribution along the vertical dimension is also peaked at the centre, but shows a clear asymmetry for the top and bottom parts of the screen because humans are literally footed in the ground plane.

In the same figure, the spatial distribution of extracted improved Dense Trajectory descriptors is also presented. These correspond to moving features in the scene

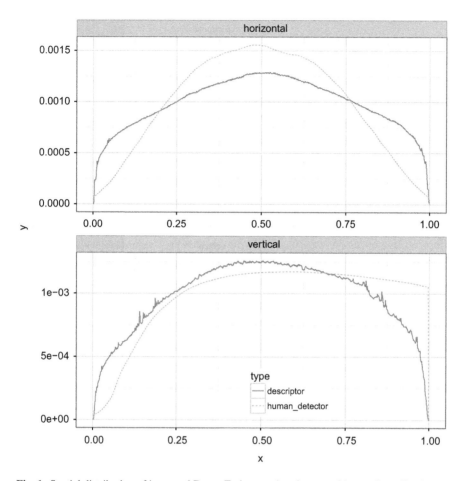

Fig. 1 Spatial distribution of improved Dense Trajectory descriptors and human bounding boxes in Hollywood2. Particularly for the locations of detected humans, there is a clear central bias along the horizontal axis (*top*); along the vertical axis, this bias is less pronounced and the distribution of bounding boxes is also skewed towards the bottom of the screen (*bottom*)

and while the distributions are also peaked near the screen centre, the central bias is not as clearly pronounced as for human detections, particularly along the horizontal dimension.

The analytical saliency measures S and K should also respond strongly to moving image features. Nevertheless, their central bias is weaker than for iDT descriptors (Fig. 2) and it is more in line with the biases exhibited by oculomotor behaviour, empirical saliency (ES), and smooth pursuit (SP) saliency.

Surprisingly, the peaks of the distributions of empirical saliency are slightly shifted left and down from the peaks of the image-based saliency measures and the image centre, and smooth pursuit eye movements seem less prone to the central bias than fixations.

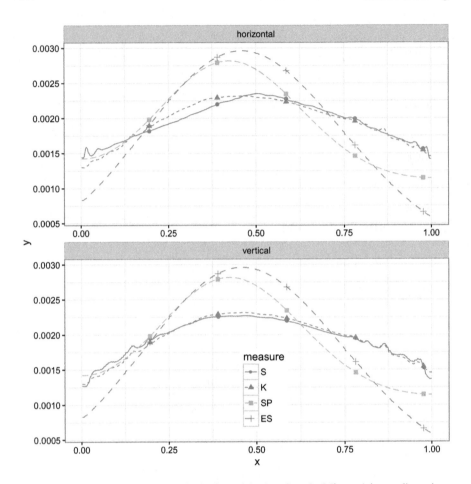

Fig. 2 Marginal distributions along the horizontal (*top*) and vertical (*bottom*) image dimensions of empirical and analytical saliency measures. The geometrical invariant K, which corresponds to intrinsically three-dimensional features and is thus less redundant and more informative than the i2D features represented by S, is more centrally biased than S. Among the eye movement-based measures, smooth pursuit (SP) episodes are less centrally biased than regular empirical saliency (ES)

4.2 Data Set Comparability

Results for our evaluation of the similarity of the two independently collected gaze data sets for Hollywood2 are shown in Fig. 3. The highest coherence across observers can be found for the "active" condition in the Mathe data set (median NSS score 6.21), where subjects explicitly performed the action recognition task. The "free" condition constrained subjects less and showed very comparable NSS scores as the Vig data set (median NSS scores of 5.05, and 4.65, respectively). Notably, the "cross-free" condition, which assessed the similarity of subjects from the Vig

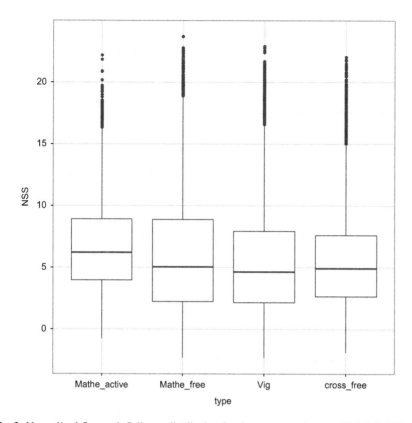

Fig. 3 Normalized Scanpath Saliency distribution for the two gaze data sets "Mathe" [25] and "Vig" [42]. Eye movements are most coherent in the active condition of the Mathe data set where subjects had to explicitly solve an action recognition task. The free-viewing condition has similar NSS scores as the Vig data set, where subjects were only told to look for the actions, but not to expressly report them. The inter-data set NSS distribution ("cross_free") is very similar to both intra-data set NSS distributions ("Mathe_free" and "Vig"), indicating that there is no fundamental difference between the eye movement data sets recorded by different groups and with different hardware setups

data set to those in the Mathe "free" condition and vice versa, had similar NSS scores (median 4.93) as the two within-group comparisons, indicating no substantial differences between the data sets despite the differences in hardware setup and protocol.

4.3   Descriptors, Human Detections, and Saliency

Figure 4 shows the relationship of both empirical and analytical saliency measures on the one hand and human bounding boxes on the other hand. Because the distributions of raw saliency value follow a power law and the strong peaks at zero

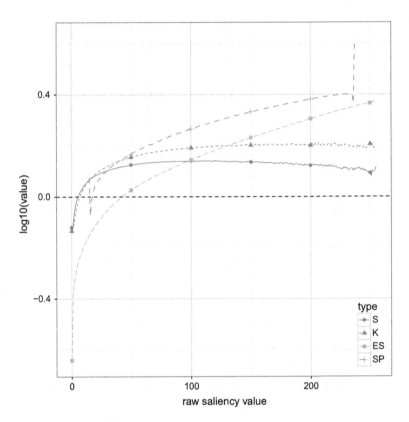

Fig. 4 Relationship of saliency values and detected humans in Hollywood2. Shown here is the histogram of log-ratios of saliency values within the detected bounding boxes and at random locations. Higher saliency values have log-ratios greater than zero, indicating that humans are classified as salient by all measures. Eye movements-based measures capture the saliency of humans better than analytical measures, and smooth pursuit (SP) performs better than empirical saliency (ES) does

make it hard to discern any differences, we here chose a different visualization: for each raw saliency value (or histogram bin) between 0 and 255, we plot the log-ratio of the number of pixels with that value within human bounding boxes versus the number of pixels with that value at random locations. If human bounding boxes and saliency were unrelated, we would therefore expect a flat line around zero (log of unit ratio). For all saliency measures, there is a clear trend towards higher ratios for higher saliency values, i.e. a systematic correlation between the presence of humans in the scene and their associated saliency. This effect is particularly strong for the empirical saliency measure based on smooth pursuit; the analytical saliency measures S and K capture bottom-up saliency such as edges and corners rather than semantics and are therefore less correlated.

A similar analysis is shown in Fig. 5, but for the saliency values at the locations of extracted descriptors. There is a systematic relationship between the analytical

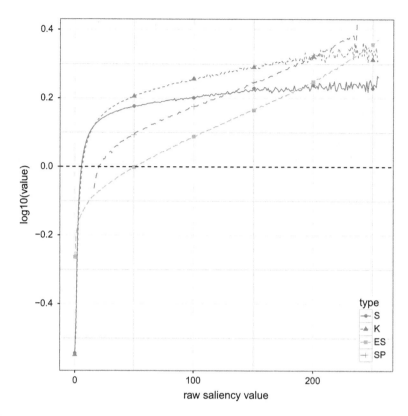

Fig. 5 Relationship of saliency values and iDT descriptors in Hollywood2. Shown here is the histogram of log-ratios of saliency values at extracted feature locations and at random locations. The intrinsically three-dimensional measure K shows a stronger relation to iDT descriptors than the intrinsically two-dimensional measure S

saliency measures and descriptors, which is to be expected given that they both are functions of local image structure. However, there is also a strong effect on the empirical saliency measures; in other words, descriptors are doing a good job of selecting informative image regions (as determined by the attention of human observers) already.

4.4   Baseline Action Recognition Performance

Without descriptor pruning, the iDT pipeline with human detection and the Bag of Words encoding resulted in a mean average precision of 62.04%. This is in line with expectations based on [48] and the increased number of codebook vectors.

4.5   Performance of Image-Based Saliency

Effects of descriptor pruning based on the image-based, analytical saliency measures are shown in Fig. 6. The dashed line indicates baseline performance for the standard pipeline without descriptor pruning. Successively pruning descriptors based on different thresholds for the analytical saliency measure K maintains baseline performance up to about 20% discarded descriptors, but then performance quickly drops. For S, subtle pruning of less than 10% slightly improves performance (62.48% at 90.6% retained descriptors), but higher pruning levels also substantially reduce performance. The "central" measure, which is independent of image content and exploits the central bias in professional movie making, outperforms the baseline by nearly one percentage point and reaches an mAveP of 62.9% using 73.4%

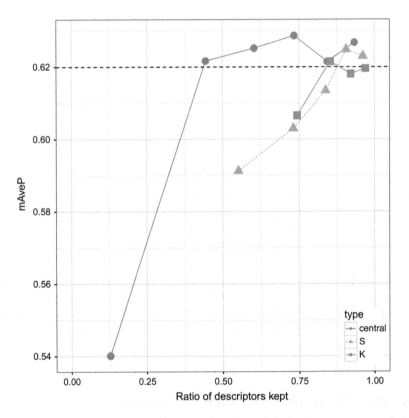

Fig. 6 Effect of saliency-based descriptor pruning for analytical saliency measures; *dashed horizontal line* indicates baseline performance for the full descriptor set (=100%). For the image-based measures S and K, performance quickly deteriorates below baseline; S may give a very small benefit for a pruning of descriptors by about 10% only. However, central saliency, which exploits the central bias in professionally directed Hollywood video clips, improves upon baseline performance for moderate pruning levels and maintains baseline performance for a pruning by almost 60%

of descriptors (all descriptors in a radius of 0.3 around the image centre). Even with 44.4% of descriptors (radius 0.2), performance is still slightly above baseline (62.17%).

4.6 Performance of Empirical Saliency

Figure 7 shows action recognition performance if descriptors are pruned based on empirical saliency measures, i.e. an implicit human labelling of informative image regions. Because smooth pursuit episodes are rare, the measure based on smooth pursuit alone ("SP-pure" in Fig. 7) captures less than a third of all descriptors even with a low threshold and strong spatio-temporal blurring (see Sect. 3.6). At these

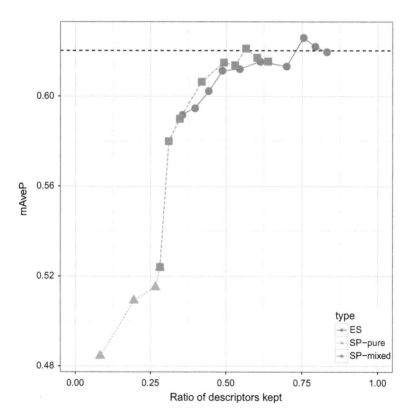

Fig. 7 Effect of saliency-based descriptor pruning for empirical saliency measures; *dashed horizontal line* indicates baseline performance for the full descriptor set (=100%). Because of the sparsity of smooth pursuit eye movements, more than two thirds of descriptors are pruned for the "SP-pure" measure, and action recognition performance is substantially worse than baseline. Augmenting the descriptor set by additionally sampling outside of the SP regions ("SP-mixed") brings performance back to baseline, but does not improve upon it. The empirical saliency measure ES, which is based on raw gaze samples, performs better than SP, but yields only very little improvement relative to baseline

pruning levels, performance of SP is substantially worse than both baseline and centre-based pruning. In order to increase the number of retained descriptors, we increased Θ, i.e. the sampling density in "peripheral", non-salient regions. Because of the (differently weighted) mixture of salient and non-salient regions, this strategy is labelled "SP-mixed" in Fig. 7. Using this approach, roughly baseline performance (62.13%) can be reached using 56.5% of all descriptors.

Finally, baseline performance can only moderately be improved by descriptor pruning based on the ground truth human attention map ES. At 75.4% of descriptors retained, mAveP reaches 62.6%.

4.7 Combinations of Image-Based Metrics

We also evaluated the performance of combinations of different image-based metrics; results are shown in Fig. 8. For reference purposes, results for the "central"

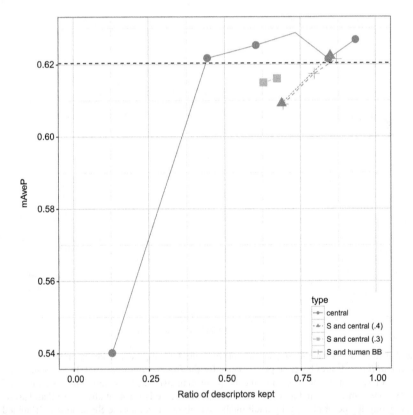

Fig. 8 Performance for combinations of analytical saliency S with a central bias or human detection. Performance decreases relative to the central bias alone

measure are repeated from Fig. 6. A combination of human detections with analytical saliency S is actually slightly worse than S alone (62.14% at 86.9% retained descriptors). Simultaneously pruning based on S and the "central" measure (with radii 0.3 and 0.4, respectively) also reduces performance relative to the central measure alone.

5 Discussion

Action recognition in unconstrained videos remains a challenge for computer vision algorithms, but is a task easily solved by human observers. Unlike current computer algorithms, humans employ selective attention to fully process only parts of the scene at any one time. Because of the space-variant resolution of the retina, the deployment of attention can easily be observed by a recording of eye movements. The fundamental question then is whether it is possible to mimic human attention in computer vision algorithms.

Here, we evaluated several aspects of both analytically generated and empirically obtained attention maps as a preprocessing step in a state-of-the-art action recognition pipeline.

First, we looked at two gaze data sets independently collected by two different groups of researchers, and found substantial similarities between them. Notably, however, gaze behaviour differed between sub-conditions with different instructions given to the participants. Even though participants in the Vig et al. study were asked to recognize the actions, their gaze patterns were more similar to those in the Mathe et al. study that free-viewed the videos than those who had to select the correct action(s) after each video clip presentation. This finding underlines the importance of task instructions for gaze-recording experiments [6, 36].

The original Dense Trajectories pipeline significantly benefited from pruning of descriptors in non-salient regions [25, 42]. Our results indicate that the camera motion compensation in the improved Dense Trajectories pipeline [48] already suppresses irrelevant descriptors very effectively, and performance cannot be improved by using the generic, image-based analytical saliency measures that we evaluated. Strikingly, however, performance was also only marginally improved when human eye movements were used for descriptor pruning, and smooth pursuit eye movements were even detrimental to action recognition. Arguably, human attention should precisely highlight those image regions that are relevant for video understanding; however, the human brain likely integrates information both in time across several eye movements as well as over the whole visual field, despite the lower resolution of the periphery. The exact nature of this information processing, and how to mimic it in computer algorithms, therefore remains an open field of study.

Importantly, pruning descriptors simply based on their distance to the screen centre still improved results, as in the original Dense Trajectories pipeline. We ran further analyses and demonstrated that there are several levels of central bias in the Hollywood2 data set, which we consider mostly artefacts. Truly unconstrained video, such as that potentially encountered by robots or autonomous vehicles, thus will likely pose future challenges.

Acknowledgements Our research was supported by the Elite Network Bavaria, funded by the Bavarian State Ministry for Research and Education.

References

1. Agtzidis, I., Startsev, M., Dorr, M.: Smooth pursuit detection based on multiple observers. In: Proceedings of the Ninth Biennial ACM Symposium on Eye Tracking Research & Applications, ETRA'16, pp. 303–306. ACM, New York (2016)
2. Borji, A., Itti, L.: State-of-the-art in visual attention modeling. IEEE Trans. Pattern Anal. Mach. Intell. **35**(1), 185–207 (2013)
3. Buso, V., Benois-Pineau, J., González-Díaz, I.: Object recognition in egocentric videos with saliency-based non uniform sampling and variable resolution space for features selection. In: CVPR 2014 Egocentric (First-Person) Vision Workshop (2014)
4. Bylinskii, Z., Judd, T., Borji, A., Itti, L., Durand, F., Oliva, A., Torralba, A.: MIT Saliency Benchmark (2016). http://saliency.mit.edu
5. Bylinskii, Z., Judd, T., Oliva, A., Torralba, A., Durand, F.: What do different evaluation metrics tell us about saliency models? arXiv preprint arXiv:1604.03605 (2016)
6. Castelhano, M.S., Mack, M.L., Henderson, J.M.: Viewing task influences eye movement control during active scene perception. J. Vis. **9**(3), 6 (2009)
7. Cerf, M., Frady, P., Koch, C.: Faces and text attract gaze independent of the task: experimental data and computer model. J. Vis. **9**(12:10), 1–15 (2009)
8. Chaabouni, S., Benois-Pineau, J., Zemmari, A., Amar, C.B.: Deep saliency: prediction of interestingness in video with CNN. In: Benois-Pineau, J., Le Callet, P. (eds.) Visual Content Indexing and Retrieval with Psycho-Visual Models. Springer, Cham (2017)
9. Ciregan, D., Meier, U., Schmidhuber, J.: Multi-column deep neural networks for image classification. In: Proceedings of the IEEE Conference on Computer Vision and Pattern Recognition (CVPR), pp. 3642–3649 (2012)
10. Donahue, J., Anne Hendricks, L., Guadarrama, S., Rohrbach, M., Venugopalan, S., Saenko, K., Darrell, T.: Long-term recurrent convolutional networks for visual recognition and description. In: Proceedings of the IEEE Conference on Computer Vision and Pattern Recognition, pp. 2625–2634 (2015)
11. Dorr, M., Martinetz, T., Gegenfurtner, K., Barth, E.: Variability of eye movements when viewing dynamic natural scenes. J. Vis. **10**(10), 1–17 (2010)
12. de Souza, C.R., Gaidon, A., Vig, E., López, A.M.: Sympathy for the details: Dense trajectories and hybrid classification architectures for action recognition. In: Proceedings of the European Conference on Computer Vision, pp. 697–716. Springer, Cham (2016)
13. Ester, M., Kriegel, H.P., Sander, J., Xu, X.: A density-based algorithm for discovering clusters in large spatial databases with noise. In: KDD Proceedings, vol. 96, pp. 226–231 (1996)
14. Feichtenhofer, C., Pinz, A., Wildes, R.P.: Dynamically encoded actions based on spacetime saliency. In: Proceedings of the IEEE Conference on Computer Vision and Pattern Recognition, pp. 2755–2764 (2015)
15. Goldstein, R.B., Woods, R.L., Peli, E.: Where people look when watching movies: Do all viewers look at the same place? Comput. Biol. Med. **3**(7), 957–64 (2007)
16. Harel, J., Koch, C., Perona, P., et al.: Graph-based visual saliency. In: Advances in Neural Information Processing Systems, vol. 1, p. 5 (2006)

17. Hasson, U., Landesman, O., Knappmeyer, B., Vallines, I., Rubin, N., Heeger, D.J.: Neurocinematics: the neuroscience of film. Projections **2**(1), 1–26 (2008)
18. Hooge, I., Holmqvist, K., Nyström, M.: The pupil is faster than the corneal reflection (CR): are video based pupil-CR eye trackers suitable for studying detailed dynamics of eye movements? Vis. Res. **128**, 6–18 (2016)
19. Judd, T., Ehinger, K., Durand, F., Torralba, A.: Learning to predict where humans look. In: Proceedings of IEEE International Conference on Computer Vision (ICCV), pp. 2106–2113 (2009)
20. Karpathy, A., Toderici, G., Shetty, S., Leung, T., Sukthankar, R., Fei-Fei, L.: Large-scale video classification with convolutional neural networks. In: Proceedings of the IEEE Conference on Computer Vision and Pattern Recognition (2014)
21. Koch, K., McLean, J., Segev, R., Freed, M.A., II, M.J.B., Balasubramanian, V., Sterling, P.: How much the eye tells the brain. Curr. Biol. **16**, 1428–34 (2006)
22. Lan, Z., Lin, M., Li, X., Hauptmann, A.G., Raj, B.: Beyond Gaussian Pyramid: Multi-skip feature stacking for action recognition. In: Proceedings of the IEEE Conference on Computer Vision and Pattern Recognition, pp. 204–212 (2015)
23. Marat, S., Rahman, A., Pellerin, D., Guyader, N., Houzet, D.: Improving visual saliency by adding 'face feature map' and 'center bias'. Cogn. Comput. **5**(1), 63–75 (2013)
24. Marszalek, M., Laptev, I., Schmid, C.: Actions in context. In: Proceedings of the IEEE Conference on Computer Vision and Pattern Recognition, pp. 2929–2936 (2009)
25. Mathe, S., Sminchisescu, C.: Dynamic eye movement datasets and learnt saliency models for visual action recognition. In: Proceedings of the European Conference on Computer Vision, pp. 842–856. Springer, Berlin (2012)
26. Mathe, S., Sminchisescu, C.: Actions in the eye: dynamic gaze datasets and learnt saliency models for visual recognition. IEEE Trans. Pattern Anal. Mach. Intell. **37**(7), 1408–1424 (2015)
27. Mital, P.K., Smith, T.J., Hill, R., Henderson, J.M.: Clustering of gaze during dynamic scene viewing is predicted by motion. Cogn. Comput. **3**(1), 5–24 (2011)
28. Peng, X., Wang, L., Wang, X., Qiao, Y.: Bag of visual words and fusion methods for action recognition. Comput. Vis. Image Underst. **150**(C), 109–125 (2016)
29. Peters, R.J., Iyer, A., Itti, L., Koch, C.: Components of bottom-up gaze allocation in natural images. Vis. Res. **45**(8), 2397–2416 (2005)
30. Prest, A., Schmid, C., Ferrari, V.: Weakly supervised learning of interactions between humans and objects. IEEE Trans. Pattern Anal. Mach. Intell. **34**(3), 601–614 (2012)
31. Sapienza, M., Cuzzolin, F., Torr, P.H.: Learning discriminative space-time actions from weakly labelled videos. In: Proceedings of the British Machine Vision Conference, vol. 2, p. 3 (2012)
32. Sapienza, M., Cuzzolin, F., Torr, P.H.: Learning discriminative space–time action parts from weakly labelled videos. Int. J. Comput. Vis. **110**(1), 30–47 (2014)
33. Shapovalova, N., Raptis, M., Sigal, L., Mori, G.: Action is in the eye of the beholder: eye-gaze driven model for spatio-temporal action localization. In: Advances in Neural Information Processing Systems, pp. 2409–2417 (2013)
34. Shi, F., Petriu, E., Laganiere, R.: Sampling strategies for real-time action recognition. In: Proceedings of the IEEE Conference on Computer Vision and Pattern Recognition, pp. 2595–2602 (2013)
35. Simonyan, K., Zisserman, A.: Two-stream convolutional networks for action recognition in videos. In: Advances in Neural Information Processing Systems, pp. 568–576 (2014)
36. Smith, T.J., Mital, P.K.: Attentional synchrony and the influence of viewing task on gaze behavior in static and dynamic scenes. J. Vis. **13**(8), 16–16 (2013)
37. Spering, M., Schütz, A.C., Braun, D.I., Gegenfurtner, K.R.: Keep your eyes on the ball: smooth pursuit eye movements enhance prediction of visual motion. J. Neurophysiol. **105**(4), 1756–1767 (2011)
38. Sultani, W., Saleemi, I.: Human action recognition across datasets by foreground-weighted histogram decomposition. In: Proceedings of the IEEE Conference on Computer Vision and Pattern Recognition, pp. 764–771 (2014)

39. Tatler, B.W.: The central fixation bias in scene viewing: Selecting an optimal viewing position independently of motor biases and image feature distributions. J. Vis. **7**(14), 1–17 (2007). http://journalofvision.org/7/14/4/
40. Tseng, P.H., Carmi, R., Cameron, I.G.M., Munoz, D.P., Itti, L.: Quantifying center bias of observers in free viewing of dynamic natural scenes. J. Vis. **9**(7), 1–16 (2009). http://journalofvision.org/9/7/4/
41. Vig, E., Dorr, M., Cox, D.D.: Saliency-based selection of sparse descriptors for action recognition. In: Proceedings of International Conference on Image Processing, pp. 1405–1408 (2012)
42. Vig, E., Dorr, M., Cox, D.D.: Space-variant descriptor sampling for action recognition based on saliency and eye movements. In: Proceedings of the European Conference on Computer Vision. LNCS, vol. 7578, pp. 84–97 (2012)
43. Vig, E., Dorr, M., Martinetz, T., Barth, E.: Intrinsic dimensionality predicts the saliency of natural dynamic scenes. IEEE Trans. Pattern Anal. Mach. Intell. **34**(6), 1080–1091 (2012)
44. Vrigkas, M., Nikou, C., Kakadiaris, I.A.: A review of human activity recognition methods. Front. Robot. AI **2**, 28 (2015)
45. Wang, H., Schmid, C.: Action recognition with improved trajectories. In: Proceedings of the IEEE International Conference on Computer Vision (2013)
46. Wang, H., Kläser, A., Schmid, C., Liu, C.L.: Action recognition by dense trajectories. In: Proceedings of the IEEE Conference on Computer Vision and Pattern Recognition (CVPR), pp. 3169–3176. IEEE, New York (2011)
47. Wang, L., Qiao, Y., Tang, X.: Action recognition with trajectory-pooled deep-convolutional descriptors. In: Proceedings of the IEEE Conference on Computer Vision and Pattern Recognition, pp. 4305–4314 (2015)
48. Wang, H., Oneata, D., Verbeek, J., Schmid, C.: A robust and efficient video representation for action recognition. Int. J. Comput. Vis. **119**, 219–38 (2016)
49. von Wartburg, R., Wurtz, P., Pflugshaupt, T., Nyffeler, T., Lüthi, M., Müri, R.: Size matters: Saccades during scene perception. Perception **36**, 355–65 (2007)
50. Zhou, Y., Yu, H., Wang, S.: Feature sampling strategies for action recognition. arXiv preprint arXiv:1501.06993 (2015)
51. Zitnick, L., Dollar, P.: Edge boxes: locating object proposals from edges. In: Proceedings of the European Conference on Computer Vision (2014)

Querying Multiple Simultaneous Video Streams with 3D Interest Maps

Axel Carlier, Lilian Calvet, Pierre Gurdjos, Vincent Charvillat, and Wei Tsang Ooi

Abstract With proliferation of mobile devices equipped with cameras and video recording applications, it is now common to observe multiple mobile cameras filming the same scene at an event from a diverse set of view angles. These recorded videos provide a rich set of data for someone to re-experience the event at a later time. Not all the videos recorded, however, show a desirable view. Navigating through a large collection of videos to find a video with a better viewing angle can be time consuming. We propose a query-response interface in which users can intuitively switch to another video with an alternate, better, view, by selecting a 2D region within a video as a query. The system would then response with another video that has a better view of the selected region, maximizing the viewpoint entropy. The key to our system is a lightweight 3D scene structure, also termed 3D interest map. A 3D interest map is naturally an extension of saliency maps in the 3D space since most users film what they find interesting from their respective viewpoints. A user study with more than 35 users shows that our video query system achieves a suitable compromise between accuracy and run-time.

A. Carlier (✉) • P. Gurdjos • V. Charvillat
IRIT, UMR 5505, Université Toulouse, 2 rue Charles Camichel, 31071 Toulouse, France
e-mail: Axel.carlier@enseeiht.fr; pgurdjos@enseeiht.fr; Vincent.Charvillat@enseeiht.fr

L. Calvet
Simula Research Laboratory, Martin Linges vei 25, 1364 Fornebu, Norvége
e-mail: lcalvet@simula.com

W.T. Ooi
School of Computing, National University of Singapore, Lower Kent Ridge Road, 119077, Singapore
e-mail: ooiwt@comp.nus.edu.sg

© Springer International Publishing AG 2017
J. Benois-Pineau, P. Le Callet (eds.), *Visual Content Indexing and Retrieval with Psycho-Visual Models*, Multimedia Systems and Applications,
DOI 10.1007/978-3-319-57687-9_6

1 Introduction

The proliferation of mobile devices, such as smartphones and tablets, that are equipped with sensors, cameras, and networking capabilities has revolutionized the way multimedia data are produced and consumed, and has posed new challenges as well as led to new, novel applications.

We consider the case of public cultural performances (dance, singing, sport, magic, theater, etc.) with a spectating crowd. It has become common for a spectator to watch a performance and film it at the same time with a mobile camera. Figure 1 depicts such a scene with an open air stage and multiple filming cameras (six of which are labelled). The recorded videos are often uploaded and shared via social networks. For instance, a search for "Chingay Parade 2014" on YouTube returns more than 3000 results; "New York Ball Drop 2014" returns more than 172,000 results.

While the large amount of simultaneous videos capturing the same event provides a rich source of multimedia data captured from a diverse angle for someone to explore and experience the captured event, navigating from one video to another is challenging. In this paper, we focus on the problem of view switching: often, a camera filming the event does not permanently get a perfect view—for instance, the object of interest on the stage might be occluded by another spectator. In this case, it will be useful for the viewer to switch to another video capturing the same instance, but with a *better* view.

Figure 2 illustrates the idea of our work. The first three images from the left show snapshots (at the same time instance) of videos filmed simultaneously by mobile devices of a song-and-dance performance. At that particular moment, the lead singer (with a white bow on her head) is singing alone and other performers are dancing by her side. The rightmost image in Fig. 2 shows a user interface on the mobile phone, where the user is watching a video stream of a performance filmed from the right

Fig. 1 A performance filmed by seven cameras (Jiku dataset): six of the cameras are located just around the scene, and the seventh is out of the scope of this image but its field of view is shown as a *red rectangle* (Color figure online)

Fig. 2 Images of three synchronized videos from the **Fukuoka** dataset (*top row*), and an example of two possible queries (*bottom row*) materialized by a *red rectangle* and a *blue circle* on the image (Color figure online)

side of the stage and is not able to view the lead singer clearly. Using our system, the user can request to switch to a better view of the lead singer, by either tapping on the lead singer on his screen (the blue circle) or clicking and dragging a rectangle surrounding the lead singer on his screen (the red rectangle). This action generates a query that is sent to the server. The server then determines that, say, the video stream that corresponds to the first image from the left, provides the best view of the lead singer, and switches to transmitting this stream to the user.

It is important to note that this query is not interpreted as a content-based image retrieval problem (CBIR). We do not look for something similar to queried region in appearance, but we rather want to make a 3D interpretation of the query. In our use case, the user might orientate his mobile camera towards the important part of the scene but he has a partially occluded/contaminated viewpoint.

While the user interface above is intuitive, we face a few questions. First, we need to efficiently identify the regions containing the objects of interest in the videos. Our approach exploits the fact that, the cameras naturally film objects that are of interest to the viewers. For instance, a camera usually zooms into or points at interesting events on the stage. Thus, objects that appear in multiple cameras can be assumed to be of high interest. (e.g., the lead singer in Fig. 2).

Second, we need to relate what is captured between different videos to tell if they are depicting the same scene. Traditional content-based analysis would fail, due to high variations in appearance of the same object captured from different angles. To address this issue, we need to reconstruct the scene captured by the cameras in 3D, using multiple view geometry. We limit the reconstruction to regions that are in the intersection of the views of multiple cameras. As a result, 3D points around objects of high interest naturally become denser.

Third, we need to perform the reconstruction and answer the query efficiently, with a target response time of 1 s. To this end, we chose to perform a coarse yet discriminative reconstruction, using a modified version of the multiview stereopsis algorithm [7] that is less sensitive to camera parameters and is tuned to run in real-time. We model these objects of interest and the associated clusters of 3D points as a collection of 3D ellipsoids, providing a fairly coarse representation of the objects in the scene, but that are sufficient to support our view switching application. For instance, in Fig. 2, each 3D ellipsoid would fit each performer visible in all three images. We also choose to use only simple features to identify potential objects of interest. While these features alone may not lead to accurate inference of the object of interest, we found that combining the features from multiple cameras improves the accuracy.

Finally, we need to define and quantify what does a "better" view mean. In this work, we adopt the notion of viewpoint entropy [25] and choose the video depicting the same scene with the largest entropy with respect to the current video to switch to.

The chapter is organized into seven sections. We first review the related work in Sect. 2. Section 3 introduces the 3D query principles. Section 4 describes how we reconstruct the set of 3D ellipsoids. The experiments and evaluation results are presented in Sect. 5. Finally, the Sect. 6 concludes the paper.

2 Related Work

Our literature review is broken down in two parts. We first review some recent work on visual computing with mobile phones. Then we explain how the proposed system based on multiple simultaneous video streams relates to several similar applications.

2.1 Visual Computing with (Mobile Phone) Camera Networks

Visual computing on mobile phones equipped with cameras is moving in two directions: the visual computation power is increasing on-device and, simultaneously, the tremendous amount of deployed devices leads to large scale camera networks. The first aspect is perfectly illustrated by Tanskanen et al. [22] in which a complete on-device live 3D reconstruction pipeline using monocular hand-held camera along with inertial sensors is presented. In the second direction, structure-from-Motion (SfM) algorithms can also be centralized taking as input images acquired by many mobile cameras: the famous SfM pipeline used in the Photo Tourism project and called Bundler [20] allows to reconstruct jointly 3D cameras and a set of 3D points from unordered image collections. An even more challenging set-up consists in synchronizing [18] many mobile phone cameras to make them cooperating in near real time. If we already enjoy many location-based-services exploiting sensor network of mobile phones (real-time applications reporting flooded roads for instance), we identify only a few efforts fusing simultaneous mobile phone camera captures. In their work [9], Kansal and Zhao consider an audio-visual sensor network that potentially exploits millions of deployed mobile phones. The visual data from those mobile cameras help overcoming limitations of classical location techniques (cell-tower/WLAN triangulations, GPS, etc.). The proposed hybrid location technique includes matching methods between un-located images and images with known location. Another example is the PhonéCam project [3]: with sufficient synchronization and calibration, multiple mobile phone cameras might play the role of HD video sources for 3D and tele-immersion. It is an example where smartphones replace cameras connected to a computer leading to an emerging type of smart camera networks made of relatively cheap distributed computational nodes with network interconnections and links to one or more central servers. Our contribution is similar in nature but address another challenging application supporting switches between simultaneous video streams with a centralized lightweight 3D reconstruction computed in near real-time. Our task-oriented reconstruction is clearly a compromise between the two aforementioned 3D reconstruction techniques: one camera, real-time on-device reconstruction [22] and distributed cameras, centralized and time consuming reconstruction [20].

2.2   Applications Based on Simultaneous Video Streams

Video clips recorded by multiple users during the same crowded event can be used for several purposes. For instance, these videos can be automatically edited to produce a new *mashup* video similar to how a TV director would switch between different cameras to produce the show. Shresta et al. [19] address this problem and select the cameras by maximizing video quality. They also explain in [18] how to synchronize multiple cameras from the available multimedia content. Saini et al. [16] expand this effort about video mashups with live applications in mind. They try to make decisions about cameras without any reference to future information. Their improved model jointly maximizes the video signal quality but also the diversity and quality of the view angles as well as some aesthetic criteria about shot lengths, distances from the stage etc. These works add to the abundant literature about best view selection as explained in the recent paper introducing the Jiku mobile video dataset [17]. We also address this issue in our video switching application. In the camera networks community, one often aims at selecting the *optimal* viewpoint in order to control data redundancy while saving resources [6, 24] or in order to identify view(s) with task-oriented criteria for sport [14] or surveillance [12] applications. In this paper we follow a popular approach to this problem leading to the *most informative* viewpoint [26]. Finally our video query system offers social media interactions during live events. Dezfulli et al. [5] also investigate a live scenario for mobile video sharing during a soccer match. Their prototype, called CoStream, has been designed to evaluate both the production and the consumption of videos. Indeed, a close-up video showing a goal can be produced by users located next to the goal in the stadium and be requested (e.g., consumed) by some friends seating in other aisles far apart from the place where the goal was scored. During CoStream design sessions, the participants stressed the need of a pointing gesture for immediate interaction. Pointing their mobile device in the direction of an interesting event should naturally allow a query of existing multiple video streams. In this work, we try to give a sound technical answer to this specific and open problem.

3   3D Query in Simultaneously Captured Videos

In this section, we define formally what we meant by *3D query* and *better view*. To simplify the explanation, we will present our algorithm in the context of a set of J images $I_j, j = 1 \ldots J$, corresponding to video frames taken from the same time instance from J cameras filming the same scene from different angles. We denote the cameras as $\mathscr{C}_j$ and we know the projection matrices of the cameras.

Let I_q be the image currently viewed by the user, in which the user will specify a region of interest (ROI) R_q. We call I_q the query image and R_q the query region.

For now, we assume that we have a set of K 3D shapes, representing the interesting objects in the scene (how we obtained this will be described in the next section). We back-project R_q onto 3D space, forming a query volume V_q that is a generalized viewing cone through R_q. We then compute the intersection between V_q and the 3D shapes.

After this step, the algorithm selects a subset of 3D shapes $\mathscr{O}_q$ that intersects with V_q (we consider V_q intersects with a 3D shapes if more than 40% of a shape is within V_q). Note that, it is possible to select a shape corresponding to an object that does not appear in I_q.

The set $\mathscr{O}_q$ represents 3D shapes selected by the user through R_q, and ideally, would correspond to the set of objects of interest in the scene that the user is interested in. What remains is for the algorithm to return an image that depicts these objects in the "best" way. To compute this, we use the notation of *viewpoint entropy*, as inspired by Vázquez et al. [25].

For each image I_j, we compute its viewpoint entropy. We adapt the notion of viewpoint entropy by Vazquez et al. to handle a finite set of 3D shapes and the restricted region of background visible from I_j. The viewpoint entropy $E(I_j)$ represents the amount of visual information about the selected 3D shapes $\mathscr{O}_q$ in I_j. Let $\mathscr{A}_o$ be the projected area of shape o on I_j, normalized between 0 and 1 with respect to the area of I_j. We define $\mathscr{A}_{bg}$ as the normalized area in I_j that is not covered by any shape (i.e., the background). We define the viewpoint entropy as

$$E(I_j) = -\mathscr{A}_{bg} \log_2 \mathscr{A}_{bg} - \sum_{o \in \mathscr{O}_q} \mathscr{A}_o \log_2 \mathscr{A}_o \tag{1}$$

An image that depicts all the requested shapes with the same relative projected area would have the highest entropy. Since the relative projected areas $\mathscr{A}_i$ form a probability distribution, the relative visibility of the background at maximum entropy $(\log_2(|\mathscr{O}_q| + 1))$ should be also comparable to the visibility of each shape. In practice, we do not reach this upper bound and simply maximize $E(I_j)$ over j.

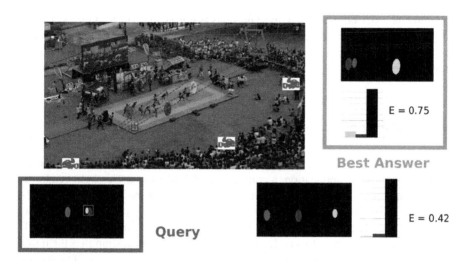

Fig. 3 A 3D query volume V_q intersecting $K_q = 2$ shapes and $J = 2$ candidate viewpoints

We return the image with the highest entropy as the result of our query. The system then switches the video stream to the one corresponding to the resulting image.

As clearly stated by Vazquez et al. the intervention of $\mathscr{A}_0$ helps to handle various zoom levels (or various distances between the cameras and the scene) among the J candidate images. The use of the background visibility level gives nearer shapes a higher entropy. In Fig. 3, a larger projection of the requested yellow shape increases the entropy of the best viewpoint (by limiting the information brought by the background).

Several efficient implementations can be used to compute $E(I_j)$ ranging from immediate rendering on graphics hardware to specialized algebraic methods for 3D shapes and their images. We use an algebraic method which is out of the scope of this chapter.

Figure 3 shows a small example illustrating this process. The small red square inside the image represents the query R_q region. The corresponding query volume V_q intersects two shapes, shown in blue and yellow, out of three 3D shapes. The image with the highest entropy (0.75) is selected out of two candidate images.

4   Lightweight Reconstruction of 3D Ellipsoids: 3D Interest Maps

As previously described, the proposed novel video interaction is actually a 3D query, i.e. a query that is performed on a 3D reconstruction of the scene. The proper functioning of the query is conditioned by three main requirements: (1) we need an automatic detection of the important objects a user may wish to query; (2) we need a 3D reconstruction that makes those objects identifiable from any viewpoint; (3) we need a very fast reconstruction to typically get a one-second-duration query-response cycle.

4.1 Motivation and Method Overview

In the previous section we have introduced a mid-level 3D representation of the scene guided by the application: a collection of 3D ellipsoids. This lightweight 3D scene structure is a simplified version of our 3D interest maps introduced in [2]. A 3D interest map is an extension of saliency maps in the 3D space since most users film what they find interesting from their respective viewpoints. In this paper, 3D interest maps are reduced to a collection of 3D ellipsoids which simplifies the initial mathematical formulation (a mixture of 3D Gaussians). This simpler 3D structure is rather coarse but well adapted to the query-response mechanism. In this section, we detail our lightweight 3D reconstruction method which is fast, discriminative enough and which can be seen as an important contribution of this work along with the query. It is later evaluated through task oriented experiments.

The input data of the reconstruction problem are classical: at any time instant we have at our disposal a collection of J high definition images $\mathscr{I} = \{I_j\}_{j=1...J}$ and the associated camera matrices $\{P_j\}_{j=1...J}$. In our set-up, the environment and the cameras are supposed to be equipped enough to have, at least approximately, a synchronization between the videos and an estimation of the camera parameters. This assumption is also evaluated in the experimental section.

Under these conditions, the most popular state-of-the-art 3D reconstruction technique [7] is publicly available as a software named PVMS. Taking our data as input, PMVS outputs the rigid structure of the scene visible in the images. Unfortunately, if we use PVMS with our data, we do not satisfy all three previous requirements: the set of reconstructed points is not restricted to the important objects (the human performers in our use-case). Those important objects are mingled with the rest of the scene (ground, stage, background etc.) and cannot be easily identified from an arbitrary (query) viewpoint. And even worse, the reconstruction is too slow for our application: a reconstruction typically lasts 40 s on a powerful machine with $J = 7$ HD images.

In order to overcome those issues we take advantage of the modularity offered by PMVS, which accepts as additional (and facultative) inputs, some 2D masks, that limit the space in which PMVS works at reconstructing points. In other words, if we want PMVS to reconstruct points only on important objects, then the challenge is to build masks that will force PMVS to do so. It is essential to understand that this step of the algorithm is actually the most important one, and is the main contribution of this chapter. One easy way to build the masks would be to use existing 2D region-of-interest detection algorithms (e.g. saliency detectors) but, as will be shown in the experiments, this method would lead to poor results as the 3D consistency of the detected 2D regions of interest is not guaranteed! This is why we introduce an alternative method based on the computation of the intersection of visibility cones, in 3D. We therefore build a 3D mask, from which we use the 2D re-projections as additional inputs for PMVS. This step is detailed in the following subsection.

4.2 Computation of 3D Masks

In this subsection we explain how to compute 3D masks which, once reprojected in the cameras frame, will be used as an input to PMVS to limit the reconstruction to the important objects. We choose to look at the quantity of motion observed in the videos as an indicator of the strategy to apply when computing 3D masks (the quantity of motion is any indicator computed from M_k, the motion map associated to camera k see also [2]).

We consider two scenarios, depending on the quantity of motion observed in the videos.

Scenario #1: Low Apparent Motion
If the quantity of motion is less than a chosen and fixed threshold, without moving objects and without semantic object detectors, it is difficult to detect the potential objects of interest in the available 2D views $I_j, j = 1 \ldots J$. We can only assume that the user's region of interest (UROI) in the image could be an elliptic region centered at the principal point (i.e., at the point where the optical axis meets the image plane, supposedly coinciding with the image centre). This makes sense as it seems natural that the user tends to shoot by steering the camera optical axis towards the scene hotspots [23]. Such regions are illustrated in blue in the first row of Fig. 5. Let us call *visual cone* the back-projection in 3-space of the ellipse associated with the UROI i.e., the cone through the ellipse which has the camera centre as vertex. Our idea is to generate a cloud of 3D points in the expected 3D ROIs by basically intersecting the visual cones of all the cameras. This is illustrated in Fig. 4where the

Fig. 4 Default

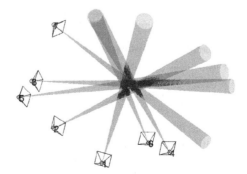

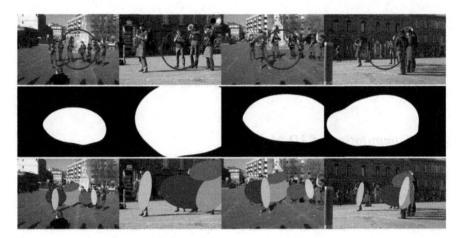

Fig. 5 Results on the **Brass Band** dataset: on *top*, *ellipses* detected based on the central focus assumption and used for the cones intersection. *Below*, reconstructed *ellipsoids* reprojected into the images

positions of the cameras are the ones estimated for the **Brass Band** dataset (see also Fig. 5). Let C^j be the ellipse associated with the UROI in image j and let Λ^j be the visual cone back-projecting C^j.

We first describe an algorithm for intersecting two visual cones, related to cameras i and j.

1. In image i, generate R random points inside the ellipse C^i and back-project each of these points p as a 3D line L_p^i, through p and the camera centre.
2. Compute the two intersection points where line L_p^i meets the PCoI Λ^j associated with image j.
3. If such intersection points exist, discretise the line segment, whose endpoints are these two points, into S points so image i yields RS 3D points.
4. Repeat 1–3 by switching the roles of cameras i and j.

Given now a sequence of J views, we can apply the above algorithm for each of the $\frac{1}{2}J(J-1)$ distinct image-pairs that can be formed in order to eventually obtain $J(J-1)RS$ 3D points of interest for the sequence.

Scenario #2: Significant Apparent Motion

In that case, we assume that the interesting video objects are correlated with the motion in the video. This is particularly true for examples such as sport or dance. We start by computing a motion map, which we get by computing the distance in RGB color space between two consecutive images in a video. Many solutions exist and the reader's favorite one will be satisfactory. Since we handle many views simultaneously, the motion detection can fail for a few viewpoints without any significant impact on the final result. Our motion map computation is primarily simple and rapid. With our motion maps, we use an unsupervised 2D clustering

Fig. 6 Results on the **Jiku** dataset: on *top*, *ellipses* detected based on the motion and used for the cones intersection. *Below*, reconstructed *ellipsoids* reprojected into the images

technique (Mean-Shift, [4]) in order to form clusters of apparent motion, and estimate an ellipse for each cluster. A result of our motion analysis can be seen in the first row of Fig. 6 for the **Jiku** dataset. It is worth noticing that we output elliptical independent moving regions in each view *without any matching between them*. We then use a generalization of the intersection of visual cones dealing with all pairs of detected ellipses and all pairs of available views. We also get the expected 3D ROIs as a pool of 3D elliptical clusters. Those 3D ROIs can be projected and binarized to form the 2D masks shown in the second row of Fig. 6.

4.3   Lightweight Reconstruction as a Set of Ellipsoids

In this subsection we describe our method to obtain the final set of 3D ellipsoids, as can be visualized on the third row of Figs. 5 and 6.

We run PMVS with all needed inputs: the images, the masks and the camera projection matrices. We set the *level* parameter to 4, in order to lower the resolution of the images and therefore obtain a sparse reconstruction.

At this point we get a 3D points cloud and those points should be concentrated on important objects. It is then very intuitive to cluster the points, and to associate an ellipsoid with each cluster.

We use, once again, the Mean-Shift clustering algorithm [4] to cluster the points. This choice is motivated by the fact that we do not know the number of important objects that are present in the scene, so we need an unsupervised clustering technique in order to automatically discover the number of objects. The Mean-Shift algorithm takes a parameter as input, that defines a radius of search for neighbouring points. This parameter is called the bandwidth, and because we aim at separating objects that are in fact persons, we choose a bandwidth equal to 50 cm.

Finally we need to create an ellipsoid to model a cluster of points. We set the ellipsoid center to the mean value of the coordinates of all points. Then, by computing the eigenvectors of the covariance matrix of the points coordinates we get the directions of the three axes of the ellipsoid.

4.4 Efficient Implementation

In order to boost real-time intersection of visual cones, we suggest a problem statement in matrix form with projective geometry as theoretical background. On the one hand, matrix operations can be implemented in a very efficient way. On the other hand, one key advantage of such a projective representation is that one can avoid to deal with special cases, as two objects that do not intersect in affine space intersect at complex points in projective space.

We now give some modeling details (using the same writing conventions as in [8]) that can be eventually skipped. If the camera is seen as a pinhole device, then it can be represented by a 3×4 projection matrix P. We show next that the *input data* only consist in the set of projection matrices and the set of ellipses associated with the UROIs; *no image features are required*.

An ellipse is given by 3×3 symmetric homogeneous matrix C so any image point (u, v) on the ellipse satisfies the quadratic equation $(u, v, 1)\mathsf{C}(u, v, 1)^T = 0$. The back-projection of an image ellipse C is a visual cone (which is a degenerate quadric in projective 3-space) with 4×4 matrix

$$\Lambda = \mathsf{P}^T \mathsf{C} \mathsf{P}.$$

The back-projection of an image point p is a 3D line, through p and the camera centre, whose Plücker matrix [8, p. 197] is

$$\mathsf{L}_p = (\mathsf{P})^T [\mathbf{p}]_\times \mathsf{P},$$

where $\mathbf{p} = (u, v, 1)^T$ is the homogeneous vector of pixel p with coordinates (u, v) and $[\mathbf{p}]_\times$ is the order-3 skew-symmetric matrix associated with $\mathbf{p}$ [8, p. 581].

The two 3D intersection points A and B where line L_p meets the cone are given in closed form by the rank-2 order-4 symmetric matrix

$$\mathbf{AB}^T + \mathbf{BA}^T \sim \mathsf{L}_p^* \Lambda \mathsf{L}_p^*,$$

where L_p^* is the dual Plücker matrix of L_p, $\mathbf{A}$ and $\mathbf{B}$ are the homogeneous 4-vectors of points A and B, and the operator $\sim$ means 'proportional to'. Due to lack of space, the proof is not given here but it can be shown that (1) the two points are real if the two non-zero eigenvalues of $\mathbf{AB}^T + \mathbf{BA}^T$ are of different signs and complex otherwise, and (2) A and B can be straightforwardly obtained by a simple decomposition of $\mathbf{AB}^T + \mathbf{BA}^T$.

Now consider the special case of a circular UROI centered at the principal point. It can be shown that a visual cone through such a circle only depends on the camera centre and the optical axis (through it). In this special case, errors on the rotation around the optical axis, which are computed in the projection matrix, have no effect on the matrix of the visual cone.

4.5 Summary

To wrap up this section, we list here the steps required to obtain a lightweight reconstruction of the scene.

- Apply the OpenCV blob tracker to find 2D Regions of Interest.
- Intersect back-projection of the 2D ROI, sample these cones intersection, and estimate a 3D mask.
- Project the 3D mask back into 2D masks, and apply PMVS with these masks on a sub-sampled version of the images.
- Cluster the set of 3D points thus obtained using Mean-Shift, and then associate one ellipsoid to every cluster.

5 Experiments

Before we present the evaluation of our proposed lightweight reconstruction and the associated query system, we first introduce three datasets that we used for evaluation, and briefly explain our experimental set-up. The 3D objects obtained from our experiments are then compared against saliency maps in the 2D image space (since a comparison in 3D is difficult to visualize). Finally, we report the major results from our study to evaluate the query mechanism.

5.1 Datasets

We use three datasets to evaluate our approach.

BrassBand The BrassBand dataset is one that we recorded ourselves to match perfectly our purpose. This dataset serves as a baseline to evaluate our algorithm. It consists of three videos captured with fixed cameras; four videos captured with smartphones with little or no movement, and one video from a smartphone that moved around the scene and for which we also recorded its accelerometers and GPS values. The dataset depicts an outdoor scene, where eight musicians stand close to each other and move according to the instrument they are playing. We drew concentric circles on the floor so that we can reconstruct the cameras pose more easily.

Fukuoka This dataset consists of five high resolution video clips of a 5-min dance show captured by fixed cameras. The video clips capture a complex scene with multiple performers, wearing the same uniform, standing close to each other, and often moving and occluding each other. The floor of the stage, however, is composed of colored concentric circles, easing the camera parameter estimation process.

RagAndFlag The RagAndFlag dataset is the most challenging one. It consists of a set of videos shot from seven cameras, including mobile devices, surrounding an open air stage. The videos captured an event with many dancers moving in a highly dynamic outdoor scene. The videos are shaky and have a variable lighting. Furthermore, the lack of information on camera calibration makes this dataset a challenging input to our algorithms.

5.2   Calibration and Synchronization

In our experiments, we have performed 3D reconstructions of cameras and structure associated to each dataset via a structure-from-motion pipeline. The pipeline is based on a factorization scheme of projective reconstruction [13] upgraded to a metric one using the self-calibration method proposed in [15]. The cameras and structure are then refined through a final metric bundle adjustment. Image feature correspondences are manually selected in each view and consist of a set of about 30 points. Because all image features are visible in all views, such a procedure provides very accurate results. For this reason, we used computed cameras and structure as the ground truth in the evaluation of the camera calibration performed on *Fukuoka* and *BrassBand* datasets.

Usual assumptions about internal parameters such as cameras with square pixels whose principal point coincides with the origin of the pixel coordinate are made and the only unknown internal parameter is the focal length. External parameters, also called the *camera pose*, consist in six degrees of freedom (DOF), three are associated to its orientation and three—to its position. Thus, in our application, we consider cameras as having seven DOF.

Fukuoka As mentioned in Sect. 5.1, planar patterns can be used for internal and external calibration. In fact, it suffices to know the plane-to-image homography associated to a given plane in the scene to compute the focal length [8] and the camera pose [21]. In our case, the considered plane is the platform on which

Table 1 Results obtained for the internal and external camera calibration on *Fukuoka* and *BrassBand* datasets

Sequence	Fukuoka	BrassBand
Sensor	No	Yes
Orientation error (degree)	0.13	0.48
Position error (%)	1.45	5.74
Focal length error (%)	1.59	5.91
Reprojection error (pixels) on 1920 × 1080 pixels image	2.25	2.15
Reprojection error (pixels) on 240 × 135 pixels image (as input for PMVS level 3)	0.28	0.27

performers are moving. The plane-to-image homography is computed from ellipses, images of concentric circles, as proposed in [11]. Pose estimation is then performed similarly to the method presented in [1].

BrassBand With seven DOF in our camera model, if we consider the problem of the camera calibration based on 2D-3D correspondences, also called *camera resectioning*, at least four points are needed, each point providing two independent equations. Thus, in this dataset, camera calibration is performed using only the minimal number of four points (randomly chosen from the image features available) to artificially damage the accuracy of the estimated camera parameters and thus verifying how does the system respond in such challenging situations. In this case, orientation sensors of the smartphones such as accelerometer and magnetometer are used as initial orientation. Global Positioning System (GPS) provides positioning but in our cases, its accuracy is not sufficient because the area to cover is too small.

RagAndFlag In this dataset, camera matrices are those provided by the structure-from-motion pipeline and are not subject to evaluation of the camera calibration.

The results of parameter estimation are expressed in the Table 1. We provided the mean errors on the orientation (in degrees), the relative 3D error on the position (in percent) and the relative error on the focal length (in percent). Reprojection errors are also mentioned since, in our application, this factor is crucial for both making sub-sampled 3D reconstructions using PMVS (cf. row associated with the 240 × 135 pixels resolution) and querying.

Synchronization We evaluated an algorithm [10] for automatic synchronization of the video from the Fukuoka dataset using the audio streams. Table 2 shows that the algorithm performs fairly well, scoring an average error of 7.25 frames (circa 0.25 s). This result, while being good considering the state of the art in this domain, offers a challenge to our system as coping with such delay makes 3D reconstruction very hard. This result motivates again our choice introduced in Sect. 5.1 to perform a sub-sampled reconstruction in order to reduce the impact of noise on the results.

Table 2 Frame offset between videos computed by Ke et al. [10] and obtained manually

Videos	Offset given by Ke et al. [10]	Manually defined offset
#1–#5	48	55
#2–#5	1578	1570
#3–#5	890	899
#4–#5	1241	1248

Fig. 7 Query on the Fukuoka dataset. On the *left* the queried region (in *red*) and on the *right*, the top answer of both our algorithm and the users (Color figure online)

5.3 Queries

To evaluate the quality of the resulting video that the system provide in response to a query, we conducted a user study with the following setup.

Videos We selected 15 sequences, 1 from Fukuoka, 1 from RagAndFlag and 13 from BrassBand. Since we only have captors data on the BrassBand dataset, most of the sequences used in the study are taken from this dataset.

Methodology For each sequence, one of the images is considered as the query image. On this image, we define five spatial regions corresponding to the actual query we want to evaluate. For each query, we ask the users which of the remaining videos they think is the best answer to the query. In order to avoid any bias, the order of presentation of the videos is randomized, as well as the order of the sequences and the order of the queries.

We have set up a web-based interface, displaying the query (as a red rectangle on one of the images) and the entire set of videos. Users were asked to look at the query, identify the objects of interest that were queried and find, among the set of videos, the one that they think shows the queried objects of interest the best. They then voted for this video by clicking on it, and moved on to the next query.

Participants The study involved 35 participants (13 females, 22 males) with ages ranging from 20 to 60 (average age is 30). Each of the 35 participants answered 75 queries, giving a total of 2625 votes.

Results We show some qualitative results in Figs. 7 and 8.

Fig. 8 Query on the BrassBand dataset. On the *left* the queried region (in *red*), on the *middle* the top answer of our algorithm and on the *right* the top answer of the users (Color figure online)

Table 3 Percentage of the users satisfied with the top two answers to the query

Method	First answer (%)	Second answer (%)
Best possible	56	78
Our method (real time)	44	62
PMVS	30	41
Our method (no time constraints)	49	68

Figure 7 shows a scenario where our algorithm performs exactly as user did. The top answer of our algorithm allows to see a clear view of the queried region, which is the lead singer of the band. This answer was also chosen by all users but one.

Figure 8 shows a scenario where our algorithm is not consistent with users' answers. A majority of users chose the rightmost image, as it allows to see all performers clearly without occlusion. Our algorithm on the other hand gave the middle image as the best answer. The main reason for that is that even if some of the ellipsoids are occluded, the background weight is less important than in others images, which results in a larger viewpoint entropy.

We now introduce quantitative results, based on the user study. We say that a user is satisfied by the answer to a query if the answer given by our algorithm is the same as the one voted by the user during the user study. This hypothesis assumes that users would be satisfied with one answer only, which is not true in general. For example, in the *BrassBand* dataset, some of the cameras were located pretty close to each other, which means that in some cases users would have been satisfied by both videos as an answer to a query.

Table 3 shows the percentage of users that are satisfied by the top answer, and the top two answers, to the query. The first row of Table 3 indicates the highest percentage of users that it is possible to satisfy. These relatively low numbers are explained by the dispersion of the users answers to the query during the user study. There are often several suitable images that answer a query, and this fact is reflected by the users' choice.

Our results are introduced in the second row of Table 3. Almost half of the users (44%) would be satisfied on average by the answer provided by our algorithm, and more than 60% would be satisfied by one of our top two answers. The remaining users chose different views, which does not necessarily mean they would not have been pleased with our answer. In fact, in the case of the Fukuoka and BrassBand datasets, there are often multiple views that would give acceptable answers to a query, as some cameras are close to each other.

It is common in CBIR to evaluate an algorithm by computing the Average Rank of the answers to a query. To obtain this value, we rank the videos according to the number of users' votes for each query. Let $rank(I, q)$ be the rank of image I associated to the query q. The Average Rank of the first answer to a query (or $AR(1)$) is defined as

$$AR(1) = \frac{1}{card(Q)} \sum_{q \in Q} rank(A_q^1, q) \tag{2}$$

where A_q^1 is the first answer to query q from our algorithm, and Q is the set of all queries that were evaluated during the user study.

Table 4 shows the Average Rank of the first four answers to the query from various algorithms. The first row shows that our method performs well: $AR(1) = 1.95$ reflects that the first answer given by our algorithm is often either the best or the second best one. Another interesting aspect of the result is that the average rank of each answer is correlated to the rank of the answers from the user study. Indeed, we observe that $AR(1) < AR(2) < AR(3) < AR(4)$. This observation means that our algorithm can rank the possible answer in a comparable way as real users would.

Our algorithm sacrifices some accuracy for efficiency. To study this effect, the third row of the table shows the results of a query that is performed on a scene reconstructed without time constraints, using the full resolution images but with our masks. The results, as expected, are better than our method since no accuracy is sacrificed. Note that the percentage of users satisfied by the two best answers computed with this method (Table 3) is also quite high compared to the best possible result.

Finally, the second row of the Table 4 and the third row in Table 3 show the results of a query performed on a scene reconstructed by PMVS without any masks. Not only does not the algorithm run in real time, but the query results are poor. This result is due to the fact that PMVS reconstructs more objects than just those that are needed to perform the query. This result validates our masks construction step as a necessary contribution to perform the querying.

Table 4 Average Rank (AR) of the first four answers to the query implemented using our real-time method (first line), PMVS (second line) and our method without time constraints (third line)

Method	$AR(1)$	$AR(2)$	$AR(3)$	$AR(4)$
Our method (real time)	1.95	2.7	3.6	4.5
PMVS	2.9	3.7	3.1	3.9
Our method (no time constraints)	1.5	2.6	3.7	4.4

6 Conclusion

In this paper, we have investigated and validated a new interest-based and content-based mechanism for users to switch between multiple cameras capturing the same scene at the same time. We devised a query interface that allows a user to highlight objects of interest in a video, in order to request video from another camera with a closer, non-occluded, and interesting view of the objects. The answer to the query is computed based on a 3D interest map [2] automatically inferred from the available simultaneous video streams. Such a map can be reconstructed very efficiently with our approach if the environment is equipped enough to have a reasonably precise calibration and synchronization of the cameras. During our user study, we have shown that the system responses fit well with users' expectations. We have also seen that our original 3D interest map is a rich combination of the simultaneous visual sources of information as well as a consistent generalization of the more conventional 2D saliency maps.

In the future, we want to precisely evaluate each component of our system. In order to respect the end-to-end delay, the 3D interest map reconstruction should be performed in real-time on the server side. We expect a cycle between the query and the video-switch to be done in about one or two seconds. The precise performances of both the cones intersection and the finer reconstruction technique must be known.The spatio-temporal coherence of the maps could also be taken into account to improve the computations. More generally, using more of content analysis for improving the masks and the maps would probably be interesting. Finally, we also aim at further studying the ergonomics of the client interface: for instance, it is not clear so far if we should provide the requester with an interactive overview of the good available streams or simply switch to the best one.

References

1. Calvet, L., Gurdjos, P., Charvillat, V.: Camera tracking using concentric circle markers: paradigms and algorithms. In: ICIP, pp. 1361–1364 (2012)
2. Carlier, A., Calvet, L., Nguyen, D.T.D., Ooi, W.T., Gurdjos, P., Charvillat, V.: 3D interest maps from simultaneous video recordings. In: Proceedings of the 22nd ACM International Conference on Multimedia, MM '14, pp. 577–586 (2014)
3. Chandra, S., Chiu, P., Back, M.: Towards portable, high definition multi-camera video capture using smartphone for tele-immersion. In: IEEE International Symposium on Multimedia (2013)
4. Comaniciu, D., Meer, P.: Mean shift: a robust approach toward feature space analysis. IEEE Trans. Pattern Anal. Mach. Intell. **24**(5), 603–619 (2002)
5. Dezfuli, N., Huber, J., Olberding, S., Mühlhäuser, M.: CoStream: in-situ co-construction of shared experiences through mobile video sharing during live events. In: CHI Extended Abstracts, pp. 2477–2482 (2012)
6. Ercan, A.O., Yang, D.B., Gamal, A.E., Guibas, L.J.: Optimal placement and selection of camera network nodes for target localization. In: IEEE DCOSS, pp. 389–404 (2006)

7. Furukawa, Y., Ponce, J.: Accurate, dense, and robust multiview stereopsis. IEEE Trans. Pattern Anal. Mach. Intell. **32**(8), 1362–1376 (2010)
8. Hartley, R.I., Zisserman, A.: Multiple View Geometry in Computer Vision, 2nd edn. Cambridge University Press, Cambridge (2004). ISBN: 0521540518
9. Kansal, A., Zhao, F.: Location and mobility in a sensor network of mobile phones. In: ACM Network and Operating Systems Support for Digital Audio and Video (2007)
10. Ke, Y., Hoiem, D., Sukthankar, R.: Computer vision for music identification. In: CVPR (1), pp. 597–604 (2005)
11. Kim, J.S., Gurdjos, P., Kweon, I.S.: Geometric and algebraic constraints of projected concentric circles and their applications to camera calibration. IEEE Trans. Pattern Anal. Mach. Intell. **27**(4), 637–642 (2005)
12. Lee, H., Tessens, L., Morbée, M., Aghajan, H.K., Philips, W.: Sub-optimal camera selection in practical vision networks through shape approximation. In: ACIVS, pp. 266–277 (2008)
13. Oliensis, J., Hartley, R.: Iterative extensions of the sturm/triggs algorithm: convergence and nonconvergence. IEEE Trans. Pattern Anal. Mach. Intell. **29**(12), 2217–2233 (2007)
14. Philip Kelly, C.O.C., Kim, C., O'Connor, N.E.: Automatic camera selection for activity monitoring in a multi-camera system for tennis. In: ACM/IEEE International Conference on Distributed Smart Cameras (2009)
15. Pollefeys, M., Gool, L.J.V., Vergauwen, M., Verbiest, F., Cornelis, K., Tops, J., Koch, R.: Visual modeling with a hand-held camera. Int. J. Comput. Vis. **59**(3), 207–232 (2004)
16. Saini, M.K., Gadde, R., Yan, S., Ooi, W.T.: MoViMash: online mobile video mashup. In: ACM Multimedia, pp. 139–148 (2012)
17. Saini, M., Venkatagiri, S.P., Ooi, W.T., Chan, M.C.: The Jiku mobile video dataset. In: Proceedings of the Fourth Annual ACM SIGMM Conference on Multimedia Systems, MMSys, Oslo (2013)
18. Shrestha, P., Barbieri, M., Weda, H., Sekulovski, D.: Synchronization of multiple camera videos using audio-visual features. IEEE Trans. Multimedia **12**(1), 79–92 (2010)
19. Shrestha, P., de With, P.H.N., Weda, H., Barbieri, M., Aarts, E.H.L.: Automatic mashup generation from multiple-camera concert recordings. In: ACM Multimedia, pp. 541–550 (2010)
20. Snavely, N., Seitz, S.M., Szeliski, R.: Photo tourism: exploring photo collections in 3D. ACM Trans. Graph. **25**(3), 835–846 (2006)
21. Sturm, P.F.: Algorithms for plane-based pose estimation. In: CVPR, pp. 1706–1711 (2000)
22. Tanskanen, P., Kolev, K., Meier, L., Camposeco, F., Saurer, O., Pollefeys, M.: Live metric 3D reconstruction on mobile phones. In: ICCV (2013)
23. Tatler, B.W.: The central fixation bias in scene viewing: selecting an optimal viewing position independently of motor biases and image feature distributions. J. Vis. **7**(14), 1–17 (2007)
24. Tessens, L., Morbée, M., Lee, H., Philips, W., Aghajan, H.K.: Principal view determination for camera selection in distributed smart camera networks. In: IEEE ICDSC, pp. 1–10 (2008)
25. Vázquez, P.P., Feixas, M., Sbert, M., Heidrich, W.: Viewpoint selection using viewpoint entropy. In: Proceedings of VMV 2001, pp. 273–280 (2001)
26. Wang, C., Shen, H.W.: Information theory in scientific visualization. Entropy **13**(1), 254–273 (2011)

Information: Theoretical Model for Saliency Prediction—Application to Attentive CBIR

Vincent Courboulay and Arnaud Revel

Abstract This work presents an original informational approach to extract visual information, model attention and evaluate the efficiency of the results. Even if the extraction of salient and useful information, i.e. observation, is an elementary task for human and animals, its simulation is still an open problem in computer vision. In this article, we define a process to derive optimal laws to extract visual information without any constraints or a priori. Starting from saliency definition and measure through the prism of information theory, we present a framework in which we develop an ecological inspired approach to model visual information extraction. We demonstrate that our approach provides a fast and highly configurable model, moreover it is as plausible as existing models designed for high biological fidelity. It proposes an adjustable trade-off between nondeterministic attentional behavior and properties of stability, reproducibility and reactiveness. We apply this approach to enhance the performance in an object recognition task. As a conclusion, this article proposes a theoretical framework to derive an optimal model validated by many experimentations.

1 Introduction

Bio-inspired population-based algorithms can be used effectively to develop software systems for computer vision and image analysis, for applications in complex domains of high industrial and social relevance as information and saliency extraction in images or videos. For example, it is crucial to find as rapidly as possible what is interesting in multimedia documents. The problem, however, is not finding information but finding *relevant* information. But, how can we quantify the quality of an information? and before answering this question, how can we define visual information? As mentioned in [10], the problem concerning a definition of visual information is *further aggravated by a long-lasting stance borrowed from the biological vision research that assumes human-like information processing as*

V. Courboulay (✉) • A. Revel
L3i - University of La Rochelle, 17000 La Rochelle, France
e-mail: vcourbou@univ-lr.fr; arevel@univ-lr.fr

© Springer International Publishing AG 2017
J. Benois-Pineau, P. Le Callet (eds.), *Visual Content Indexing and Retrieval with Psycho-Visual Models*, Multimedia Systems and Applications,
DOI 10.1007/978-3-319-57687-9_7

an enigmatic mix of perceptual and cognitive vision faculties. Consequently, it is more important than ever to adopt a coherent strategy that would allow measuring, characterizing and processing *interesting* information. Of course, *interesting* is a subjective term, which is driven by many factors such as volition and the task at hand. In this article, interest will refer to regions that attract human gaze when looked at purposelessly, without any a priori.

Finally, regarding the context, what is the *salient information* I have to measure, analyze, characterize, transmit, present?

In this chapter, *visual attention* is defined as the cognitive or computational process of selectively focusing on one region while ignoring other ones whereas *salience* is the state or quality by which region stands out relative to its neighbors [27, 29]. Both of these concepts are strongly correlated.

This chapter deals with the problem of defining how to optimally extract information from images.

The novelty of the proposed work is to present an application of Frieden's well established information framework [20] that answers to the question: *how to optimally extract salient information based on the low level characteristics that the human visual system provides?* **We integrate our biologically inspired framework into a real time visual attention model and we propose an evaluation which demonstrate the quality of our model**.

The outline of this chapter is as follows: the next section gives a brief overview of salience modeling presented from an information theory point of view. Section 3 presents the concepts of a general framework called *extreme physical information* (EPI). In Sect. 4, we demonstrate that the equation family that has to be used to optimally extract visual information is the biologically inspired predator-prey equation (or general growth law). Then, in Sect. 5, we apply this result to build a visual attention system based on predator-prey equations. Finally in Sect. 6, we propose to position our model in an up-to-date benchmark. We used this benchmark because according to the author, this is the largest data set with so many viewers per image. They calculate the performance of many models at predicting ground truth fixations using multiple metrics. In this section, we also present an attentive CBIR approach based on our model.

2 Salience Through the Prism of the Information Theory

While machine vision systems are becoming increasingly powerful, in most regards they are still far inferior to their biological counterparts. In human, the mechanisms of evolution have generated the visual attention system which selects the relevant information in order to reduce both cognitive load and scene understanding ambiguity.

This most widespread visual attention theory is referred to as an *early selection model* because irrelevant messages are filtered out before the stimulus information is processed for meaning [3, 50, 53]. In this context, attention selects some information in order not to overload our cognitive system. This is also the basic premise of a large number of computational models of saliency and visual attention [23, 27, 41]. Besides these well known models, we would like to mention here the theory of *simplexity* [1] which also places attention among the key mechanisms to simplify complexity.

In this section, we have decided to focus our *attention* on a particular family of computational visual attention models, those based on information theory. Directly related to probabilistic theories, models based on information theory postulate that the brain uses its attentional mechanisms to maximize the amount of information extracted. Estimated locally, it can then be used to define image saliency. Different approaches to compute this amount of information are available.

Gilles [24] proposes an explanation of salience in terms of local complexity, which can be measured by the Shannon entropy of local attributes of the image. Kadir [28] takes this definition and expands the model using the maximum entropy to determine the scale of the salient features in a multi-scales analysis.

Bruce [4] proposes to use a measure of self-information to build non-linear filtering operators, used to normalize singularity maps, before merging them, in a similar architecture to that proposed in [27]. In [5, 6], he combines an independent component analysis [42] and a measurement of self-information in order to obtain an estimation of the salience of an image.

Mancas [36] proposes a very comprehensive approach based on the salience of self-information. He presents models to suit different conditions: $1D$ (audio), $2D$ (images) and $2D + t$ (video). His approach also includes attention with or without a priori information (top-down or bottom-up).

Finally, we want to mention the outlying works of Diamant [10–12]. He proposes a new definition of information, derived from Kolmogorov's complexity theory and Chaitin's notion of algorithmic information. He presents a unifying framework for visual information processing, which explicitly accounts for the perceptual and cognitive image processing peculiarities.

Interestingly, all of these approaches (except the last one) consider image and pixels as isolated entities, linked by statistical bottom-up or top-down properties without any biological plausibility. They only focus on salience and forget attention (cognitive or computational).

In the next section, we present a framework which keeps the advantages of informational theory approaches and at the same time provides strong explanatory capacity: the extreme physical information (EPI).

In EPI, *observation* is seen as an active process which extracts information from a measured object to increase the knowledge of an observer (human or computer). In this framework, *salience* and *visual attention* can be linked by a flow of information coming *from* a scene *to* its cognitive or computational representation.

We propose that EPI provides an optimal way of extracting visual information. Based on this assumption, EPI has already been used to optimally represent information held in an image [8, 25]. In this chapter, we extend these previous works by considering an open system, i.e. a system that can acquire or loose a priori information; for instance an observation of an image or a video shot by an observer. But let's make a brief presentation of the theoretical framework: the EPI.

3   Extreme Physical Information

Over the past 20 years, Roy B. Frieden has developed a very powerful and complete
theory which proposes a unified approach of physics and exploratory analysis
[19, 20]. In his work, both theory and applications are presented, from the derivation
of the *Schrödinger* equation to the theory of social change and numerous other
various topics. Recently, EPI has been extended to universal cognitive models via
a confident information first principle [58]. In this part, we briefly present the EPI
principle.

The main objective of Frieden's approach is to develop *a theory of measurement
that incorporates the observer into the phenomenon under measurement* based on
Fisher Information.

In our particular case of interest, where we have to deal with images and videos,
if $\mathbf{p}(\mathbf{x})$ denotes the probability density functions for the noise vector $\mathbf{x}$ intrinsic to
the nD measurement and $\mathbf{q}^2$ the real probability amplitudes defined as $\mathbf{p} = \mathbf{q}^2$ (see
[19] for a more complete and proper approach), I can be expressed as:

$$I[\mathbf{q}] = 4 \sum_i \int dx_i \sum_v \left(\frac{\partial q_i}{\partial x_{iv}} \right)^2, \tag{1}$$

where $q_i \equiv q_i(x_i)$ is the ith probability amplitude for the measure fluctuation $x_i = (x_{i1}, \dots, x_{ip})$.

Using Fisher information, instead of Shannon or Boltzmann information, and
taking into account the observer allow to derive among the best-known laws of
physics, statistical mechanics, quantum mechanics, thermodynamics and quantum
gravity [19]. Frieden defined a unique principle of physics, that of EPI. As
previously mentioned, the main characteristic of this approach is the inclusion as
integral part of the measurement of the observer, and its main aim is to find unknown
system probabilities $\mathbf{p}$.

The EPI principle is based upon the discovery that the Fisher information
I contented in data arises out of the effect under measurement where it had
the value J. Whereas information I characterizes the quality or efficiency of
the data, the information J characterizes the effect under measurement and it is
determined through an invariance principle (Fourier transform for instance). Thus,
any measurement arises from a *flow of information*:

$$J \to I \tag{2}$$

Mathematically, EPI is based on extremization of the following expression:

$$\partial(I[\mathbf{q}(\mathbf{x})] - J[\mathbf{q}(\mathbf{x})]) = 0 \quad or \quad I - J = Extrem, \tag{3}$$

where J is named the *bound information* (in the sense of being bound to the source).
Frieden also defined a coefficient κ:

$$I - \kappa J = 0 \quad 0 \le \kappa \le 1 \tag{4}$$

In the case of a **closed-system**, the flow of information is total and κ is equal to one. In the case of an **open-system** κ is equal to $\frac{1}{2}$.

Frieden defines a new quantity K called the physical information. K arises through the specifics of the particular problem as captured by I and J.

$$I - J \equiv K = extrem \tag{5}$$

K is then extremized with respect to the unknown probabilities **p** or their first derivatives.

Finally, the solutions obtained (**q** or **p**) are then interpreted as functions that allow the *best measure of information* in the chosen context [19, 20].

To briefly sum up, the EPI principle determines the functions which allow to optimize the extraction or the measure of information for a given scenario. It also determines the variational principle underlying the given scenario and by the way, differs from other approaches which often use ad hoc Hamiltonians. We voluntarily do not deeply present EPI, mainly because it is not our main objectives, and we think that the complete mathematical foundation does not provide better comprehension of our approach. For interested readers, a more complete presentation of EPI can be found for instance in [7, 14, 19, 20].

To our opinion, one of the most interesting quotation of Frieden's work is the following one [20]:

It[1] will permit us to conclude that EPI applies holistically to the observer, i.e., both to his external world and to his internal world:

(a) *externally*, defining the microscopic and macroscopic phenomena he purposely observes, including the ecology surrounding him; and
(b) *internally*, defining the growth of the competing populations (functioning, cells, bacteria, possible cancer cells, etc.) that exist within his body. These govern his ability to lie and, ultimately, to *observe*.

This quotation was the key point of our reasoning. In the next section, we propose to use it to transpose the EPI principle used in an ecological scenario into the context of visual information.

4 EPI and Visual Information

Frieden started to study closed-system phenomenon [19]. The fact that the system is closed is expressed by stating that the total number of each element is conserved, no matter what kind of molecule it may be a part of. There is no way to gain, loss or integrate a priori elements.

Yet, this closed world is obviously not adapted to visual observation, in which both environment and interior mood may affect the process. Observation clearly

---

[1] EPI used in an **open** system.

belongs to an open system, an open world. An open system is a system which continuously interacts with its environment.

At this step of this article, we would like to emphasize that there is an important difference between *seeing* and *observing*. Seeing is the action to perceive or measure with the eyes, whereas observation is to look at something with *attention*. We are not interested in seeing, which is only a flow of information between the world and our retina. We have already demonstrated that EPI could be used to model such a phenomenon [8, 26]. In this article, we are focused on observation, which is a high level processing task, a flow of information, i.e. an interaction, between the world and *our mind* through our retina and its detectors (color, orientation and intensity) [32].

The interaction can take the form of information, energy, or material transfers through of the system boundary, depending on the discipline which defines the concept. An open system should be contrasted with the concept of an isolated system which exchanges neither energy, matter, nor information with its environment. The Cramer-Rao lower bound is a limit below which the variance of an unbiased estimator cannot be found, but nothing is said so far about whether or not this bound can be reached; and that is exactly what happens in an open system.

The objective of this section is to provide an analogy that will allow us to transpose EPI in the field of vision.

4.1 Hypothesis

In this part, we present the hypothesis on which we rely in order to apply the EPI framework.

- First of all, we assume that visual observation leads to a global and optimal representation built from different and well-known features extracted by our eyes (**color, intensity, orientation, motion**) [32].
- Secondly, our main assumption is that each measured or perceived feature (color, intensity and orientation) behaves like a *mind particles population* [33]. Every feature is *fed* by the observed scene. Since the capacity of information that exists on the retina is obviously limited, we state that our mind contains N kinds of *particles* which represent the population of the features measured. Let $m_n = 1, \ldots, N$ the level of population of these particles, the total number of *particles* in the retina is:

$$M \equiv \sum_n m_n$$

Considering these assumption, we can re-use the work made in [20] concerning *Growth and transport processes*.

The framework is clearly discrete and dynamic. As time elapses populations interact, grow and die. Hence, the population size m_n vary with the time.

We define relative particles population:

$$m_n/M \equiv p_n,$$

and $\mathbf{p} = [p_1, \ldots, p_N]$.

- Our last hypothesis is to consider that our system involves four different populations, $N = 4$, with three families of populations that represents basics inputs (color, intensity orientation) and one population that represents *interest*, but we can easily increase the number of particles, which is a very interesting part of our approach.

  - The three inputs we used here was proposed by Koch and Ullman [29]. It is related to the so-called *feature integration theory*, explaining human visual search strategies. Visual input is thus decomposed into a set of three features.
  - the output, i.e. interest is considered as a population that consumes low-level features [33]. In this chapter, authors explained that *interests compete for attention, which they consume* but also *interests are consumed by the activity they engender.*

  With such an approach authors modeled development of interest system.

  Once these three hypothesis made, we can reuse the work of Fath and Frieden [14, 15, 20] in order to derive a set of optimal equations that rule the observation process.

4.2 EPI Derivation of Evolution Law

In this section, we do not present the entire computation of optimal laws but only the main steps and results, interested readers can refer to [14, 15, 20].

For our discrete problem, Fisher information at time t is given by Frieden [20]:

$$I(t) = \sum_n \frac{z_n^2}{p_n}, \qquad p_n \equiv p(n|t), \qquad z_n \equiv \frac{dp_n}{dt} \equiv p_n(g_n + d_n) \qquad n = 1, \ldots, 4,$$

(6)

where

$$g_n = \sum_n g_{nk} p_k, \qquad g_{nk} \equiv g_{nk}((p), t)$$

(7)

$$d_n = d_n((p), t), \qquad n = 1, \ldots, 4$$

The g_n, d_n are change coefficients called *growth* and *depletion* respectively. These functions are assumed to be known functions that effectively drive the differential equations, acting as EPI source terms. In Sect. 3, we have seen that:

$$I - \kappa J = 0 \quad 0 \leq \kappa \leq 1 \tag{8}$$

In *a classical* open system (in the sense of non-relativistic context), $\kappa = \frac{1}{2}$ (see [20] Chap. 5 for more details).

Frieden have also shown that Fisher bound information J can be written as:

$$J \equiv \sum_n J_n(\mathbf{g}, \mathbf{p}, \mathbf{z}, t), \quad \mathbf{g} \equiv (g_n(\mathbf{p}, t), d_n(\mathbf{p}, t), n = 1, \dots, 4) \tag{9}$$

As a consequence, extremum solution K is given by:

$$K \equiv \sum_m \left[\frac{z_m^2}{p_m} - J_m(\mathbf{g}, \mathbf{p}, \mathbf{z}, t) \right] = extrem \tag{10}$$

Differentiating $\partial / \partial z_n$ (define in Eq. (6)), Eq. (10) gives:

$$2 \frac{z_n}{p_n} - \sum_m \frac{\partial J_m}{\partial z_n} = 0, \quad n = 0, \dots, 4. \tag{11}$$

Using Eq. (3) in previous equation leads to

$$\sum_n \left(\frac{z_n^2}{p_n} - \frac{1}{2} J_n \right) = 0. \tag{12}$$

This is satisfied by the microlevel EPI conditions

$$\frac{z_n^2}{p_n} - \frac{1}{2} J_n = 0, \quad n = 1, \dots, 4 \tag{13}$$

Combining Eqs. (11) and (13) and eliminating their common parameters p_n gives

$$p_n = \frac{2 z_n}{\sum_m \frac{\partial J_m}{\partial z_n}} = 2 \frac{z_n^2}{p_n} \tag{14}$$

After cancellation this reduces to

$$\sum_m \frac{\partial J_m}{\partial z_n} = \frac{J_n}{z_n} \tag{15}$$

Some others considerations presented in [20], lead to

$$J_n = f_n(\mathbf{g}, \mathbf{p}, t) z_n \tag{16}$$

in terms of new functions f_n that have to be found.

Combining results gives:

$$z_n \equiv \frac{1}{2} f_n(\mathbf{g}, \mathbf{p}, t) p_n \tag{17}$$

where:

$$f_n(g, p, t) = 2 \left[g_n(\mathbf{p}, t) + d_n(\mathbf{p}, t) \right], \tag{18}$$

then we finally obtain:

$$\frac{dp}{dt} = \left[g_n(\mathbf{p}, t) + d_n(\mathbf{p}, t) \right] p_n, \quad n = 1, \ldots, 4, \tag{19}$$

where:

- $\mathbf{p}$ represents the optimal evolution process of interest,
- g_n represents a *growth* function,
- d_n represents a *depletion* function.

This equation is the optimal growth process equation [39]. Considering previous hypothesis and Lessers' definitions previously presented (*interests compete for attention, which they consume*; *interests are consumed by the activity they engender*), we can simplified this general equations in order to obtain the well known **Volterra-Lotka equations** [14], where the *growth function* is known as *growth rate* and *depletion* as *mortality*. Hence, our goal of deriving an optimal evolution process to extract information via EPI has been met. This general equation is usually presented as a pair of first-order, nonlinear, differential equations presented next.

4.3 Solution

Volterra-Lotka equations are used in order to model predator-prey systems. These systems were originally built to simulate the evolution and the interactions of some colonies of preys and predators [38, 39].

Traditionally, the evolution of predator-prey systems is governed by a small set of simple rules [55]:

- the growth rate of preys is proportional to their population C and to a growth factor b;
- the growth rate of predators I is proportional to their predation rate CI (rate at which preys and predators encounter) and to a predation factor s;
- the mortality rate of predators is proportional to their population I and to a mortality factor m_I;
- the mortality rate of preys is proportional to the predation rate CI and a mortality factor s';

Growth and mortality rates were previously presented as g_n and p_n functions respectively.

Formalizing these rules lead to Volterra-Lotka equations:

$$\begin{cases} \frac{dC}{dt} = bC - s'CI \\ \frac{dI}{dt} = sCI - m_I I \end{cases} \tag{20}$$

It is very interesting to mention that these results are totally coherent with works of Lesser [33] in which they assume that it exists a **competition** between different sources in our brain in order to define what we have to focus. The authors of this model propose that mind is a noisy far from equilibrium dynamical system of competing interests. The system comprises two spatially discretized differential equations similar to a chemical diffusion reaction model. These equations belong to the same family of equations than Volterra-Lotka equations. In the next section, we present how to exploit such a result to model visual attention.

5 Preys/Predators Visual Attention Model

As previously mentioned, we have demonstrated that modeling visual attention with a biologically inspired competitive dynamical system is an optimal way of extracting information. The general architecture on this model is shown in Fig. 1. We have represented the flow of information from the upper part of the figure to the lower part. Starting from the information included in the basic inputs of the scene (color, intensity and orientation) and finishing by the interest generated by scene observation (predators).

Starting from this *basic* version of predator-prey equations, we have decided to enrich the model in several ways:

- the number of parameters can be reduced by replacing s' by s. Indeed, mortality rate differences between preys and predators can be modeled by an adjustment of factors b and m_I
- the original model represents the evolution of a single quantity of preys and predators over time. It can be spatially extended in order to be applied to 2D maps where each point represents the amount of preys or predators at a given place and time. Preys and predators can then *move* on this map using a classical diffusion rule, proportional to their Laplacian $\triangle_C$ and a diffusion factor f.
- natural mortality of preys in the absence of predation is not taken into account. If the model only changes temporally, mortality is negligible when compared to predation. However, when the model is applied to a 2D map (which is the case in our system), some areas of the map may not contain any predator. Natural mortality of preys can no longer be considered negligible. A new mortality term $-m_c$ needs to be added to the model.

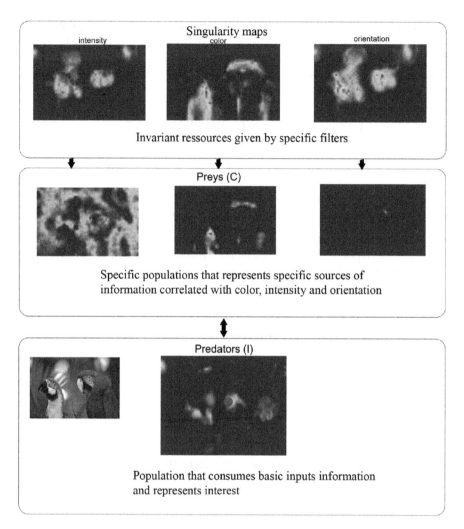

Fig. 1 Competitive preys/predators attention model. Singularity maps are the resources that feed a set of preys which are themselves eat by predators. The maximum of the predators map represents the location of the focus of attention at time t (*red circle*) (Color figure online)

- in order to generalize this work to video, we can easily include a new population of preys which represents the information included in motion.

This yields to the following set of equations, modeling the evolution of prey and predator populations on a two dimensional map:

$$\begin{cases} \frac{dC_{x,y}}{dt} = bC_{x,y} + f \triangle_{C_{x,y}} - m_C C_{x,y} - sC_{x,y}I_{x,y} \\ \frac{dI_{x,y}}{dt} = sC_{x,y}I_{x,y} + sf \triangle_{P_{x,y}} - m_I I_{x,y} \end{cases} \tag{21}$$

A last phenomenon can be added to this model: a positive feedback, proportional to C^2 or I_2 and controlled by a factor w. This feedback models the fact that (provided that there are unlimited resources) the more numerous a population is, the better it is able to grow (more efficient hunting, higher encounter rates favoring reproduction, etc.). The new predator-prey system is now:

$$\begin{cases} \frac{dc_{x,y}}{dt} = b(C_{x,y} + w(C_{x,y})^2) + f \triangle_{C_{x,y}} - m_C C_{x,y} - \\ \qquad\quad s C_{x,y} I_{x,y} \\ \frac{dI_{x,y}}{dt} = s(C_{x,y} I_{x,y} + w(I_{x,y})^2) + sf \triangle_{P_{x,y}} - m_I I_{x,y} \end{cases} \qquad (22)$$

In order to simulate the evolution of the focus of attention, we propose a predator-prey system (as described above) with the following features:

- the system is comprised of four types of prey and one type of predator;
- these four types of prey represent the spatial distribution of the curiosity generated by our four types of conspicuity maps (intensity, color, orientation and motion);
- the predators represent the interest generated by the consumption of curiosity (preys) associated to the different conspicuity maps;
- the global maximum of the predators maps (interest) represents the focus of attention at time t.

The equations described in the next sub-section are obtained by building a predator-prey system which integrates the above cited features but also an information of motion.

5.1 Simulating the Evolution of the Attentional Focus with a Predator-Prey System

For each of the four conspicuity maps (color, intensity orientation, motion), the preys population C evolution is governed by the following equation:

$$\frac{dC_{x,y}^n}{dt} = hC_{x,y}^{*n} + hf \triangle_{C_{x,y}^{*n}} - m_C C_{x,y}^n - s C_{x,y}^n I_{x,y} \qquad (23)$$

with $C_{x,y}^{*n} = C_{x,y}^n + w C_{x,y}^{n\,2}$ and $n \in \{c, i, o, m\}$, which mean that this equation is valid for C^c, C^i, C^o and C^m which represent respectively color, intensity, orientation and motion populations.

C represents the curiosity generated by the image's intrinsic conspicuity. It is produced by a sum h of four factors:

$$h = b(1 - g + gG)(a * R + (1 - a) * SM_n)(1 - e) \qquad (24)$$

where:

- the image's conspicuity SM_n (with $n \in \{c, i, o, m\}$) is generated using our real time visual system, previously described in [43, 45]. Its contribution is inversely proportional to a;
- a source of random noise R simulates the high level of noise that can be measured when monitoring our brain activity [18]. Its importance is proportional to a. The equations that model the evolution of our system become stochastic differential equations. A high value for a gives some freedom to the attentional system, so it can explore less salient areas. On the contrary, a lower value for a will constrain the system to only visit high conspicuity areas;
- a Gaussian map G which simulates the central bias generally observed during psycho-visual experiments [32, 49]. The importance of this map is modulated by g
- the entropy e of the conspicuity map (color, intensity, orientation or motion). This map is normalized between 0 and 1. C is modulated by $1 - e$ in order to favor maps with a small number of local minimums. Explained in terms of predator-prey system, we favor the growth of the most organized populations (grouped in a small number of sites). This mechanism is the predator-prey equivalent to the feature maps normalization presented above.

The population of predators I, which consume the four kinds of preys, is governed by the following equation:

$$\frac{d_{I_{x,y}}}{dt} = s(P_{x,y} + wI_{x,y}^2) + sf \, \Delta_{P_{x,y} + wI_{x,y}^2} - m_I I_{x,y} \tag{25}$$

with $P_{x,y} = \sum_{n \in \{c,i,o\}} (C_{x,y}^n) I_{x,y}$.

As already mentioned, the positive feedback factor w enforces the system dynamics and facilitates the emergence of chaotic behaviors by speeding up saturation in some areas of the maps. Lastly, please note that curiosity C is consumed by interest I, and that the maximum of the interest map I at time t is the location of the focus of attention.

5.2   System Architecture

In this part, we will present the bottom-up attentional systems that model the principal of human selective attention we derived. This model aims to determine the most relevant parts within the large amount of visual data. As we mentioned, it uses psychological theories like "Feature Integration theory" [51, 52] and "Guided Search model" [57]. Four features have been used based on these theories in computational models of attention: intensity, color and orientation and motion. The first complete implementation and verification of attention model was proposed by

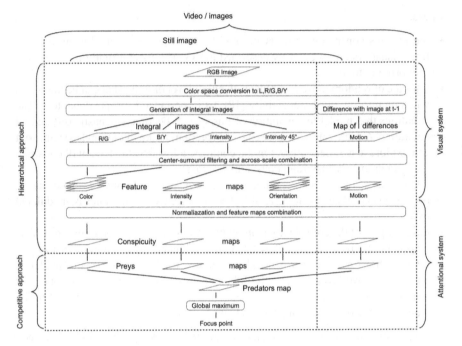

Fig. 2 Architecture of the computational model of attention

Itti et al. [27] and was applied to synthetic as well as natural scenes. Its main idea was to compute features and to fuse their saliencies in a representation which is usually called saliency map. Our approach proposes to substitute the second part of Itti's model by our optimal competitive approach. The output of this algorithm is a saliency map $S(I, t)$ computed by a temporal average of the focalization computed through a certain period of time t. The global architecture is presented in Fig. 2.

6 Validation

6.1 Benchmark

In [43], we have presented a complete evaluation of our model. Cross-correlation, Kullback-Leibler divergence and normalized scanpath saliency were used to compare six algorithms to an eye-tracking ground-truth.

In these evaluations, we have shown that our model is highly item, reproducible, exploratory (we can easily define scene exploration strategy of our model), dynamics, plausible, fast, highly configurable, reactiveness. For this latter evaluation, all measures were done on two image databases. The first one is proposed in [6].[2] It is made up of 120 color images which represent streets, gardens, vehicles or buildings, more or less salients. The second one, proposed in [32][3] contains 26 color images. They represent sport scenes, animals, building, indoor scenes or landscapes. For both databases, eye movements recordings were performed during a free viewing task.

Regarding the numerous models that exist in literature, we have decided to confront our generic model to a larger amount of algorithm. However, it is hard to make immediate comparisons between models. To alleviate this problem, Tilke Judd have proposed a benchmark data set containing 300 natural images with eye tracking data from 39 observers to compare model performances (http://saliency. mit.edu/). As she write, *this is the largest data set with so many viewers per image.* She calculates the performance of ten models at predicting ground truth fixations using three different metrics: a receiver operating characteristic, a similarity metric, and the Earth Mover's Distance. We have downloaded the database, have runned our model to create saliency maps of each image and have submitted our maps. We present the results in Fig. 3. References of algorithms can be found in the web page of the benchmark.

Model Name	Area under ROC curve (higher is better)	Similarity (higher is better)	Earth mover's distance (lower is better)
Chance	0.503	0.327	6.352
Achanta	0.523	0.297	6.854
Itti&Koch	0.562	0.284	5.067
SUN saliency	0.672	0.34	5.088
Hou & Zhang	0.682	0.319	53368
Torralba	0.684	0.343	7.715
Context-Aware saliency	0.742	0.39	4.9
Preys/predators model	0.7496 (7)	0.4147 (8)	4.7735 (11)
Itti&Koch 2	0.75	0.405	4.56
Bruce and Tsotsos AIM	0.751	0.39	4.236
Random Center Surround Saliency (Narayan model)	0.753	0.42	3.465
RARE2012	0.7719	0.4363	4.1019
Saliency for Image Manipulation	0.774	0.439	4.137
Center	0.783	0.451	3.719
CovSal	0.7999	0.4869	3.4224
Graph Based Visual Saliency (GBVS)	0.801	0.472	3.574
Judd et al.	0.811	0.506	3.13
Humans	0.922	1	0

Fig. 3 Comparison of several models of visual attention. The number inside parenthesis is the rank of our method

---

[2]Bruce database is available at http://www-sop.inria.fr/members/Neil.Bruce.

[3]Le Meur database is available at http://www.irisa.fr/temics/staff/lemeur/visualAttention.

We can make several comments.

Firstly, it is clear that new deep learning models are better than ours, but these models needs thousands of training pictures to perform. Our model do not need any training image.

Secondly, our model perform either on image than video or depth images [9], without any difficulties to enrich inputs.

Thirdly, it works in real time even for videos [43]. In the next subsection, we present one of the numerous applications of our model we have proposed.

6.2 Application to an Attentive Content Bases Image Retrieval

6.2.1 Introduction

The domain of Content Based image retrieval (CBIR) is considered as one of the most challenging domain in computer vision and it has been an active and fast advancing research area over the last years. Most retrieval white boxes methods[4] are based on extracting points of interest using interest points detectors [54] as Harris, Harris/Laplace and described it by multi dimensional feature vectors using SIFT [35]. The set of these feature vectors is known as bag-of-features [13] and a retrieval can be performed. Although these approaches have demonstrated a high efficiency, some weakness may be mentioned. The first limitation is represented in the interest point detectors. Most of these detectors are based on geometric forms as corners, blobs or junctions and consider that the interest of the image is correlated with the presence of such features. This constraint is well known as semantic gap [47]. The second constraints mentioned in the literature concerns SIFT descriptors. Although SIFT shows a high efficiency, scalability remains an important problem due to the large number of features generated for each image [17]. Many of them are outliers.

An alternative way for extracting region of interests is derived from visual attention domain. This domain had been investigated intensely in the last years and many models had been proposed [2]. In this section, we focus on bottom-up visual attention models [27, 44].

Recently, many works have been proposed to combine these domains, given what we called "Attentive Content Based Image Retrieval (Attentive C.B.I.R)". This idea was introduced earlier in [40], who indicate that object recognition in human perception consists of two steps: "attentional process selects the region of interest and complex object recognition process restricted to these regions". Based on this definition, Walther [56] proposed an algorithm for image matching: his algorithm detects SIFT key-points inside the attention regions. These regions determine a search area whereas the matching is on SIFT key-points. This approach

---

[4]White Box Testing is a software testing method in which the internal structure/design/implementation of the item being tested is known to the tester.

Fig. 4 Attention-CBIR
relationship

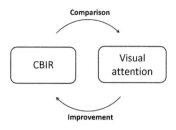

was successful since they used very complex objects and those which not change viewpoint. Others as Frintrop and Jenselft [22] applied directly SIFT descriptors to the attention regions. They applied their approach on robot localization: the robot has to determine its position in a known map by interpreting its sensor data which was generated by a laser camera. Although this approach achieved an improvement in the detection rate for indoor environment, it fails in the outdoor environment and opens areas.

In this section, we hypothesize that attention can improve object recognition systems in query-run time and information quality since these models generate salient regions on large scales, considering the context information. This property of attentional models permits to generate fewer salient points regardless interest point detector. Or, these detectors extract regions of interest on small scales, resulting several hundreds or thousands of points. This idea was presented previously by Frintrop [21] who indicated that the task of object recognition become easier if an attentional mechanism first cued the processing on regions of potential interest; thus is because of two reasons: first, it reduces the search space and results in computational complexity. Second, most recognition and classification methods works best if the object occupies a dominant portion of the image.

6.2.2 A Classical CBIR Architecture

Many challenges have been proposed to test the efficiency and robustness of the recognition methods. One of the most popular challenges is the Visual Object Classes Challenge. VOC was proposed for the first time in 2005 with one objective: recognizing objects from number of visual object classes in realistic scenes [13]. Since then, it has been organized every year and integrates new constraints in order to provide a standardized database to the researchers.

In 2005, twelve algorithms have been proposed to compete for winning the challenge; it is interesting to mention that all algorithms were based on local features detection. We propose taxonomy in Table 1. Finally, INRIA-Zhang appeared to be the most efficient white-box method. We decide to take it as the reference algorithm for object recognition. The algorithm shown in Fig. 5 consists of extracting an invariant image representation and classifying this data with non-linear support

Table 1 Taxonomy of methods proposed in VOC2005

Category	Description
Distribution of local image feature	Images are represented by probability distributions over the set of descriptors, basing on two methods. Bags of words [48] in which image is represented by a histogram over a dictionary, recording either the presence of each word. Alternative way is based on kernel as Bhattacharyya kernel [30]. Finally, the model is learned using classification methods as SVM
Recognition of individual local feature	In this approach, interest points detector are used to focus the attention on a small number of local patches. Then each patch in each image is associated with a binary label. Vectors are built by grouping these labels. A parametric model of the probability that the patch belongs to a class is built. Finally the output is the posterior class probability for a patch feature vector
Recognition based on segmented regions	This method combines the features extracted from the image and the regions obtained by an image segmentation algorithm. The Self Organizing Maps (SOM) [31] are defined on the different feature spaces that were used to classify the descriptors resulting from the segmented regions and the whole image
Classifications by detection	It extracts patches in an image using interest points detector. A codebook is built using a clustering method. A new object class is detected using matching method. Then a hypothesis on which accept or refusal is defined

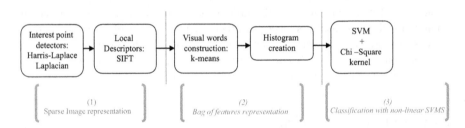

Fig. 5 Architecture of Zhang algorithm

vector machines (SVM) with an χ^2-kernel. This algorithm can be divided in three parts:

1. Sparse image representation: this part extract a set of SIFT keypoints $K_{Zhang}(I)$ from an image $I(x, y)$ which was provided before as input. It consists of two steps:

   • Interest points detectors: Zhang uses two complementary local region detectors to extract *interesting* image structures: Harris-Laplace detector [37], dedicated to corner-like region and Laplacian detector [34] dedicated to blob-like regions. These two detectors have been designed to be scale invariant.

- Local descriptor: To compute appearance-based descriptor on the extracted patches, Zhang used the SIFT descriptor [35]. It computes descriptors less sensitive to scale variations and invariant to illumination changes.

2. Bag-of-features representation: Zhang builds a visual vocabulary by clustering the descriptors from the training set. Each image is represented as a histogram of visual words drawn from the vocabulary. He randomly selects a set of descriptors for each class extracted from the training set and he clusters these features using k-means to create 1000-elements vocabulary. Finally, each feature in an image is assigned to the closest word and a histogram that measures the frequency of each word in an image is built for each image.

3. Classification: Zhang uses a non-linear SVM in which the decision function has the following form:

$$g(x) = \sum \alpha_i y_i k(x_i, x) - b \tag{26}$$

with $k(x_i, x)$ the kernel function value for the training sample x_i and the test sample x. α_i is the learned weighted coefficient for the training sample x_i, and b is the learned threshold. Finally, to compute the efficiency of the algorithm, SVM score has been considered as a confidence measure for a class.

6.2.3 Proposed Architecture

As mentioned before, Attentive CBIR is a combination of attentional systems and CBIR algorithms. We have chosen Zhang algorithm as the reference of our proposal mainly because its code is available and easy to split in different white boxes methods. Analyzing the different steps of the algorithms, it can be noticed that the first step consists in using the interest point detectors. According to [17], not all of those points are useful to categorize the image. On the contrary, we assume the idea that non relevant "noisy" information can also be detected. Thus, the idea is that attentional system can be used to select among all the keypoints only those which are the most salient. Given the selection of salient keypoints, the rest of Zhang's algorithm could stay unchanged for a CBIR application (see Fig. 6).

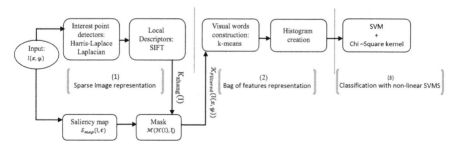

Fig. 6 Architecture of our model

Practically speaking, the process we propose consists in providing both Zhang's and our systems the same image $I(x, y)$. After step 2 of Zhang's framework, a first set of $K_{Zhang}(I)$ of keypoints is obtained. In parallel, for the same image $I(x, y)$, our system provides a saliency map $S_{map}(I, t)$ which evolves with time. In order to emphasize the visual regions the systems mainly focuses on, $S_{map}(I, t)$ is integrated along the time axis to get what is usually known as a "heatmap". Formally, the heatmap can be defined as: $H(I) = \int_0^T \mathscr{S}_{map}(I, t).dt$, with T the integration window.

To take advantage of the saliency map within the context of Zhang's framework, the idea is to generate a mask $M(H(I), \xi)$ that is used as a filter of the SIFT keypoints set, with the minimum level of saliency considered in the image. Formally, the generated mask could be defined as:

$$M(H(I), \xi) = \begin{cases} 1 \ if \ H(x_h, y_h) > \xi \\ 0 \ otherwise \end{cases} \tag{27}$$

The filtering process by itself consists of selecting the subset $K_{Filtered}(I)$ of keypoints in $K_{Zhang}(I)$ for which the mask $M(H(I), \xi)$ is on:

$$\begin{aligned} K_{Filtered}(I(x, y)) = \\ \{Key_j \in K_{Zhang}(I(x_h, y_h)) \mid M(H(I), \xi) = 1\} \end{aligned} \tag{28}$$

This subset $K_{Filtered}(I)$ serves as input for the next parts of Zhang algorithm for object recognition. In the following, we will verify if the Attentive CBIR can produce an meaningful enhancement.

To validate our hypothesis, we implemented our approach and evaluated it on the VOC 2005 database. The VOC challenge proposed two images subsets, the subset S_1 with selected images and another subset S_2 with Google image randomly selected. Thus, our approach can be performed independently during learning and for the test process. We evaluate the binary classification using Receiver Operating Characteristic (ROC) curve [16]. With this curve, it is easy to observe the trade-off between two measures: proportion of false positives plotted on the x-axis showing how many times a method says the object class is present when it is not; proportion of true-positives plotted on the y-axis showing how many times a method says the object class is present when it is.

In Fig. 7, some ROC curves are shown. As it can be seen in Table 2, the value of the threshold parameter ξ has a great impact on the decimation of the keypoints: the higher it is, the least number of keypoints are kept. These curves present the results of our evaluation method, for two computational attention models: Itti and ours. The idea, here, is to develop two Attentive CBIR models and to test its efficiency, not to evaluate all the existing methods:

- P/P+Zhang: this system represents the combination of our models with Zhang's nominal algorithm.
- Itti+ Zhang: this system represents the combination of Itti models with Zhang's nominal implementation.

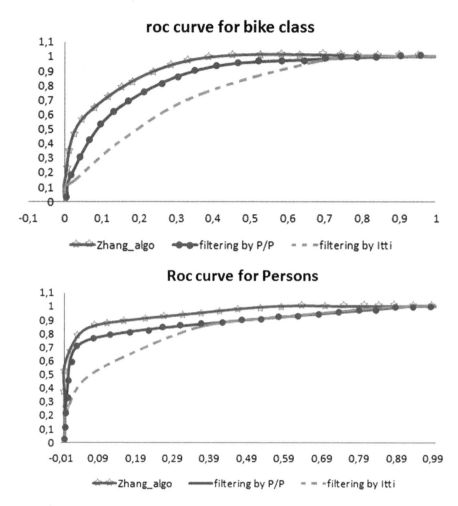

Fig. 7 ROC curve with and without our filter approach for two different classes

Finally, three curves were drawn, representing our implementation of Zhang's algorithm and two attentive CBIR models. Examples of results are summarized in Tables 3, 4, 5 and 6. They present results for different classes with, respectively, Zhang's original score as reported in the challenge summary, our implementation of Zhang's algorithm without filtering and several filtering.

Furthermore, we tested also the usefulness of attentive CBIR towards object recognition domain. Our test consists on using our system as a mask to select among all the SIFT keypoints only those which are the most salient. Results are shown in Fig. 8 representing, respectively, our implementation of Zhang algorithm without filtering and with several filtering. For reason of clarity, we don't present the tests

Table 2 Percentage of decreasing SIFT keypoint with threshold=0

	Classes	Zhang+ Itti (%)	Zhang+P/P (%)		Zhang+Itti (%)	Zhang+ P/P (%)
Train	Persons	−87	−60	Test	−86	−58
	Bike	−80	−58		−83	−42
	Motorbikes	−82	−41		−83	−42
	Cars	−86	−55		−83	−59

Table 3 AUC/EER values for Persons class

AUC/EER	S_1			
	Zhang	Reimpl.of Zhang	40%,40%	40%,10%
	0.97/0.91	0.93/0.87	0.92/0.86	0.79/0.77
	S_2			
	Zhang	Reimpl.of Zhang	10%,30%	40%,10%
	0.813/0.728	0.67/0.56	0.69/0.62	0.58/0.47

Table 4 AUC/EER values for cars class

AUC/EER	S_1			
	Zhang	Reimpl.of Zhang	30%,40%	30%,10%
	0.98/0.93	0.95/0.90	0.94/0.87	0.83/0.79
	S_2			
	Zhang	Reimpl.of Zhang	30%,20%	10%,40%
	0.802/0.720	0.73/0.73	0.76/0.76	0.61/0.44

Table 5 AUC/EER values for bikes class

AUC/EER	S_1			
	Zhang	Reimpl.of Zhang	30%,40%	40%,10%
	0.98/0.93	0.94/0.90	0.93/0.86	0.72/0.64
	S_2			
	Zhang	Reimpl.of Zhang	10%,30%	40%,10%
	0.813/0.728	0.67/0.56	0.69/0.69	0.58/0.44

Table 6 AUC/EER values for motorbikes class

AUC/EER	Zhang	Reimpl.of Zhang	40%,40%	40%,10%
	0.99/0.96	0.98/0.94	0.98/0.93	0.89/0.83

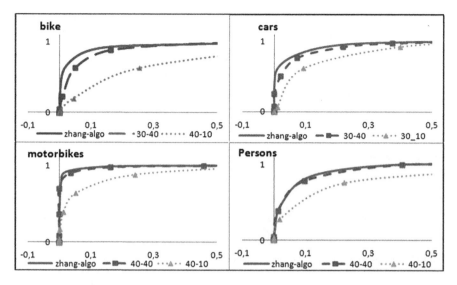

Fig. 8 ROC curve with and without our filter approach for the different classes-S_1

we did exhaustively: we selected only the "best" and "worst" curves. They present results for each class with, respectively, Zhang's original score as reported in the challenge summary, our implementation of Zhang's algorithm without filtering and several filtering. In this section, we have shown that Attentive CBIR can improve the query-run time and information quality in object recognition. Therefore, we proposed our approach for selecting the most relevant SIFT keypoints according to human perception, using our visual attention system. Testing this approach on VOC 2005 demonstrated that we can maintain approximately the same performance by selecting only 40% of SIFT keypoints. Based on this result, we propose this approach as a first step to solve problems related to the management of memory and query run-time for recognition systems based on white boxes detectors.

7 Conclusion and Perspectives

In this article, we have introduced an optimal approach to extract visual information. We have presented a state of the art through the prism of information theory. We have stressed the weaknesses and advantages of existing approaches, and proposed to use a physical framework to derive optimal laws to extract visual information: the EPI. We have presented this framework and proposed an adaptation of the *growth and transport processes* derivation. We have demonstrated that optimal visual information extraction can be obtained thanks to a predator-prey equations system, in which preys are linked to low level visual features (intensity, color, orientation and motion) and predator is interest. Thanks to our model it is very easy to include some new features such as texture, and top-down information (skin, face, car, hand gesture [46] ...) actually, it is just a new kind of prey. We finally have presented new and complementary evaluation of our approach: an up to date benchmark and an attentive CBIR approach.

Nevertheless, as say the fox in the little Prince: *It is only with the heart that one can see rightly; what is essential is invisible to the eye...*

References

1. Berthoz, A.: La simplexité, odile jacob edn. Paris (2009)
2. Borji, A., Itti, L.: State-of-the-art in visual attention modeling. IEEE Trans. Pattern Anal. Mach. Intell. **99**(Xxx) (2012). doi: 10.1109/TPAMI.2012.89. http://doi.ieeecomputersociety.org/10.1109/TPAMI.2012.89?utm_source=dlvr.it&utm_medium=feed
3. Broadbent, D.E.: Perception and Communication. Pergamon Press, Elmsford, NY (1958)
4. Bruce, B., Jernigan, E.: Evolutionary design of context-free attentional operators. In: Proceedings of ICIP'03, pp. 0–3. Citeseer (2003)
5. Bruce, N.D.B., Tsotsos, J.K.: Spatiotemporal saliency: towards a hierarchical representation of visual saliency. In: Proceedings of the 5th International Workshop on Attention in Cognitive Systems, pp. 98–111. Springer, Heidelberg (2008)
6. Bruce, N.D.B., Tsotsos, J.K.: Saliency, attention, and visual search: an information theoretic approach. J. Vis. **9**(3), 5 (2009)
7. Cabezas, H., Fath, B.D.: Towards a theory of sustainable systems. Fluid Phase Equilib. **194–197**, 3–14 (2002)
8. Courboulay, V.: Une nouvelle approche variationnelle du traitement d'images. Application à la coopération détection-reconstruction. Ph.D. thesis, La Rochelle (2002)
9. Courboulay, V., Mancas, M.: CuriousMind photographer: distract the robot from its initial task. EAI Endorsed Trans. Creative Technol. **2**(2), 1–9 (2014). doi:10.4108/ct.2.2.e4. https://hal.archives-ouvertes.fr/hal-01062621
10. Diamant, E.: Modeling human-like intelligent image processing: an information processing perspective and approach. Signal Process. Image Commun. **22**(6), 583–590 (2007). doi:10.1016/j.image.2007.05.007 http://linkinghub.elsevier.com/retrieve/pii/S0923596507000781
11. Diamant, E.: Unveiling the mystery of visual information processing in human brain. Brain Res. **1225**, 171–178 (2008). doi:10.1016/j.brainres.2008.05.017. http://www.ncbi.nlm.nih.gov/pubmed/18585686
12. Diamant, E., Box, P.O., Ono, K.: Does a plane imitate a bird? Does computer vision have to follow biological paradigms? In: Vision, and Artificial Intelligence, First International Symposium Proceedings. Lecturer Notes in Computer Science, pp. 108–115. Springer, Berlin/Heidelberg (2005)
13. Everingham, M., Gool, L., Williams, C.K.I., Winn, J., Zisserman, A.: The Pascal visual object classes (VOC) challenge. Int. J. Comput. Vis. **88**(2), 303–338 (2009). doi:10.1007/s11263-009-0275-4. http://www.springerlink.com/index/10.1007/s11263-009-0275-4
14. Fath, B.: Exergy and Fisher Information as ecological indices. Ecol. Model. **174**(1-2), 25–35 (2004). doi: 10.1016/j.ecolmodel.2003.12.045. http://linkinghub.elsevier.com/retrieve/pii/S0304380003005660
15. Fath, B.D., Cabezas, H., Pawlowski, C.W.: Regime changes in ecological systems: an information theory approach. J. Theor. Biol. **222**, 517–530 (2003)

16. Fawcett, T.: An introduction to ROC analysis. Pattern Recogn. Lett. **27**(8), 861–874 (2006). doi:10.1016/j.patrec.2005.10.010. http://linkinghub.elsevier.com/retrieve/pii/S016786550500303X

17. Foo, J.J.: Pruning SIFT for scalable near-duplicate image matching. In: Australasian Database Conference, Ballarat, p. 9 (2007)

18. Fox, M.D., Snyder, A.Z., Vincent, J.L., Raichle, M.E.: Intrinsic fluctuations within cortical systems account for intertrial variability in human behavior. Neuron **56**(1), 171–184 (2007). doi:10.1016/j.neuron.2007.08.023

19. Frieden, B.R.: Physics from Fisher Information: A Unification. Cambridge University Press, Cambridge (1998)

20. Frieden, B.R.: Science from Fisher Information: A Unification, Cambridge edn. Cambridge University Press, Cambridge (2004). http://www.amazon.com/Science-Fisher-Information-Roy-Frieden/dp/0521009111

21. Frintrop, S.: Towards attentive robots. Paladyn. J. Behav. Robot. **2**, 64–70 (2011). doi:10.2478/s13230-011-0018-4, http://dx.doi.org/10.2478/s13230-011-0018-4

22. Frintrop, S., Jensfelt, P.: Attentional landmarks and active gaze control for visual slam. IEEE Trans. Robot. **24**(5), 1054–1065 (2008). doi:10.1109/TRO.2008.2004977

23. Frintrop, S., Klodt, M., Rome, E.: A real-time visual attention system using integral images. In: 5th International Conference on Computer Vision Systems (ICVS). Applied Computer Science Group, Bielefeld (2007)

24. Gilles, S.: Description and Experimentation of Image Matching Using Mutual Information. Robotics Research Group, Oxford University (1996)

25. Histace, A., Ménard, M., Courboulay, V.: Selective image diffusion for oriented pattern extraction. In: 4th International Conference on Informatics in Control, Automation and Robotics (ICINCO), France (2008). http://hal.archives-ouvertes.fr/hal-00377679/en/

26. Histace, A., Ménard, M., Cavaro-ménard, C.: Selective diffusion for oriented pattern extraction: application to tagged cardiac MRI enhancement. Pattern Recogn. Lett. **30**(15), 1356–1365 (2009). doi:10.1016/j.patrec.2009.07.012. http://dx.doi.org/10.1016/j.patrec.2009.07.012

27. Itti, L., Koch, C., Niebur, E., Others: A model of saliency-based visual attention for rapid scene analysis. IEEE Trans. Pattern Anal. Mach. Intell. **20**(11), 1254–1259 (1998)

28. Kadir, T., Brady, M.: Saliency, scale and image description. Int. J. Comput. Vis. **45**(2), 83–105 (2001)

29. Koch, C., Ullman, S.: Shifts in selective visual attention: towards the underlying neural circuitry. Hum. Neurobiol. **4**(4), 219–227 (1985)

30. Kondor, R., Jebara, T.: A kernel between sets of vectors. Mach. Learn. 361–368 (2003)

31. Laaksonen, J.: PicSOM? Content-based image retrieval with self-organizing maps. Pattern Recogn. Lett. **21**(13/14), 1199–1207 (2000). doi:10.1016/S0167-8655(00)00082-9. http://linkinghub.elsevier.com/retrieve/pii/S0167865500000829

32. Le Meur, O., Le Callet, P., Dominique, B., Thoreau, D.: A coherent computational approach to model bottom-up visual attention. IEEE Trans. Pattern Anal. Mach. Intell. **28**(5), 802–817 (2006)

33. Lesser, M., Dinah, M.: Mind as a dynamical system: implications for autism. In: Psychobiology of Autism: Current Research & Practice (1998). http://www.autismusundcomputer.de/mind.en.html

34. Lindeberg, T.: Feature detection with automatic scale selection. Comput. Vis. **30**(2), 96 (1998)

35. Lowe, D.G.: Distinctive image features from scale-invariant keypoints. Int. J. Comput. Vis. **60**(2), 91–110 (2004). doi:10.1023/B:VISI.0000029664.99615.94. http://www.springerlink.com/openurl.asp?id=doi:10.1023/B:VISI.0000029664.99615.94

36. Mancas, M.: Computational attention: towards attentive computers. Ph.D., Faculté Polytechnique de Mons (2007)

37. Mikolajczyk, K.: Scale & affine invariant interest point detectors. Int. J. Comput. Vis. **60**(1), 63–86 (2004). doi:10.1023/B:VISI.0000027790.02288.f2. http://www.springerlink.com/openurl.asp?id=doi:10.1023/B:VISI.0000027790.02288.f2

38. Murray, J.D.: Mathematical Biology: An Introduction. Springer, Berlin/Heidelberg (2003)

39. Murray, J.D.: Mathematical Biology: Spatial Models and Biomedical Applications. Springer, New York (2003)
40. Neisser, U.: Cognitive Psychology. Appleton-Century-Crofts, New York (1967)
41. Ouerhani, N., Hugli, H.: A model of dynamic visual attention for object tracking in natural image sequences. Lecture Notes in Computer Science, pp. 702–709. Springer, Berlin (2003)
42. Park, S.J., An, K.H., Lee, M.: Saliency map model with adaptive masking based on independent component analysis. Neurocomputing 49(1), 417–422 (2002)
43. Perreira Da Silva, M., Courboulay, V.: Implementation and evaluation of a computational model of attention for computer vision. In: Developing and Applying Biologically-Inspired Vision Systems: Interdisciplinary Concepts, pp. 273–306. IGI Global, Hershey (2012)
44. Perreira Da Silva, M., Courboulay, V., Estraillier, P.: Objective validation of a dynamical and plausible computational model of visual attention. In: IEEE European Workshop on Visual Information Processing, Paris, pp. 223–228 (2011)
45. Perreira Da Silva, M., Courboulay, V., Estraillier, P.: Une nouvelle mesure de complexité pour les images basée sur l'attention visuelle. In: GRETSI, Bordeaux (2011)
46. Pisharady, P., Vadakkepat, P., Loh, A.: Attention based detection and recognition of hand postures against complex backgrounds. Int. J. Comput. Vis. 1–17 (2012). doi:10.1007/s11263-012-0560-5. http://dx.doi.org/10.1007/s11263-012-0560-5
47. Santini, S., Gupta, A., Jain, R.: Emergent semantics through interaction in image databases. IEEE Trans. Knowl. Data Eng. 13(3), 337–351 (2001). doi:10.1109/69.929893. http://dx.doi.org/10.1109/69.929893
48. Sivic, J., Russell, B.C., Efros, A.A., Zisserman, A., Freeman, W.T.: Discovering objects and their location in images. In: Proceeding of the International Conference on Computer Vision, vol. 1, pp. 370–377 (2005)
49. Tatler, B.W.: The central fixation bias in scene viewing: selecting an optimal viewing position independently of motor biases and image feature distributions. J. Vis. 7, 1–17 (2007). doi:10.1167/7.14.4.Introduction
50. Treisman, A.: Strategies and models of selective attention. Psychol. Rev. 76, 282–299 (1969)
51. Treisman, A., Gelade, G.: A feature-integration theory of attention. Cogn. Psychol. 136(12), 97–136 (1980)
52. Treisman, A.M., Kanwisher, N.G.: Perceiving visually presented objets: recognition, awareness, and modularity. Curr. Opin. Neurobiol. 8(2), 218–226 (1998). http://linkinghub.elsevier.com/retrieve/pii/S0959438898801438
53. Tsotsos, J.K., Culhane, S.M., Kei Wai, W.Y., Lai, Y., Davis, N., Nuflo, F.: Modeling visual attention via selective tuning. Artif. Intell. 78(1-2), 507–545 (1995)
54. Tuytelaars, T., Mikolajczyk, K.: Local invariant feature detectors: a survey. Found. Trends Comput. Graph. Vis. 3(3), 177–280 (2007). doi:10.1561/0600000017. http://www.nowpublishers.com/product.aspx?product=CGV&doi=0600000017
55. Volterra, V.: Variations and fluctuations of the number of individuals in animal species living together. ICES J. Mar. Sci. 3(1), 3–51 (1928)
56. Walther, D.: Selective visual attention enables learning and recognition of multiple objects in cluttered scenes. Comput. Vis. Image Underst. 100(1-2), 41–63 (2005). doi:10.1016/j.cviu.2004.09.004
57. Wolfe, J.M., Cave, K.R., Franzel, S.L.: Guided search: an alternative to the feature integration model for visual search. J. Exp. Psychol. Hum. Percept. Perform. 15(3), 419–433 (1989). http://www.ncbi.nlm.nih.gov/pubmed/2527952
58. Zhao, X., Hou, Y., Song, D., Li, W.: Extending the extreme physical information to universal cognitive models via a confident information first principle. Entropy 16(7), 3670–3688 (2014)

Image Retrieval Based on Query by Saliency Content

Adrian G. Bors and Alex Papushoy

Abstract This chapter outlines a content based image retrieval (CBIR) methodology that takes into account the saliency in images. Natural images are depictions of real-life objects and scenes, usually set in cluttered environments. The performance of image retrieval in these scenarios may suffer because there is no way of knowing which parts of the image are of interest to the user. The human visual system provides a clue to what would be of interest in the image, by involuntarily shifting the focus of attention to salient image areas. The application of computational models of selective visual attention to image understanding can produce better, unsupervised retrieval results by identifying perceptually important areas of the image that usually correspond to its semantic meaning, whilst discarding irrelevant information. This chapter explores the construction of a retrieval system incorporating a visual attention model and proposes a new method for selecting salient image regions, as well as embedding an improved representation for salient image edges for determining global image saliency.

1 Introduction

Visual information retrieval is one of basic pursuits required by people in the current technology driven society. Whether from mobile devices or whilst browsing the web, people search for information and a significant part of such information is visual. Many image retrieval approaches use collateral information, such as keywords which may be or not associated with the images. Content-based image retrieval (CBIR) considers a user-provided image as a query, whose visual information is processed and then used in a content-based search [11, 38]. CBIR is based on the notion that visual similarity implies semantic similarity, which is not always the case, but is in general a valid assumption. Due to the ambiguous nature of images, for a given query, a set of candidate retrieval images are sorted based on their relevance/similarity to the query.

A.G. Bors (✉) • A. Papushoy
Department of Computer Science, University of York, York YO10 5GH, UK
e-mail: adrian.bors@york.ac.uk

© Springer International Publishing AG 2017
J. Benois-Pineau, P. Le Callet (eds.), *Visual Content Indexing and Retrieval with Psycho-Visual Models*, Multimedia Systems and Applications,
DOI 10.1007/978-3-319-57687-9_8

171

The main challenge in CBIR systems is the ambiguity in the high-level (semantic) concepts extracted from the low-level (pixels) features of the image [5, 43, 44]. The second obstacle is the sensory gap which can be interpreted as the incompleteness of the object information captured by an imaging device. The problem stems from the fact that the same object, photographed under different illumination conditions, different view angles, located at various depths or which may be occluded by other objects, appears differently due to changes in its acquisition context [38]. Whilst the semantic concept remains unchanged, the visual information results in a different interpretation that may negatively affect the performance of a CBIR system. Moreover, there is ambiguity within the user's intent itself. Generally, it is difficult for image retrieval systems to search for broad semantic concepts because it is hard to limit the feature space without broadening the semantic gap.

The majority of research studies during the early years of CBIR research have focused on the extraction and succinct representation of the visual information that facilitates effective retrieval. Narrow image domains usually contain domain-specific images such as medical scans or illustrations, where the set of semantic concepts is restricted and the variability of each concept is rather small. On the other hand, broad domains, such as natural images on the web, contain a large set of semantic concepts with significant variabilities within them. Producing a system that can cope well with a broad image domain is much more challenging than one for the narrow domain [38]. Images are ambiguous and the user of an image retrieval system is usually only interested in specific regions or objects of interest and not the background. Early works extracted a single signature based on the global features of the image, but the background concealed the true intent. In the later approaches, in order to capture the finer detail, the images were segmented into regions from which signatures were extracted.

There are four categories of CBIR methods, [11]: bottom-up, top-down, relevance feedback and those based on image classification. Those that rely purely on the information contained in the image are bottom-up approaches such as [33], while top-down approaches consider the prior knowledge. In image classification approaches, the system is presented with training data from which it learns a query [8]. Systems involving the user in the retrieval process via relevance feedback mechanisms are a mixture of bottom-up and top-down approaches [35].

Some of the earliest examples of CBIR systems is QBIC (Query by Image Content) [2, 13] developed at IBM, and Blobworld [5]. Images are represented as scenes or objects, and videos are converted into small clips from which motion features are extracted. These distinctions enable the system to be queried in several ways: the user may search for objects (such as round and red), scenes (by defining colour proportions), shots (defined by some type of motion), a combination of the above, and based on user-defined sketches and query images. In order to query by objects, the user must use a mask indicating the objects in the image. Image segmentation was used for the automatic extraction of the object boundaries in simpler images, but user tools are also provided for manual and semi-automatic extraction. The downside of such systems is the use of global colour representations (histograms), which preserve the colour distributions but have the tendency to hide information relating to smaller areas of interest that may carry a lot of importance. In addition, in order to take full advantage of the retrieval by object, the user is heavily involved in the database population. The later versions of QBIC included the automatic segmentation of the foreground and background in order to improve the retrieval.

CANDID (Comparison Algorithm for Navigating Digital Image Databases) [25] image retrieval represented the global colour distribution in the image as a probability density function (pdf) modelled as a Gaussian mixture model (GMM). The idea originated in text document retrieval systems, where the similarity measure was simply the dot product of two feature vectors [39]. For images, the local features such as colour, texture and shape were computed for every pixel and then clustered with the k-means algorithm which defined the GMM's components and parameters. The similarity measure was then based on the dot product, representing the cosine of the angle between the two vectors. The background was considered as another pdf which was subtracted from each signature during the similarity computation. This method was applied in narrow image domains such as for retrieving aerial data and medical greyscale images.

The Chabot [27] system combined the use of keywords and simple histograms for the retrieval task. The system was highly interactive and utilized a relational database that would eventually store around 500,000 images. For the retrieval performance, the RGB colour histograms were quantised to 20 colours, which was sufficient for qualitative colour definition during query with the keywords as the primary search method. The MIT Photobook [32] system took an entirely different approach to the retrieval of faces, shapes and textures. The system performed the Karhunen-Loeve transform (KLT) on the covariance matrix of image differences from the mean image of a given training set, while extracting the eigenvectors corresponding to the largest eigenvalues. These vectors would represent the proto-typical appearance of the object category and images can be efficiently represented as a small set of coefficients. The similarity between objects is computed as an Euclidean distance in the eigenspaces of the image representations. The VisualSEEk [37] system combines image colour feature-based querying and spatial layouts. The spatial organisation of objects and their relationships in an image are important descriptive features that are ignored by simple colour histogram representation methods. VisualSEEk identifies areas in a candidate image, whose colour histogram is similar to that of the query.

Certain top-down, CBIR approaches employ machine learning techniques for the relevance feedback such as the support vector machine (SVM) [4] or multiple instance learning [33]. Image ranking for retrieval systems has been performed by using integrated region matching (IRM) [44] and the Earth Mover's Distance (EMD) [23, 34]. Deep learning, emerged lately as a successful machine learning approach to a variety of vision problems. This application of deep learning to CBIR was discussed in [42, 45].

The focus of this work is to analyze and evaluate the effectiveness of a bottom-up CBIR system that employs saliency in order to define the regions of interest in order to perform localised retrieval in the broad image domain. Visual saliency was considered for CBIR in [14, 30] as well. This chapter is organized as in the following. In Sect. 2 we introduce the modelling framework for visual attention while in Sect. 3 we present the initial processing stages for the Query by Saliency Content Retrieval (QSCR) methodology. The way how saliency is taken into account by QSCR is explained in Sect. 4. The ranking of images based on their content is outlined in Sect. 5. The experimental results are provided in Sect. 6 and the conclusions of this study in Sect. 7.

2 Modelling Visual Attention

The process of meaningful information processing from images by the human brain is very complex and it is not fully understood. Human reaction to the perceived information from images takes into account previous experiences and memories, as well as eye contact and fixation. The human visual system aims to focus on interesting regions in images, which coincide with the fixation points chosen by saccades, corresponding to random eye movements, at the pre-attentive stage for foveation, representing conscious acquisition of detail. These regions are characterized by local discontinuities, features and parts of images that attract the visual attention determining them to stand out from the rest. Such salient regions tend to correspond to important semantic concepts and are useful for image understanding while the rest of image content is ignored. In Fig. 1 we present some examples of visual saliency in images.

Salient regions can be defined in two ways. Bottom-up attention is instinctive and involuntary. It is entirely driven by the image, usually by specific features, such as colour, size, orientation, position, motion or their scene context. This approach is almost a reflex and corresponds to the instinctive type of attention to a salient region. Top-down attention, on the other hand, is driven by memory and prior experiences.

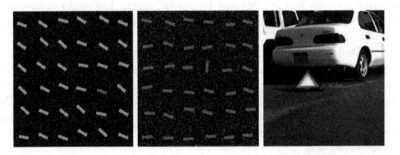

Fig. 1 Examples of visual saliency

Looking for a specific object of interest amidst many others, such as a book on a shelf or a key of a keyboard, may be defined by the previous knowledge of the title or authors of that book for example. Top-down attention driven by memories may even suppress bottom-up attention in order to reduce distraction by salient regions. Recently, memorisation studies have been undertaken in order to identify the reasoning behind the visual search [40, 41].

Visual attention is a diverse field of research and there are several models that have been proposed. Visual attention can be defined as either space-based or object-based. Spatial-based attention selects continuous spatial areas of interest, whereas object-based attention considers whole objects as driving the human attention. Object-based attention aims to address some of the disadvantages of spatial models such as their imprecision in selecting certain non-salient areas. Spatial models may select different parts of the same object as salient which means that the attention focus is shifted from one point to another in the image, whereas object-based attention considers a compact area of the image as the focus of attention. Applications of spatial-based attention to Content Based Image Retrieval tasks have been prevalent whilst those of object-based attention have not received a similar attention from the Image Retrieval community.

One of the main computer vision tasks consists of image understanding which leads to attempting to model or simulate the processing used by the human brain. Computational attention models aim to produce saliency maps that identify salient regions of the image. A saliency map relies on firstly finding the saliency value for each pixel. Salient region identification approaches fall into two main categories. The first category is based on purely computational principles such as the detection of interest points. These are detected using corner detectors and are robust under some image transformations, but are sensitive to image texture and thus would generalize poorly. Textured regions contain more corners but there are not necessarily more salient. Other computational approaches are based on image complexity assuming that homogeneous regions have lower complexity than regions of high variance. Some computational methods use either the coefficients of the wavelet transform or the entropy of local intensities [24]. Once again, such approaches assume that textured regions are more salient than others, which is not necessarily true. A spectral approach was used in [19], while [17] proposed a bottom-up model based on the maximisation of mutual information. A top-down classification method was proposed in [17] by employing the classification into either interesting or non-interesting areas.

The biologically influenced computational models of attention represent the second category of saliency models. This category further splits into two sub-categories: biologically plausible and biologically inspired. Biologically plausible models are based on actual neurological processes occurring in the brain, whereas biologically inspired models do not necessarily conform to the neurological model. Generally, these models consist of three phases: the feature extraction, the computation of activation maps, and the normalization and recombination of the feature maps into a single saliency map [20].

The Itti-Koch saliency model [21, 22] is a well-known biologically plausible method modelling rapid changes of visual attention in scene which is based on neurological processes occurring in the brains of primates. The algorithm analyses colour, intensity and orientation information within nine different scale spaces by using dyadic Gaussian pyramids calculating center-surround differences using Difference of Gaussians (DoG) in order to detect local spatial discontinuities. From these, feature conspicuity maps (CM) are produced by recombining the multi-scale images and normalizing. A further linear combination produces the final saliency map. Among the salient regions, some are more salient than others. When the human brain is presented with the fixation points defining salient regions, the order in which it chooses the focus of attention (FOA) is determined by the saliency of a specific point. This principle is modelled by the algorithm by assigning each pixel in the saliency map to an input neuron in a feed-forward winner-take-all (WTA) neural network. In simulated time, the voltage in the network is increased until one of the input neurons fires, moving the FOA to the salient location represented by that neuron. After firing, the network is reset and the inhibition of return (IOR) is applied for a certain time in order to prevent the previous winner neuron from firing repeatedly. This mechanism produces a sequence of attended locations, where the order is driven by their saliency. The luminance image is produced from the average of the result for the red, green, blue image components. Orientation features are obtained from filtering the image with a bank of Gabor filters at different orientations. Image scales represent the image from original size down to 1/256th of the original image. During across-scale map combinations, low-resolution feature maps are upscaled and the final saliency map is downscaled to 1/256th of the original image. Given the amount of rescaling and Gaussian filtering occurring during the process, the saliency map produced by this model removes 99% of the high frequencies, [1]. This produces blurred edges of the salient regions after the map is upscaled to the original image size. The map only shows the peaks in saliency having high precision at low recall, which quickly drops off, [1]. Other criticism is directed at the lack of a clear optimisation objective of the system. The research study from [15] used different centre-surround difference calculations in order to optimise the Itti-Koch framework. The method proposed in [18] uses the biologically plausible model of Itti-Koch but applies a graph-based method for producing feature activation maps followed by normalisation.

Another biologically inspired hybrid method is the SUN model proposed in [47]. This model relies on a Bayesian framework based on the statistics of natural images collected off-line. The training set of natural images is decomposed though independent component analysis (ICA), yielding 326 filters, which are convolved with the image feature maps to produce the activations. This approach was shown to outperform the DoG when computing activation maps, albeit at the increase of the computational cost, as 326 filters are used in convolutions instead of 12.

3 Content Based Image Retrieval Framework

Content based image retrieval (CBIR) involves using an image as a model or query in order to search for similar images from a given pool of images. CBIR relies on the image content as a base of information for search, whilst defining image similarity remains a challenge in the context of human intent. In bottom-up computational analysis of images, the content is considered as being represented by statistics of image features. In this chapter we explain the Query by Saliency Content Retrieval (QSCR) method, which considers that the visual attention is a determinant factor which should be considered when initiating the image search. Firstly, we have a training stage in which characteristic image features are extracted from image regions corresponding to various categories of images from a training set. In the retrieval stage we rank the images, which are available from a database, according to a similarity measure. The scheme of the proposed QSCR system is provided in Fig. 2. The main parts of the QSCR system consists of image segmentation, feature extraction, saliency modelling and evaluating the distance in the feature space between a query image and a sample image from the given pool of images [29].

3.1 Image Segmentation

The mean shift segmentation algorithm is a well known clustering algorithm relying on kernel density estimation. This algorithm is a density mode-finding algorithm [9, 10] without the need to estimate explicitly the probability density. A typical kernel density estimator is given by

$$f(\mathbf{x}) = \frac{c_{k,d}}{nh^d} \sum_{i=1}^{n} K\left(\frac{\mathbf{x} - \mathbf{x}_i}{h}\right) \tag{1}$$

where n is the number of data points, h is the bandwidth parameter, d is the number of dimensions, $c_{k,d}$ is a normalizing constant and $K(\mathbf{x})$ is the kernel. The multivariate Gaussian function is considered as a kernel in this study. The mode of this density estimate is defined by $\nabla f(\mathbf{x}) = 0$. A density gradient estimator can be obtained by taking the gradient of the density estimator. In case of multivariate Gaussian estimator, it will be

$$\nabla f(\mathbf{x}) = \frac{2c_{k,d}}{nh^d} \sum_{i=1}^{n} (\mathbf{x} - \mathbf{x}_i) K\left(\frac{\mathbf{x} - \mathbf{x}_i}{h^{d+2}}\right) \tag{2}$$

and then derive a center updating vector called the mean shift vector:

$$\mathbf{m}_{h,G}(\mathbf{x}) = \frac{\sum_{i=1}^{n} \mathbf{x}_i K\left(\frac{\mathbf{x} - \mathbf{x}_i}{h}\right)}{\sum_{i=1}^{n} K\left(\frac{\mathbf{x} - \mathbf{x}_i}{h}\right)} - \mathbf{x} \tag{3}$$

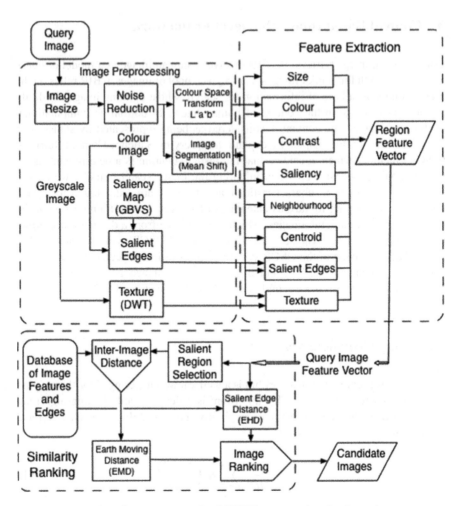

Fig. 2 The query by saliency content retrieval (QSCR) system using visual attention

Rearranging, yields the mean shift vector as:

$$\mathbf{m}_{h,G}(\mathbf{x}) = \frac{h^2 c}{2} \frac{\nabla f(\mathbf{x})}{f(\mathbf{x})} \qquad (4)$$

The mean shift algorithm stops when the mean shift becomes zero and consequently there is no change in the cluster center defining the mode. In the case when the algorithm starts with too many initial clusters, several of these would converge to the same mode and consequently all, but the ones corresponding to the real modes, can be removed.

In order to segment images, colour is transformed to the perceptually uniform CIELUV space. The two pixel coordinates defining their spatial location, and the colour values are combined into a single 5D input vector, which are then clustered using the mean-shift algorithm. Clusters, defining image regions correspond to the set of points that fall within the basin of attraction of a mode. The number of clusters, each characterizing a segmented region, is selected automatically by the algorithm based on the data depending only on the bandwidth parameter h [3].

3.2   Image Features Used for Retrieval

Each image is resized and then segmented into regions as described in the previous section. For each image region a characteristic feature vector is calculated, with entries representing statistics of colour, contrast, texture information, the region neighbourhood information and region's centroid.

Firstly, six entries characterizing the colour are represented by the median values as well as the standard deviations for the L*a*b* colour components calculated from the segmented regions. The median estimator is well known as a robust statistical estimator, whilst the variance represents the variation of that feature in the image region. The L*a*b* is well known as a colour space defining the human perception of colours. The Daubechies 4-tap filter (Db4) is used as a Discrete Wavelet Transform (DWT) [26] function for characterizing texture in images. 4 from Db4 indicates the number of coefficients used for describing the filter having two vanishing points. A larger numbers of coefficients would be useful when analysing signals with fractal properties which are also characterized by self-similarity. Db4 wavelets are chosen due to their good localisation properties, very good texture classification performance [6], high compactness, low complexity, and efficient separation between image regions of high and low frequency. Moreover Daubechie wavelet functions are able to capture smooth transitions and gradients much better than the original Haar wavelets, which are not continuous and are sensitive to noise. The lower level decompositions are up-scaled to the size of the image by using bicubic interpolation and then by averaging the pixel values across the three scales and for each direction. Three entries represent the texture energy measured as the average of the absolute values of the DWT coefficients of the region in the horizontal, vertical and oblique directions across the three image scales, [6].

The human visual system is more sensitive to contrast than to absolute brightness. Generally, the contrast is defined as the ratio between the difference in local brightness and the average brightness in a region. In order to increase its robustness, the contrast is computed as the ratio between the inter-quartile range and the median of the L* (luminance) component for each segmented region. The locations of the centers for each region are calculated as the averages of pixel locations from inside each compactly segmented region. These values are normalised by the image dimension in order to obtain values in the interval [0,1]. By giving more importance to the centroid locations, candidate images that best satisfy the spatial layout of the query image can be retrieved. However, placing too much importance on the location may actually decrease the precision and this is the reason why this feature is considered, together with the region neighbourhood, as a secondary feature, characterised by a lower weight in the calculation of the similarity measure. The region neighbourhood can provide very useful information about the image context. The neighbourhood consistency is represented by the differences between the L*, a* and b* values of the given region and those of its most important neighbouring regions located above, below, left and right, where the neighbouring significance is indicated by the size of the boundary between two regions, [33].

4 Defining the Saliency in Images

Based on the assumption that salient regions capture semantic concepts of an image, the goal of computing visual saliency is to detect such regions of interest so that they can be used as a search query. Saliency maps must concisely represent salient objects or regions of the image. In Fig. 3 we present an example of retrieving the Translucent Bowl (TB) image in SIVAL database without visual attention models compared to when visual attention models is used, assuming identical image features. As it can be observed, when using visual attention models, all first six retrieved images and the eight out of the total of nine correspond to the TB category, while when not using the visual attention models only the seventh image is from the correct category but none of the other eight images.

Saliency is used to identify which image regions attract the human visual attention and consequently should be considered in the image retrieval. Saliency is defined in two ways: at local and at the global image level, [29]. The former is defined by finding salient regions, while the latter is defined by the salient edges in the entire images. The regions which are salient would have higher weights

Fig. 3 Retrieving images with salient object when not using visual attention (*top image*) and when using the visual attention (*bottom images*) from SIVAL database. The query image is located at the *top left image* in each case

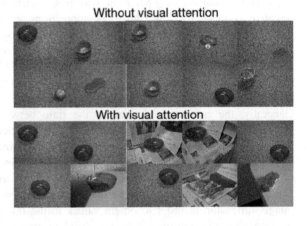

when considering their importance for retrieval while the salient edges are used as a constraint for evaluating the similarity of the query image to those from the given pool of images as shown in Fig. 2.

4.1 Salient Edges

In order to capture the global salient properties of a given image we consider the salient edges as in [14]. Firstly, the image is split into 16×16 pixels blocks, called sub-images. Salient edges are represented by means of the MPEG-7 Edge Histogram Descriptor (EHD) which is translation invariant. This represents the distribution along four main directions as well as the non-directional edges occurring in the image. Edges corresponding to each of these directions are firstly identified and then their density is evaluated for each sub-image region. The EHD histogram is represented by five values representing the mean of the bin counts for each edge type across the 16 sub-images. Each value represents the evaluation of the statistics for each of the edge orientations: vertical, horizontal, the two diagonal directions at 45 and 135 deg and the non-directional. The bin counts correspond to a specific directional edge energy and consequently the mean is an estimate that would capture it without any specific image location constraint.

4.2 Graph Based Visual Saliency

Known computational models of visual saliency are the Itti-Koch (IK) [22], Graph-Based Visual Saliency (GBVS) [18], which is the graph-based normalisation of the Itti-Koch model, the Saliency Using Natural statistics (SUN) [47], and the Frequency-Tuned Saliency (FTS) [1]. The first three methods produce low-resolution saliency blur maps that do not provide clear salient region boundaries. FTS, on the other hand, produces full resolution maps with clear boundaries, however, unlike the first three methods it only uses colour information, so it may fail to identify any salient regions when all objects in the image have the same colour.

The Graph-Based Visual Saliency (GBVS) method [18] was chosen due to its results for modelling saliency in images. The GBVS saliency extraction method is a computational approach to visual saliency based on the Itti-Koch model, but it takes a different approach to the creation of activation maps and their normalisation. Unlike the Itti-Koch model, which computes activation maps by center-surround differences of image features [22], GBVS applies a graph-based approach [18]. Generally, saliency maps are created in three steps: feature vectors are extracted for every pixel to create feature maps, then activation maps are computed, and finally the activation maps are normalized and combined. The image is converted into a representation suitable for the computation of the feature contrasts. Feature dyadic Gaussian pyramids are produced at three image scales of 2:1, 3:1, and 4:1. Gaussian pyramids are created for each channel of physiologically based DKL colour space [12], which has similar properties to L*a*b*. Orientation maps are then produced after applying Gabor filters at the orientations of $\{0, \pi/4, \pi/2, 3\pi/4\}$ degrees for every scale of each colour channel. The outputs of these Gabor filters represent the features which are then used as inputs in the GBVS algorithm.

In the first level of representation in GBVS, adjacency matrices are constructed by connecting each pixel of the map to all the other pixels, excluding itself, by using the following similarity function $\phi_1(\mathbf{M_x}, \mathbf{M_y})$ between feature vectors corresponding to the pixels located at $\mathbf{x}$ and $\mathbf{y}$:

$$\phi_1(\mathbf{M_x}, \mathbf{M_y}) = \left| \log \frac{\mathbf{M_x}}{\mathbf{M_y}} \right| \exp \left[-\frac{\|\mathbf{x} - \mathbf{y}\|^2}{2\sigma^2} \right] \tag{5}$$

where $\sigma \in [0.1, 0, 2]D$, D representing the given map width. A Markov chain is defined over this adjacency matrix, where the weights of outbound edges are normalized to $[0, 1]$, by assuming that graph nodes are states, and edges are transition probabilities. By computing the equilibrium distribution yields an activation map, where large values are concentrated in areas of high activation and thus indicate the saliency in the image. The resulting activation map is smoothed and normalized. A new graph is constructed onto this activation map, with each node connected to all the others including itself and which has the edge weights given by:

$$\phi_2(\mathbf{M_x}, \mathbf{M_y}) = A(\mathbf{x}) \exp \left[-\frac{\|\mathbf{x} - \mathbf{y}\|^2}{2\sigma^2} \right] \tag{6}$$

where $A(\mathbf{x})$ corresponds to the activation map value at location $\mathbf{x}$. The normalization of the activation maps leads to emphasizing the areas of true dissimilarity, while suppressing non-salient regions. The resulting. saliency map for the entire image is denoted as $S(\mathbf{x})$, for each location $\mathbf{x}$ and represents the sum of the normalized activation maps for each colour and each local orientation channel as provided by the Gabor filters.

In Fig. 4 we show a comparison of saliency maps produced by four saliency algorithms: Itti-Koch (IK) [22], Graph-Based Visual Saliency (GBVS) [18], Saliency using Natural Statistics (SUN) [47], and Frequency-Tuned Saliency (FTS) [1]. It can be seen that IK produces small highly focused peaks in saliency that tend to concentrate on small areas of the object. The peaks are also spread across the image spatially. This is because the Itti-Koch model was designed to detect areas to which the focus of attention would be diverted. Because the peaks do no capture the whole object, but rather small areas of it, it is insufficient for representing the semantic concept of the image and is not suitable for retrieval purposes.

Fig. 4 Evaluation of saliency performance. Original images are in the *first row*, Itti-Koch saliency maps are in the *second row*, GBVS maps are in the *third row*, SUN maps are in the *fourth row*, and FTS maps are in the *fifth row*. Saliency maps are overlaid on the original images

The image selections produced by GBVS provides a good coverage of the salient object by correctly evaluating the saliency. It has a good balance between coverage and accuracy the results sit in between IK and SUN. Unlike the other three methods, GBVS provides a high-level understanding of the whole image and its environment, in the sense that it does not get distracted by the local details, which may result in false positives. It is able to achieve this because it models dissimilarity as a transition probability between nodes of a graph, which means that most of the time, saliency is provided by the nodes with the highest transition probability. It can be seen from the mountain landscape image in the last column that saliency is correctly indicated at the lake and sky, despite not having an evident object in that region of the image. In the second image where the red bus fills most of the image, GBVS recognises the area surrounding the door as most salient, compared to SUN algorithm, which considers the whole image as salient. It appears that the SUN algorithm only works well with the simplest of images such is the third image showing a snowboarder on snow. In the first image, given the image of the horse, which is only slightly more difficult, the SUN algorithm correctly identifies the head of horse, its legs, and tail. However, it also selects the trees, which are not that relevant for the retrieval of such images. The large amount of false positives, apparent bias, and lack of precision makes SUN an unsuitable choice for retrieval in the broad image domain, but perhaps it could prove itself useful in specialised applications. FTS algorithm, which represents a simple colour difference, only works well when there is a salient colour object in the image, and the image itself has little colour variation, such that the average colour value is close to that of the background. As it uses no other features than the colour, it lacks the robustness of other methods, but works extremely well when its conditions are met. As seen with the bus in the second image, its downside is that it does not cover salient objects when there is a lot of colour variation within, hence failing to capture the semantic concept. One of the problems with local contrast-based saliency algorithms is that they may misinterpret the negative space around true salient objects as the salient object.

GBVS is chosen for saliency computation in this study because of its robustness, accuracy, and coverage. One downside is that it does not produce full resolution saliency maps due to its computational complexity. During the up-scaling, blurred boundaries are produced, which means that saliency spills into adjacent regions and so marks them as salient, albeit to a smaller extent.

4.3   Salient Region Selection

In this study we consider that we segment the images using the mean-shift algorithm described in Sect. 3.1 and we aim to identify which of the segmented regions are salient. The purpose of the saliency maps is to select those regions that correspond to the salient areas of the image, which are to be given a higher importance in the querying procedure. For distinctive objects present in images, this represents selecting the object's regions, whereas for distinctive scenes it would come down to selecting the object and its neighbouring regions. Several approaches have been attempted to select an optimal threshold on the saliency energy of a region as the sum of the saliencies of all its component pixels. An optimal threshold would be the one that maximises the precision of retrieval rather than the one that accurately selects regions corresponding to salient objects. This is somewhat counter-intuitive, as one would think that specifying well-defined salient objects would improve the precision, but due to the semantic gap, this is actually not always the case. In the Blobworld image retrieval method [5], images are categorized as distinctive scenes or distinctive objects, or both. However, it was remarked that when considering CBIR in some image categories it would be useful to include additional contextual information and not just the salient object.

Firstly, we consider selecting regions that contain a certain percentage of salient pixels, where salient pixels are those defined by $S(\mathbf{x}) > \theta_p$. The average region saliency is calculated from the saliency of its component pixels as:

$$S(r_i) = \sum_{\mathbf{x} \in r_i} \frac{S(\mathbf{x})}{N_r} \tag{7}$$

where $\mathbf{x}$ is a pixel in region r_i, $i = 1, \ldots, R$, where R represents all segmented regions in the image, $S(\mathbf{x})$ is the value of the saliency for $\mathbf{x}$, and N_r is the number of pixels in the region r. In a different approach we can consider a saliency cut-off, given by $S(r) > \theta_R$, which was set at a value that would remove most of the regions defined by a small saliency. A third method of salient region selection is the one adopted in [14], where a threshold that maximizes the entropy between the two region partitions by the saliency threshold, was adopted. In [14] they set two cut-offs. The first cut-off was at 10% of the average region saliency value, calculated using the cumulative distribution function (CDF) of all region saliencies $S(r)$, as in Eq. (7) across the whole image database. This first cut-off was used to filter out large regions characterized by low saliency. The second cut-off was based on the total region saliency, representing the sum of all saliency values in the region, and was used to filter out very small regions characterised by very high saliency.

Another approach to select the salient regions consists in finding the average region saliency value corresponding to the minimum probability density in a non-monotonically decreasing pdf. This works well when there is a clear break between the saliency values in the pdf of salient regions and produces a good cut-off candidate. However, this method fails when the saliency pdf is monotonically-decreasing as the smallest saliency value is usually too high to select any regions. An adaptive method was attempted by using the density-based method for non-monotonically decreasing pdfs and the percentile-based cut-off otherwise. If the density-based method sets a cut-off that is too high, the retrieval performance is likely to decrease, so it is applied only if the first half of saliency values is non-monotonically decreasing. Another method that provided a suitable threshold was the one proposed in [28], which was shown to capture well the salient regions in several CBIR studies.

In the following experiments we consider that salient regions capture semantic concepts of an image. By computing the visual saliency we detect salient regions of interest in order to be used as a search query. In Fig. 5 we compare the saliency maps produced in 12 different images from diverse image categories of COREL 1000 database, by using different cut-off selection methods. Using Otsu's method to select the cut-off produces maps that discard the lower saliency values associated with the background preserving the medium to high saliency values. However, this method tends to produce large areas which results in too many background regions being included, which makes it less suitable when querying for distinctive objects. An example of this is in the second image from Fig. 5, representing a snow-covered landscape area. The cumulative distribution function of pixel saliency values corresponding to COREL 1000 image database is produced as shown in Fig. 6a. From this plot we can observe that almost 40% of the data have saliency values less than 0.1 and only 10% have a value above 0.62. The other half of the data (between 40th and 90th percentiles), has uniform probability as the gradient of the curve is approximately constant. Hence, we devise two salient region selection methods which set their cut-offs at the 60th and 80th percentiles of the image's saliency values, corresponding to approximately 0.3 and 0.5 cut-off

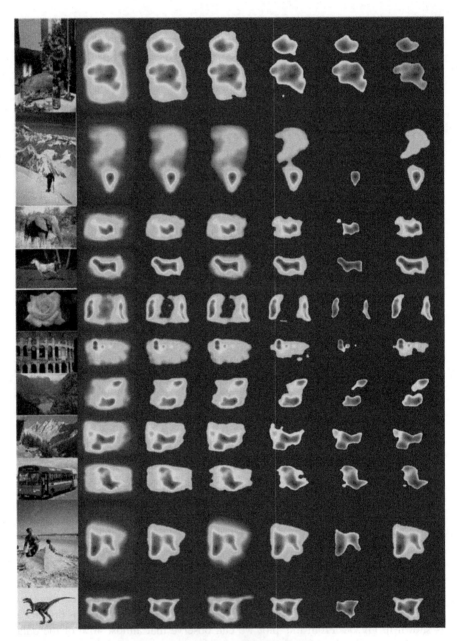

Fig. 5 Comparison of saliency cut-offs (*1*) Original image, (*2*) GBVS saliency map (SM), (*3*) Otsu's method, (*4*) Top 40%, (*5*) Top 20%, (*6*) Cut-off at 0.61, (*7*) Cut-off at twice the average saliency as in [1]

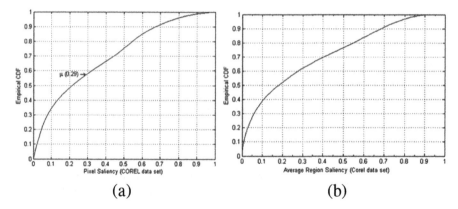

Fig. 6 Empirical cumulative distribution functions (CDF) calculated for all images from COREL 1000 database. (**a**) Pixel saliency. (**b**) Salient regions

points, respectively. The 60th percentile produces similar results to Otsu's method, but on some occasions includes too many background pixels as seen in the Beach and Dinosaur categories images, shown in the last two images from Fig. 5. The 80th percentile, representing the selection of the top 20% of data, shows a good balance between the two criteria where it selects a smaller subset of the pixels identified by Otsu's method as in the case of the Elephant and Bus categories, from the third and ninth images and at the same time captures a good amount of background pixels as in the Architecture and Beach category images from the sixth and tenth images. Obviously, it is impossible to guarantee that it will capture background information for distinctive scenes and just the object for distinctive object images, and vice versa, but at least this method is sufficiently flexible to do so. The next method is a simple fixed cut-off value set at the pixel value of 155, which corresponds to 60% precision and 40% recall. By looking at the CDF of salient pixels from COREL 1000 database, shown in Fig. 6a, this value corresponds to the 90th percentile of saliency values and so selects only the top 10% of the data. Only small portions of the image are selected and in many cases this fails to capture the background regions, resulting in lower performance. An example of this is seen in the image of the walker in the snow-covered landscape image, the Horse and the Architecture category images from second, fourth and sixth images from Fig. 5. In all these images, the most salient object has very little semantic information differentiating it from the others. For example, the walker is mostly black and very little useful information is actually contained within that region; the horse is mostly white and this is insufficient to close the semantic gap. Achieving a balance is difficult because a method that selects the regions of distinctive objects may fail when the image is both a distinctive object and a distinctive scene. An example of such a situation is the Horse category from the fourth image, where selecting the white horse by itself is too ambiguous as there are many similarly coloured regions, but by adding several background regions improves performance greatly. On the other hand, the performance would be reduced by including background regions when the image is in the category of distinctive objects. The last method, which was used in [1], sets the threshold at twice the average saliency for the image. This approximately corresponds to the top 15% of salient pixels from the empirical cumulative distribution for COREL 1000. This produces similar maps to the selection of regions with 20% salient pixels, except that it captures fewer surrounding pixels.

In the following we evaluate the segmented image region saliency by considering only those salient pixels which are among the top 20% salient pixels, which provides best results, according to the study from [29]. By considering a hard threshold for selecting salient pixels, the saliency for the rest of pixels is considered as zero for further processing. We then apply the region mask to the saliency map and consider the region saliency as given by the percentage of its salient pixels. Next, we use the saliency characteristic from all regions in the image database to construct an empirical CDF of salient regions, considering the mean-shift for the image segmentation, as explained in Sect. 3.1. The empirical CDF of the salient regions for the COREL 1000 database is shown in Fig. 6b. Now, we propose to select the most salient regions by setting the second threshold at the first point of inflexion in the CDF curve. This corresponds to the point where the gradient of the CDF curve begins to decrease. We observe that this roughly corresponds to the 35th percentile and thus our method considers the top 65% of most salient regions in the given database. We have observed that this saliency region selection threshold removes most of the regions with little saliency, while still considering some background regions containing the background information necessary for the retrieval of images of distinctive scenes. Such regions are suitable for describing the contextual semantic information.

The methods discussed above focus on selecting representative salient query regions. In the QSCR system we would segment the query image and would assume that all candidate images had been previously segmented as well. The saliency of each region in both the candidate images and the query one would then be evaluated. Once the salient query regions are determined, they could be matched with all the regions in the candidate images. Another approach could evaluate the saliency in both the query and the candidate images and the matching would be performed only with the salient regions from the candidate images. This constrains the search by reducing the number of relevant images because the query regions are searched by using only the information from the salient regions of the candidate images. Theoretically, this should improve both retrieval precision and computational speed, but in practice, the results will depend on the distinctiveness of the salient regions because the semantic gap would be stronger due to a lack of context.

5 Similarity Ranking

Given a query image, we rank all the available candidate images according to their similarity with the query image. The aim here is to combine the inter-region distance matrix with the salient edge information to rank the images by their similarity while taking into account their saliency as well. The processing stages of image segmentation, feature extraction and saliency evaluation, described in the previous section, and shown in the chart from Fig. 2, are applied initially to all images from a given database. Each region $I_j, j = 1, \ldots, N_I$, from every I image is characterized by a feature vector, and by its saliency, evaluated as described in the previous Section. Meanwhile, the energy of salient edges is evaluated for entire images. The same processing stages are applied on the query image Q, which is segmented into several regions Q_i, $i = 1, \ldots, M$ as described in Sect. 3.1. The similarity ranking becomes a many-to-many region matching problem which takes into account the saliency as well. Examples of many-to-many region matching algorithms are the Integrated Region Matching (IRM) which was used in [44] for the SIMPLIcity image retrieval algorithm and the Earth Mover's Distances (EMD), [34]. The EMD algorithm was chosen in this study due to its properties of optimising many-to-many matches, and this section of the algorithm is outlined in the lower part of the diagram from Fig. 2.

In the EMD algorithm, each image becomes a signature of feature vectors characterising each region. A saliency driven similarity measure is used between the query image Q and a given image I, represented as the weighted sum of the EMD matching cost function, considering the local saliency, and the global image saliency measure driven by the salient edges, [29]:

$$\mathscr{S}(Q, I) = W_{EMD} \frac{\text{EMD}(Q, I)}{\alpha_{EMD}} + W_{EHD} \frac{\sum_{\theta} |\text{EHD}(\theta, Q) - \text{EHD}(\theta, I)|}{5\,\alpha_E} \tag{8}$$

where $\text{EMD}(Q, I)$ is the EMD metric between images Q and I, $\text{EHD}(\theta, Q)$ represents the average salient edge energy, in five different directions of $\theta = \{0, \pi/2, \pi, 3\pi/4, \text{non-dir}\}$ for the image Q, derived as described in Sect. 4.1. The weights, found empirically, for the local region-to-region matching EMD component is $W_{EMD} = 0.7$, while for the global image component EHD, is $W_{EHD} = 0.3$. These choices indicate a higher weight for the localized saliency indicated by EMD than for the global image saliency, given by EHD, as observed in psychological studies of human visual attention. α_{EMD} and α_E represent the robust normalization factors which are set as the 95th percentile of the cumulative distribution function of the EMD and the EHD measures, respectively, calculated using a statistically significant image sample set. These robustness factors are used for normalizing the data and removing the outliers, by taking into account that the data distributions characterizing both EMD and EHD are log-normal.

EMD is an optimization algorithm which assumes a signature vector for each image, either the query image Q or any of the candidate images, I, from the database. The signature assigned to each image consists of a collection of regions, with each region represented by a feature vector and its saliency. EMD calculates a distance between the representations provided by the image signatures by transforming the matching problem into providing a solution for a known transport distribution calculation, which is solved by linear programming. The problem is a matter of transporting goods from a set of suppliers to a set of consumers by the least-cost route, defined by a flow. The intuitive idea of EMD is to assume that a certain quantity of earth is used to fill up a number of holes in the ground, [34]. The query image is associated to a specific quantity of earth, grouped on heaps, while each candidate image for retrieval is assimilated with a number of holes in the ground. Each heap and each hole correspond to a region, either in the query or in the retrieved image, respectively, while the earth corresponds to the image region feature vectors and their characteristic saliency.

We consider the distance between the two sets of features, corresponding to the regions of the query and any candidate images, as a dissimilarity cost function $D(Q_i, I_j)$:

$$D(Q_i, I_j) = \frac{\psi(S_{Q_i}, S_{I_j})}{\sqrt{\beta_P(\lambda_{cl}d_{cl}^2(i,j) + \lambda_{te}d_{te}^2(i,j) + \lambda_{co}d_{co}^2(i,j)) + \beta_S(\lambda_{nn}d_{nn}^2(i,j) + \lambda_{cd}d_{cd}^2(i,j))}}$$

(9)

where Q_i, $i = 1, \ldots, M$ from the query image Q and each region I_j, $j = 1, \ldots, N$ from the candidate retrieval image I. $\psi(S_{Q_i}, S_{I_j})$ denotes the joint saliency weight for Q_i and I_j. d_{cl}, d_{te} and d_{co} are the Euclidean distances between the primary features, weighted by β_P, corresponding to the colour, texture and contrast vectors, respectively. Meanwhile, d_{nn} and d_{cd} are the Euclidean distances between the secondary features, weighted by β_S, characterizing the colours of the nearest neighbouring regions and the centroid locations of the regions Q_i and I_j, respectively. Each feature distance component is normalized to the interval $[0, 1]$ and is weighted according to its significance for retrieval by the global weights β_P, β_S, modulating the significance for each category of features, and the individual weights, weighting the contribution of each feature as: λ_{cl}, λ_{te}, λ_{co}, λ_{nn} and λ_{cd}. The selection of primary and secondary features $\beta_P > \beta_S$, where $\beta_P + \beta_S = 1$ was performed based on computational visual attention studies [16, 46] and following extensive empirical experimentation.

The feature modelling for each segmented region is described in Sect. 3.2 and distances are calculated between vectors of features characterizing image regions from the database and those of the query image. The CIEDE2000 colour distance was chosen for the colour components of the two vectors, because it provides a better colour discrimination according to the CIE minimal perceptual colour difference, [36]. The colour feature distance d_{cl} is calculated as:

$$d_{cl}^2 = \frac{1}{6} \left[3 \left(\frac{\Delta E_{00}(i,j)}{C_{Dis}} \right)^2 + \left(\frac{\sigma_{i,L*} - \sigma_{j,L*}}{\alpha_{L*}} \right)^2 \right.$$

$$\left. + \left(\frac{\sigma_{i,a*} - \sigma_{j,a*}}{\alpha_{a*}} \right)^2 + \left(\frac{\sigma_{i,b*} - \sigma_{j,b*}}{\alpha_{b*}} \right)^2 \right] \tag{10}$$

where $\Delta E_{00}(i,j)$ represents the CIEDE2000 colour difference [36], calculated between the median estimates of $L*$, $a*$, $b*$ colour components, normalized by the largest color distance C_{Dis}, while $\{\sigma_{x,c} | x \in \{i,j\}, c \in \{L*, a*, b*\}\}$ represent the standard deviations for each colour component, and $\{\alpha_c | c \in \{L*, a*, b*\}\}$ are their corresponding 95th percentiles, calculated across the entire image database, and are used as robust normalization factors. These values are used for normalization because the cumulative distributions of these features, extracted from segmented image regions, can be modelled by log-normal functions.

The texture distance d_{te} corresponds to the Euclidean distance between the average of the absolute values of DWT coefficients corresponding to the horizontal, vertical and oblique directions for the regions Q_i and I_j, divided by their corresponding standard deviations calculated across the entire image database. The contrast difference d_{co} is represented by the normalized Euclidean distance of the contrast features for each region from I and Q, with respect to their neighbouring regions. For the sake of robust normalization, the distances corresponding to the texture features as well as those representing local contrast are divided by the 95th percentiles of the empirical cumulative distribution function of their features, computed from a representative image set. The neighbourhood characteristic difference d_{nn} is calculated as the average of the resulting 12 colour space distances to the four nearest neighbouring regions from above, below, left and right, selected such that they maximize the joint boundary in their respective direction. The centroid distance d_{cd} is the Euclidean distance between the coordinates of the regions centers.

The weight corresponding to the saliency, weighting the inter-region distances between two image regions from Q_i and I_j, from (9), is given by:

$$\psi(S_{Q_i}, S_{I_j}) = \max \left(1 - \frac{S_{Q_i} + S_{I_j}}{2}, 0.1 \right) \tag{11}$$

where S_{Q_i} and S_{I_j} represent the saliency of the query image region Q_i and that of the candidate retrieval image region I_j, where the saliency of each region is calculated, following the analysis from Sect. 4.3, and represents the ratios of salient pixels from each region. It can be observed that the distance $D(Q_i, I_j)$ is smaller when the two regions Q_i and I_j are both salient. Eventually, for all regions from Q and I, it results a similarity matrix $D(Q_i, I_j)$ which defines a set of inter-region distances between each region Q_i, $i = 1, \ldots, M$ from the query image Q and each region I_j, $j = 1, \ldots, N$ from the candidate retrieval image I. The resulting inter-region similarity matrix acts as the ground distance matrix for the EMD algorithm.

The distance matrix $D(Q_i, I_j)$ represents the cost of moving the earth energy associated with the image regions from Q to fitting the gaps of energy, represented by the image regions from I. A set of weights $\{w_{Q,i} | i = 1, \ldots, M\}$ is associated with the amount of energy corresponding to a region in the query image, while $\{w_{I,j} | j = 1, \ldots, N\}$ are the weights corresponding to the candidate image, representing the size of an energy gap. All these weights represent the ratios of each segmented region from the entire image. A unit of flow is defined as the transportation of a unit of energy across a unit of ground distance. The EMD algorithm is an optimization algorithm which minimizes the cost required for transporting the energy to a specific energy gap, [34]:

$$\min(\sum_{i=1}^{M} \sum_{j=1}^{N} f_{ij} D(Q_i, I_j)) \tag{12}$$

which is subject to the following constraints:

$$f_{ij} > 0, \ i = 1, \ldots, M, j = 1, \ldots, N \tag{13}$$

$$\sum_{j=1}^{N} f_{ij} \leq w_{Q,i}, \ i = 1, \ldots, M \tag{14}$$

$$\sum_{i=1}^{M} f_{ij} \leq w_{I,j}, \ j = 1, \ldots, N \tag{15}$$

$$\sum_{i=1}^{M} \sum_{j=1}^{N} f_{ij} = \min\left(\sum_{i=1}^{M} w_{Q,i}, \sum_{j=1}^{N} f_{ij} w_{I,j}\right) \tag{16}$$

The goal of the optimization procedure is to find the flow f_{ij} between the regions Q_i and I_j such that the cost of matching the energy from a surplus area to a deficit of energy area is minimized.

After solving this system by using linear programming, the EMD distance from (8) is calculated by normalizing the cost required:

$$\text{EMD}(Q, I) = \frac{\sum_{i=1}^{M} \sum_{j=1}^{N} f_{ij} D(Q_i, I_j)}{\sum_{i=1}^{M} \sum_{j=1}^{N} f_{ij}} \tag{17}$$

This represents the normalized cost of matching the query image signature with that of the most appropriate candidate retrieval image. The weights add up to unity only when all image regions are used. We are removing non-salient image regions, and consequently the weights would add up to a value less than one. Such signatures enable partial matching which is essential for image retrieval where there is a high likelihood of occlusion in the salient regions. The computational complexity of the proposed QSCR is contained mostly in the feature extraction stage for the given image database which is performed off-line. The computational complexity of the optimization algorithm can be substantially reduced when thresholding the distances calculated by EMD, as in [31].

6 Experimental Results

6.1 Image Retrieval Databases

In the following we apply the methodology described in the previous sections, to three different databases: COREL 1000, SIVAL and Flickr. COREL 1000 is well known for its medium-to-high image complexity and its size makes it a good choice for the development of retrieval algorithms. The database consists of ten semantic categories of natural scenes, each containing 100 images. The categories from COREL 1000 are: Africa and its people (AFR), tropical seaside and beaches (BEA), Greek and Roman architecture (ARC), buses and coaches (BUS), dinosaur illustrations (DIN), elephants in an African environment (ELE), close-ups of flowers and bouquets (FLO), brown and white horses in a natural setting (HOR), mountain landscapes and glaciers (LAN) and food and cuisine (FOO). The SIVAL (Spatially Independent, Variable Area, and Lighting) database was designed for localized image retrieval [33], by containing a large number of similar images that only differ in the salient object. It consists of 1500 images in 25 categories with 60 images per category (10 scenes, 6 photos per scene). The SIVAL categories are: chequered scarf (CS), gold medal (GM), fabric softener box (FS), coke can (CC), Julie's pot (JP), green tea box (GT), translucent bowl (TB), blue scrunge (BS), glazed wood pot (GW), felt flower rug (FF), WD40 can (WD), smiley face doll (SF), data mining book (DM), Ajax orange (AO), Sprite can (SC), apple (AP), dirty running shoe (DS), banana (BA), striped notebook (SN), candle with holder (CH), cardboard box (CB), wood rolling pin (WP), dirty work gloves (DG), rap book (RB) and large spoon (LS). The Flickr database consists of 20 categories with 100 highly diverse images in each, and 2000 images with no specific concept. The following categories are part of this database: Mexico city taxi (MC), American flag (US), New York taxi (NY), snow boarding (SB), Pepsi can (PC), fire and flames (FF), sushi (SU), orchard (OR), fireworks (FI), Persian rug (PR), waterfall (WA), Coca Cola can (CC), Canadian mounted police (MO), ostrich (OS), boat (BO), keyboard (KE), honey bee (HB), cat (CA), samurai helmet (SH) and Irish flag (IF).

6.2 Image Retrieval Performance Measures

The basic retrieval assessment is provided by precision and recall. Precision represents the number of relevant images retrieved over the total number of retrieved images, while the recall represents the number of relevant images retrieved divided by the number of relevant images in database. A precision-recall (PR) curve can be plotted by classifying all candidate images as relevant/irrelevant according to their ground truth category and then by assigning a confidence value for the decision of that classification. In this study, the confidence value is the reciprocal of the dissimilarity measure, i.e. lower dissimilarity implies more confidence. Another statistical assessment measure is the Receiver Operating Characteristic (ROC) which plots the true positive rate versus the false positive rate (false alarm) by changing a decision threshold, and can be used to select the optimal number of images to be retrieved such that both measures are maximized. The area under the ROC curve (AUC) , which corresponds to the Wilcoxon-Mann-Whitney statistic [33], is a reliable image retrieval assessment measure. This can be interpreted as the probability that a randomly chosen positive image will be ranked higher than a randomly chosen negative image. A value above 0.5 means that the image retrieval method is more likely to choose a positive image, while a value below 0.5 means that the system is more likely to choose negative images which is worse than guessing.

In this study, images are ranked based on their similarity to the query, thus producing an ordered set of results. The rank-weighted average precision (WPR) is given by, Wang et al. [44]:

$$\text{WPR} = \frac{1}{N} \sum_{k=1}^{N} \frac{n_k}{k} \tag{18}$$

where N is the number of all retrieved images and n_k is the number of matches in the first k retrieved images. This measure gives more weight to matched items occurring closer to the top of the list and takes into account both precision and ranks. Ranks can be equated to recall because a higher WPR value means that relevant images are closer to the top of the list, therefore the precision would be high at lower recall values because more relevant images are retrieved. However the WPR measure is sensitive to the ratio of positive and negative examples in the database, i.e. the total number of relevant images out of the total number of candidate images.

Quantitative tests are performed by evaluating the average performance of the proposed methodology across the whole databases considering 300 queries for COREL 1000, 600 queries for Flickr, and 750 for SIVAL. Across the graph legends in this study, μ indicates the mean value for the measure represented, calculated across all categories and followed by a $\pm\sigma$ which denotes the average of the spreads.

6.3 Visual Attention Models

Following the analysis of various image saliency selection algorithms from Sect. 4.2 we use Graph-Based Visual Saliency (GBVS) algorithm for selecting the saliency in the context of the optimization algorithm, as described in Sect. 5. Using saliency as a weight for the Euclidean distances of the feature vectors is compared against the case when salience is not used at all. The Area under the ROC curve (AUC) results for COREL 1000 database are provided in Fig. 7. From this figure it can be observed that saliency improves the performance in categories where salient objects are prominent in the image such as Flowers, Horses, Dinosaurs, and

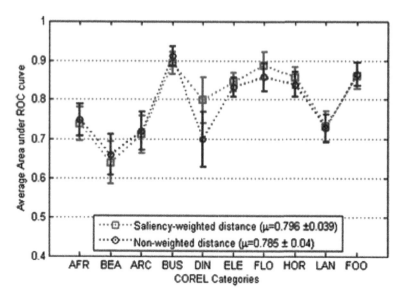

Fig. 7 Comparison between saliency weighted distances and non-weighted distances

decreases in categories where salient objects are difficult to identify, such as Beaches, Architecture, Africa, and Cuisine. This happens because in the former categories, the saliency weight gives preference to genuine candidate salient regions that correspond to a salient object well represented in that category, rather than the latter cases, where salient regions are specific in each image. Statistically, on the entire database, the mean (μ) of AUC, provided in Fig. 7, indicate that saliency is useful when used as a weighting of the distance measure.

6.4 Selecting Salient Regions from Images

In Fig. 8 we present the rank-weighted average precision results in ten image categories from COREL 1000 database when selecting the top 20% salient image data. This is compared with the case of using a fixed cut-off threshold of 0.607, which corresponds approximately to selecting the top 15% salient image data.

In Fig. 9 we provide a comparative study for the retrieval results when considering as salient regions only those corresponding to the top 65% of all salient regions from the CDF of salient regions, computed as described above. In Fig. 9a we compare the rank-weighted average precision results for the proposed image saliency region selection approach when compared to the approach which considers only the 50% most salient regions. In Fig. 9b the comparison is with a method using the maximization of entropy for the average region saliency values, proposed in [14], when using 100 saliency levels. The method based on the maximization of entropy

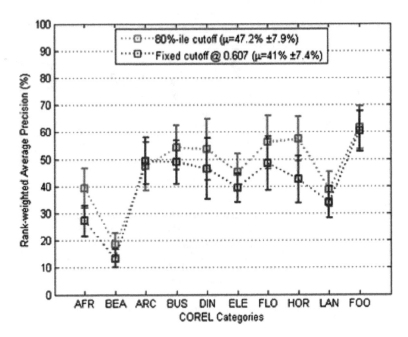

Fig. 8 Image retrieval when considering different saliency map thresholds. μ indicates the average rank-weighted precision followed by the average of the corresponding standard deviations after the $\pm$ sign. Standard deviations are indicated for each image category in the plot as well

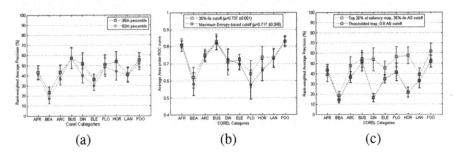

Fig. 9 Comparisons for various ways of selecting salient regions. (**a**) Rank-weighted average precision (WPR) when selecting salient regions based on the percentile of salient pixels. (**b**) Area under the ROC curve (AUC) when selecting salient regions based on the maximization of the saliency entropy. (**c**) WPR when salient regions are extracted using a thresholded saliency map

for the average region saliency values is not suitable for retrieving the images from Flower and Horse categories because it does not select enough background regions to differentiate the red/yellow flowers from buses. In both of these plots it can be observed that by selecting the top 65% salient regions outperforms the other approaches. Another method for selecting salient regions consists of binarising the saliency map using Otsu's threshold proposed in [28], then choosing the salient regions as those which have at least 80% of their pixels as salient. Figure 9c shows that this method underperforms greatly when categories have a well-defined salient object. This happens because this method selects just the salient object without including any background regions, and since those categories are classified as distinctive scenes, confusion occurs due to the semantic gap. On the other hand, the proposed QSCR method considers only the top 65% salient regions, and this was shown to be efficient in general-purpose image data sets, such as Corel and Flickr databases. However, in the case of SIVAL database, which consists entirely of distinctive objects with no semantic link to their backgrounds, salient regions are considered when they are part of the top 40% most salient regions, due to the fact that in this case the inclusion of background regions introduces false positives.

6.5   Similarity Ranking

Salient edges are extracted as explained in Sect. 4.1 and are used in the final image ranking evaluation measure from (8). The idea is that the region-to-region matching EMD distance gives a localized representation of the image while the salient edges provide a global view. Unlike in SEHD algorithm of [14], the QSCR method decouples the edge histogram from its spatial domain by considering the edge energy, corresponding to specific image feature orientations, calculated from the entire image. SEHD uses a different image segmentation algorithm and different selection of salient regions while performing the image ranking as in [7]. In Fig. 10 we compare the proposed salient edge retrieval approach, considering only the global image saliency and not the local saliency, and SEHD image retrieval method used in [14], using the average area under the ROC curve (AUC) as the comparison criterion. The categories in which the proposed approach outperforms SEHD are

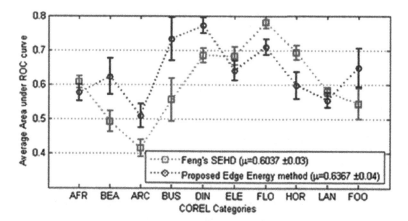

Fig. 10 Retrieval by salient edges: proposed salient edge representation compared with the Feng's SEHD approach

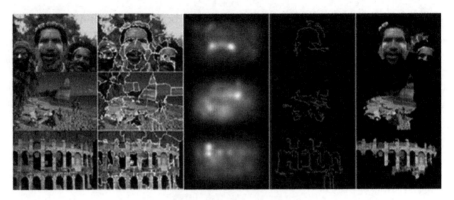

Fig. 11 Examples of extracted query information: (1) Original, (2) Image segments, (3) Saliency map, (4) Salient edges, (5) Selected salient regions

those where there is a significant amount of variation in the spatial positions of edges within the images, such as beaches and buses. The mean AUC value for SEHD and for the proposed method are 0.6037 and 0.6367, respectively. Thus, performing a two-tailed Students t-test at the highly significant 1% level with 598 degrees of freedom yields a p-value of 0.0022 which shows that the difference is statistically significant.

In Fig. 11 we provide the results for three images from three distinct image categories of COREL 1000 database after segmentation, saliency map estimation, salient edge extraction and salient region selection. These images are quite challenging due to their textured context. Examples of images from the other seven image categories from COREL database are shown in Fig. 12. It can be observed that the selected salient regions include contextual information such as in the second image from Fig. 11 and in the first, third, fifth and seventh images from Fig. 12. The salient object context is very important for image retrieval as shown in the full database results. Moreover, in the second image from Fig. 12, contextual regions are not selected since in this case they are not relevant because the main salient object is not related to its background. We have observed that the mean-shift algorithm leads to over-segmentation in some cases. However, this does not affect the salient region selection which is mainly driven by the saliency content and by the salient region selection procedure described in Sect. 4.3. Since the salient region selection is based on relative statistical measures, similar results would be obtained when using a different image segmentation algorithm.

Images are ranked according to the similarity measure $\mathcal{S}(Q, I)$ from (8), between the query image Q and a candidate retrieval image I. In Fig. 13a we present the retrieval results of 30 images for two different image categories from COREL 1000 database. In the query image, which is part of the Architecture category, from Fig. 13a it can be observed that the core of the salient region is a false positive, because the true object takes most of the image, and the most dissimilar area is a patch of sky in the middle. Nevertheless, the retrieval succeeds because the region

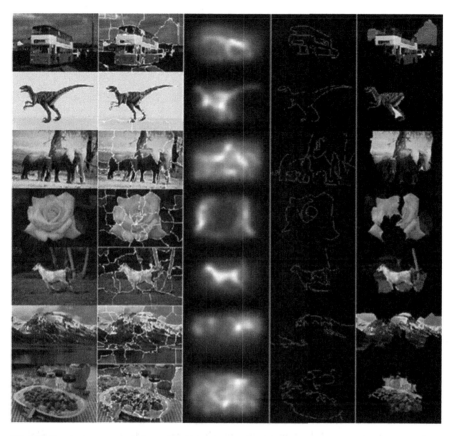

Fig. 12 Extracting query information from images for seven image categories from COREL database. The image columns indicate *from left to right*: original image, segmented regions, the GBVS saliency map, salient edges and the salient regions

selection method includes the surrounding regions in the query. The precision-recall (PR) curve corresponding to the query images is shown in Fig. 13b. Figure 14 shows a scenario where the number of positive examples in the category is much smaller, and yet the AUC value is high, as it can be observed from Fig. 14b. This means that if more positive examples were added to the database, then the precision would improve. Because all images in the category are considered relevant and the true number of positive examples is much lower, the curve underestimates the true retrieval performance. The semantic gap is evident in the retrieval of this image as the query regions contain ambiguous colours, resulting in a series of Horse and Food category images as close matches. The results when retrieving the white horse in natural habitat surroundings from Fig. 15 produces no false positives for the first 10 retrieved images, but after that creates some confusion with Africa (which basically represents people), as well as with Flowers and Elephant categories.

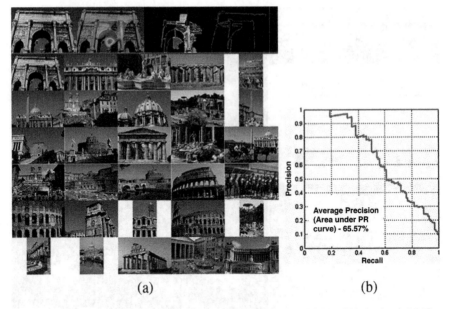

(a)   (b)

Fig. 13 Retrieval performance for Architecture category from COREL 1000 database. (**a**) The *first line* shows the query image, its saliency, selected salient regions and salient edge images while the subsequent lines displays the retrieved images in their order. In the *next six lines* are shown 30 retrieved images. (**b**) Precision-recall curve

A variety of good retrieval results are provided in Fig. 16a, b for the Bus and Flower categories from COREL 1000 database, while Fig. 16c, d shows the results for images from the Pepsi Can and Checkered Scarf categories from SIVAL database. The last two examples of more specific image categories from SIVAL database indicate very limited salient object confusion in the retrieval results.

6.6 Results for Entire Databases

Figure 17 compares the results for the proposed query by saliency content retrieval (QSCR) algorithm with SIMPLIcity from [44] when applied to COREL 1000 database. The comparison uses the same performance measures as in [44], respectively the average precision, average rank and average standard deviation of rank. As it can be observed from Fig. 17, QSCR provides better results in 4 image categories and worse in the other 6, according to the measures used. This is due to the fact that SIMPLIcity uses very selective features which are appropriate for these 6 image categories.

Figure 18 compares the results of QSCR, with the two retrieval methods proposed in [33], on Flickr database when using AUC. The results of QSCR and ACCIO are

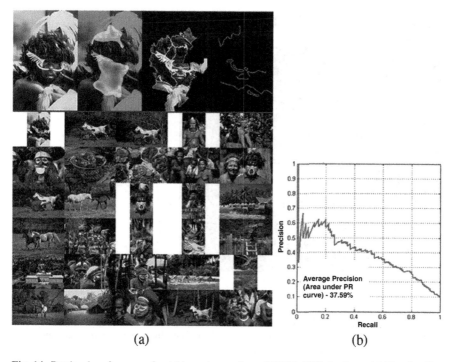

(a)   (b)

Fig. 14 Retrieval performance for Africa category from COREL 1000 database. (**a**) The *first line* shows the query image, its saliency, selected salient regions and salient edge images while the subsequent lines displays the retrieved images in their order. In the *next six lines* are shown 30 retrieved images. (**b**) Precision-recall curve

broadly similar and vary from one image category to another. However, ACCIO involves human intervention by acknowledging or not the retrieved images, while the approach described in this chapter is completely automatic. The salient edges improve the performance when the image of a certain category contain salient objects which are neither distinctive or diverse enough. This is the case with the SB category, where most of the photos depict people as salient objects, set in a snowy environment, HB, FF and FI categories, where the images are mostly close-ups, defined by mostly vertical edges.

Figure 19 provides the assessment of the retrieval results using AUC on SIVAL database when considering the retrieval of five images for each category. In this database, the objects have simple backgrounds and the saliency should highlight the main object while excluding the background which is the same for other image categories. Unlike in COREL 1000 and Flickr databases, the inclusion of the background is detrimental to the retrieval performance in this database. In the case of the images from SIVAL database we consider as salient those regions whose saliency corresponds to the top 40% of salient regions in the image instead of 35% which was used for the other two databases.

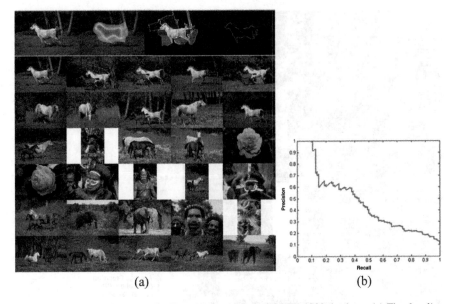

(a)   (b)

Fig. 15 Retrieval performance for Horse category from COREL 1000 database. (**a**) The *first line* shows the query image, its saliency, selected salient regions and salient edge images while the subsequent lines displays the retrieved images in their order. In the *next six lines* are shown 30 retrieved images. (**b**) Precision-recall curve

6.7 Discussion

Ideally, a larger database of millions of images should be used for assessing the image retrieval. The image segmentation currently takes about 90% of the feature extraction time. Tuning of feature weights usually came down to a decision regarding the trade-off between specificity and generality. As it can be seen from the results from Fig. 16, it is possible to obtain images that visually are highly similar to the query, in terms of colour, orientation, and position, at the cost of lower recall, since only a fraction of the category has those exact images. This may be a bad thing for the retrieval of images in general, but if the user were looking for images in a specific image sequence, then this would be the best way to achieve that goal. Qualitative tests for certain features are sensitive to the query image because some images will satisfy the criterion under evaluation and hence return better results for one specific category and at the same time reduce effectiveness in another.

Corel database is well balanced in terms of objects and scenes. Thus, maximising the average performance across all categories should produce a robust system. Nevertheless, in a few cases, the changes that improved the retrieval on the Corel database, reduced the performance on the Flickr database. Due to the varied nature of the Flickr images within each category, application of distance normalisation uncovered the true, large distances between features of the images within the category, which would otherwise have a negligible impact on ground distance

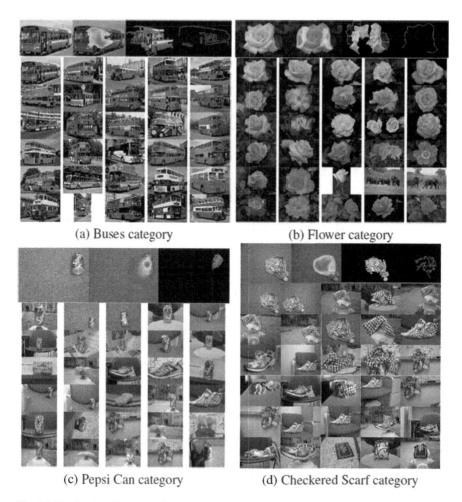

(a) Buses category   (b) Flower category

(c) Pepsi Can category   (d) Checkered Scarf category

Fig. 16 Retrieval performances for images from Corel database in (**a**) and (**b**) and from SIVAL database in (**c**) and (**d**)

because the domain of the feature values is very small. The semantic gap is most evident in this database because its images and ground truths were obtained by performing keyword search on Flickr. In addition, most of the images contain multiple salient areas, which combined with the deficiencies of computational visual attention models, result in several strong responses, which ultimately end up confusing the CBIR system.

The Corel database has also weaknesses. The categories are not entirely disjoint and it is sometimes unclear how to judge the retrieval results. When attempting to retrieve horses we may retrieve elephants as well because they are both animals and have similar relationships with their surroundings. At the lowest semantic level, this is incorrect as the retrieval is too general. Without keywords, if the user wished

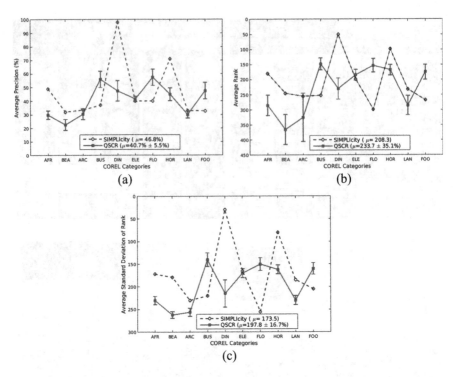

Fig. 17 Comparison results with SIMPLIcity

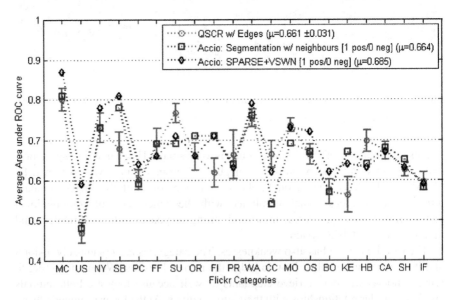

Fig. 18 Retrieval results on Flickr database and comparison with ACCIO

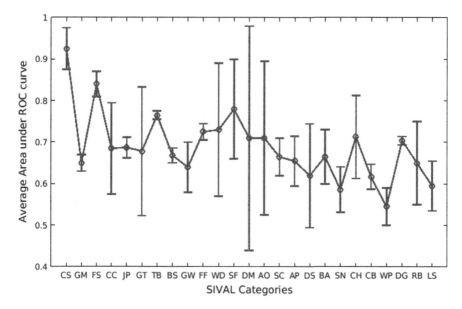

Fig. 19 Retrieval results on the SIVAL database

to search for animals, it would not be possible to specify such a query because "animal" is an abstract term. Such retrieval is only possible if the images are loosely clustered.

By considering distances using (8) between each pair of images for half of COREL 1000 database, an image classification matrix is produced, shown in Fig. 20. It shows the categories where the semantic gap is most prominent. It can be seen that Beach images are likely to get confused with Elephants, Landscapes, and Horses, whereas Elephants get mostly confused with Horses and to a lesser extent with Africa, Beaches, Architecture and Landscapes.

7 Conclusions

In this chapter we describe a visual saliency-driven retrieval system employing both local and global image saliency. Several visual attention models have been compared based on their ability to emphasise semantically meaningful areas of an image. The use of second-order moments of a region's colour distribution has been shown to improve performance considerably on occasions where the semantic gap would otherwise have a negative effect. The contrast feature was shown to provide a small boost in performance, indicating a potential for discriminative power in some types of images. The use of salient edges was shown to improve results where there

Fig. 20 Dissimilarity matrix applied on the Corel database, where *darker texture* denotes higher similarity

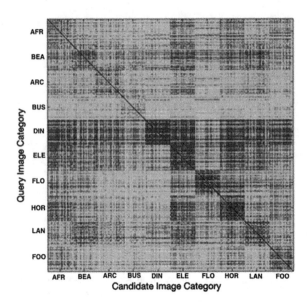

is little spatial variation of the salient object within images. A new salient region selection method, that uses the cumulative distribution of the saliency values in the database to select an appropriate threshold, was discussed in this chapter. An ideal CBIR solution would incorporate a variety of search mechanisms and would select the best choice dynamically, thus maximising its performance. The use of visual attention models would be one of the mechanisms that a CBIR solution should employ because it is indispensable in highly localized scenarios such as those found in the SIVAL database, a global ranking method would fail in SIVAL, regardless of the choices of features and distance metrics. This implies that systems must be able to distinguish between images of distinctive objects or distinctive scenes, leading to the thought of using the visual attention when searching for image content. Little work has been done before on such semantics-sensitive approaches to the retrieval task and it would be of great benefit to future CBIR systems. In their current state, computational models of visual attention are still basic because they operate on the notion of contrasting features, so they cannot accurately identify salient objects in complex images that are commonplace. Therefore, saliency models are the limiting factor for the concept of retrieval by visually salient objects and image features. In the future more reliable models of the human intent, such as those involving human memorisation processes, should be considered for CBIR systems in order to provide better retrieval results.

References

1. Achanta, R., Hemami, S., Estrada, F., Susstrunk, S.: Frequency-tuned salient region detection. In: Proceedings of IEEE International Conference on Computer Vision and Pattern Recognition, pp. 1597–1604 (2009)
2. Ashley, J.J., Barber, R., Flickner, M., Hafner, J.L., Lee, D., Niblack, C.W., Petkovic, D.: Automatic and semiautomatic methods for image annotation and retrieval in query by image content (QBIC). In: Proceedings of SPIE 2420, Storage and Retrieval for Image and Video Databases III, San Jose, CA, pp. 24–35 (1995)
3. Bors, A.G., Nasios, N.: Kernel bandwidth estimation for nonparametric modelling. IEEE Trans. Syst. Man Cybern. B Cybern. **39**(6), 1543–1555 (2009)
4. Bi J., Chen, Y., Wang, J.: A sparse support vector machine approach to region-based image categorization. In: Proceedings of IEEE International Conference on Computer Vision and Pattern Recognition, vol. 19, pp. 1121–1128 (2005)
5. Carson, C., Belongie, S., Greenspan, H., Malik, J.: Blobworld: image segmentation using expectation-maximization and its application to image querying. IEEE Trans. Pattern Anal. Mach. Intell. **24**(8), 1026–1038 (2002)
6. Chang, T., Kuo, C.-C.J.: Texture analysis and classification with tree-structured wavelet transform. IEEE Trans. Image Process. **2**(4), 429–441 (1993)
7. Chang, R., Liao, C.C.C.: Region-based image retrieval using edgeflow segmentation and region adjacency graph. In: Proceedings of International Conference on Multimedia and Expo, pp. 1883–1886 (2004)
8. Chen, Y., Wang, J.Z.: Image categorization by learning and reasoning with images. J. Mach. Learn. Res. **5**, 913–939 (2004)
9. Cheng, Y.: Mean shift, mode seeking, and clustering. IEEE Trans. Pattern Anal. Mach. Intell. **17**(8), 790–799 (1995)
10. Comaniciu, D., Meer, P.: Mean shift: a robust approach toward feature space analysis. IEEE Trans. Pattern Anal. Mach. Intell. **24**(5), 603–619 (2002)
11. Datta, R., Joshi, D., Li, J., Wan, J.Z.: Image retrieval: Ideas, influences, and trends of the new age. ACM Comput. Surv. **40**(2), 5:1–5:60 (2008)
12. Derrington, A.M., Krauskopf, J., Lennie, P.: Chromatic mechanisms in lateral geniculate. Nucleus Macaque J. Physiol. **357**, 241–265 (1984)
13. Faloutsos, C., Barber, R., Flickner, M., Hafner, J., Niblack, W., Petkovic, D., Equitz, W.: Efficient and effective querying by image content. J. Intell. Inf. Syst. **3**, 231–262 (1994)
14. Feng, S., Xu, D., Yang, X.: Attention-driven salient edge(s) and region(s) extraction with application to CBIR. Signal Process. **90**(1), 1–15 (2010)
15. Frintrop, S., Klodt, M., Rome, E.: International Conference on Computer Vision Systems (2007)
16. Frintrop, S., Rome, E., Christensen, H.: Computational visual attention systems and their cognitive foundations. A survey. ACM Trans. Appl. Percept. **7**(1), 6.1–6.46 (2010)
17. Gao, D., Han, S., Vasconcelos, N.: Discriminant saliency, the detection of suspicious coincidences, and applications to visual recognition. IEEE Trans. Pattern Anal. Mach. Intell. **31**(6), 989–1005 (2009)
18. Harel, J., Koch, C., Perona, P.: Graph-based visual saliency. In: Proceedings of Advances in Neural Information Processing Systems (NIPS), vol. 19, pp. 545–552 (2007)
19. Hou, X., Zhang, L.: Saliency detection: a spectral residual approach. In: Proceedings of IEEE International Conference on Computer Vision and Pattern Recognition, pp. 1–8 (2007)
20. Islam, M.M., Zhang, D., Lu, G.: Comparison of retrieval effectiveness of different region based image representations. In: International Conference on Information, Communications and Signal Processing, pp. 1–6 (2007)

21. Itti, L., Ullman, S.: Shifts in selective visual attention, Towards the underlying neural circuitry. Hum. Neurobiol. **4**(4), 219–227 (1985)
22. Itti, L., Koch, C., Niebur, E.: A model of saliency-based visual attention for rapid scene analysis. IEEE Trans. Pattern Anal. Mach. Intell. **20**(11), 1254–1259 (1998)
23. Jing, F., Li, M., Zhang, H.-J., Zhang, B.: An efficient and effective region-based image retrieval framework. IEEE Trans. Image Process. **13**(5), 699–709 (2004)
24. Kadir, T., Brady, M.: Saliency, scale and image description. Int. J. Comput. Vis. **45**(2), 83–105 (2001)
25. Kelly, P.M., Cannon, M., Hush, D.R.: Query by image example: the CANDID approach. In: Proceedings of SPIE 2420, San Jose, CA, pp. 238–248 (1995)
26. Mallat, S.G.: A Wavelet Tour of Signal Processing: The Sparse Way. Academic, New York (2009)
27. Ogle, V.E., Stonebraker, M.: Chabot: retrieval from a relational database of images. IEEE Comput. **28**(9), 40–48 (1995)
28. Otsu, N.: A threshold selection method from gray-level histograms. IEEE Trans. Syst. Man Cybern. **9**(1), 62–66 (1979)
29. Papushoy, A., Bors, A.G.: Image retrieval based on query by saliency content. Digital Signal Process. **36**(1), 156–173 (2015)
30. Papushoy, A., Bors, A.G.: Visual attention for content based image retrieval. In: Proceedings of IEEE International Conference on Image Processing (ICIP), Quebec City, pp. 971–975 (2015)
31. Pele, O., Taskar, B.: The tangent earth mover's distance. In: Proceedings of Geometric Science of Information. Lecture Notes on Computer Science, vol. 8085, pp. 397–404 (2013)
32. Pentland, A., Picard, R.W., Sclaroff, S.: Photobook: content-based manipulation of image databases. Int. J. Comput. Vis. **18**(3), 233–254 (1995)
33. Rahmani, R., Goldman, S.A., Zhang, H., Cholleti, S.R., Fritts, J.E.: Localized content-based image retrieval. IEEE Trans. Pattern Anal. Mach. Intell. **30**(11), 1902–1912 (2008)
34. Rubner, Y., Tomasi, C., Guibas, L.J.: The earth mover distance as a metric for image retrieval. Int. J. Comput. Vis. **402**, 99–121 (2000)
35. Rui, Y., Huang, T., Ortega, M., Mehrotra, S.: Relevance feedback: a power tool in interactive content-based image retrieval. IEEE Trans. Circuits Syst. Video Technol. **8**(5), 644–655 (1998)
36. Sharma, G., Wu, W., Dalal, E.N.: The CIEDE2000 color-difference formula: implementation notes, supplementary test data, and mathematical observations. Color Res. Appl. **30**(1), 1–24 (2005)
37. Smith, J.R., Chang, S.-F.: VisualSEEk: a fully automated content-based image query system. In: Proceedings of the ACM International Conference on Multimedia, Boston, pp. 87–98 (1996)
38. Smeulders, A., Worring, M., Santini, S., Gupta, A., Jain, R.: Content-based image retrieval at the end of the early years. IEEE Trans. Pattern Anal. Mach. Intell. **22**(12), 1349–1380 (2000)
39. Stentiford, F.W.M.: A visual attention estimator applied to image subject enhancement and colour and grey level compression. In: 17th International Conference on Pattern Recognition, vol. 3, Cambridge, pp. 638–641 (2004)
40. Tas, A.C., Luck, S.J., Hollingworth, A.: The relationship between visual attention and visual working memory encoding: a dissociation between covert and overt orienting. J. Exp. Psychol. Hum. Percept. Perform. **42**, 1121–1138 (2016)
41. Vondrick, C., Khosla, A., Pirsiavash, H., Malisiewicz, T., Torralba, A.: Visualizing object detection features. Int. J. Comput. Vis. **119**(2), 145–158 (2016)
42. Wan, J., Wang, D., Hoi, S., Wu, P., Zhu, J., Li, J.: Deep learning for content-based image retrieval: a comprehensive study. In: Proceedings of ACM International Conference on Multimedia, pp. 157–266 (2014)
43. Wang, J.Z., Wiederhold, G., Firschein, O., Sha, X.W.: Content-based image indexing and searching using Daubechies' wavelets. Int. J. Digit. Libr. **1**(4), 311–328 (1998)

44. Wang, J., Li, J., Wiederhold, G.: Simplicity: semantics-sensitive integrated matching for picture libraries. IEEE Trans. Pattern Anal. Mach. Intell. **23**(9), 947–963 (2001)
45. Wang, H., Cai,Y., Zhang, Y., Pan, H., Lv, W., Han, H.: Deep learning for image retrieval: what works and what doesn't. In: Proceedings of IEEE International Conference on Data Mining Workshop, pp. 1576–1583 (2015)
46. Wolfe, J.M.: Visual search. In: Pashler, H. (ed.) Attention. Psychology Press, Hove, East Sussex (1998)
47. Zhang, L., Tong, M.H., Marks, T.K., Shan, H., Cottrell, G.W.: SUN, A Bayesian framework for saliency using natural statistics. J. Vis. **8**(7), 32.1–32.20 (2008)

Visual Saliency for the Visualization of Digital Paintings

Pol Kennel, Frédéric Comby, and William Puech

Abstract Over the last 15 years, several applications have been developed for digital cultural heritage in the image processing and particularly in the area of digital painting. In order to help preserve cultural heritage, this chapter proposes several applications for digital paintings such as restoration, authentication, style analysis and visualization. For the visualization of digital paintings we present specific methods to visualize digital paintings based on visual saliency and in particular we propose an automatic digital painting visualization method based on visual saliency. The proposed system consists of extracting regions of interest (ROI) from a digital painting to characterize them. These close-ups are then animated on the basis of the paintings characteristics and the artist's or designer's aim. In order to obtain interesting results from short video clips, we developed a visual saliency map-based method. The experimental results show the efficiency of our approach and an evaluation based on a Mean Opinion Score validates our proposed method.

1 Introduction

The two main objectives for cultural heritage services are to preserve paintings that represent our past and to play an active role in spreading cultural knowledge [27]. For example, Giakoumis et al. presented an efficient method to detect and remove cracks in digital paintings [8]. Another interesting activity is to analyze painting styles and movements [28, 33]. This can be employed in artist identification in order to detect forgery or simply to characterize an artist's period or to study its evolution in style or technique. Specific work has also been developed to protect the content for the secure transmission of high resolution digital paintings [27]. A survey of digital painting for cultural heritage is presented in a book by Stanco et al. [7].

P. Kennel
IMFT, INPT/Univ. Toulouse, Toulouse, France
e-mail: pol.kennel@imft.fr

F. Comby • W. Puech (✉)
LIRMM, CNRS/Univ. Montpellier, Montpellier, France
e-mail: frederic.comby@lirmm.fr; william.puech@lirmm.fr

© Springer International Publishing AG 2017
J. Benois-Pineau, P. Le Callet (eds.), *Visual Content Indexing and Retrieval with Psycho-Visual Models*, Multimedia Systems and Applications,
DOI 10.1007/978-3-319-57687-9_9

The authors present several techniques, algorithms and solutions for digital imaging and computer graphics-driven cultural heritage preservation, in particular several new visualization tools are proposed [7].

In this chapter, we first present several applications for digital paintings such restoration, authentication and style analysis, secondly we present specific methods to visualize digital paintings based on visual saliency and in particular we propose an automatic digital painting visualization method based on visual saliency. The main objective of this method is to generate an animation of a digital painting, which would be close to what could be manually achieved by an artist. The three main steps are the detection of regions of interest (ROI), the ROI characterization and the order of ROI by building a path throughout the digital painting. Finally, we demonstrate how videos can be generated by following the paths with custom trajectories. In the first step, we propose to use the saliency map concept for ROI detection [13–15] a slightly modified applied on a digital painting in order to provide a map of the most valuable sites and animate them in a visualization process.

The saliency map concept was introduced by Ullman and Koch in 1985 [19]. These maps are supposed to represent salient regions in an image, i.e. regions that would capture human attention. With this knowledge, the main task is to determine human brain stimulation that would naturally detect a ROI from a scene in order to model it. Two factors are distinguished in [23] which are bottom-up and top-down factors. The first factor represents our natural instinctive sensorial attention based on factors such as color, contrast, size of objects and luminosity. For example, this mechanism allows us to detect a bright burning fire in a scene. The second factor represents a more intelligent process based on the observer's experience. We use this mechanism when we are seeking certain kinds of objects. Many techniques have been developed since the 1980s to generate such saliency maps, each of them has tried to combine speed and robustness efficiently. Three method groups can be singled out [36]: local methods [13, 15] which only deal with certain areas, global methods [1, 12, 37] which use the whole image to characterize ROI, and frequential methods [10, 26] which use the local characteristics of the spatial frequency phase.

Although saliency methods are already widely used in many domains (e.g. robotics, marketing etc.), digital paintings have not been widely studied in such a way. This could be explained by the fact that the understanding on how the brain processes work and how humans see paintings is an open problem. Gaze tracker technology has been used for this issue in [30], and shows that despite salient regions of paintings playing an important role, there is still a large variability depending on the subjects' own interests, artistic appreciation and knowledge. Conversely, Subtle Gaze Direction (SGD) process is employed in [22] to manipulate volunteers gaze on paintings. The authors succeed in improving the legibility of paintings. Especially the reading order and fixating time over panels was improved by using SGD. In this study, saliency methods are envisaged to improve the SGD, but are not currently implemented. Only a few recent studies have estimated saliency in digital paintings. In [4], the authors provide a simple saliency analysis method which helped them categorize paintings by art movement. In [18], the authors provide several valuable advancements for the study of paintings. First, they provide a large database of paintings with a wide diversity of artists and styles. State-of-the-art methods are used to categorize paintings. Moreover, the authors collected gaze fixation data for a consistent subset of paintings and applied state of the art saliency methods on the same paintings. Using Itti's framework [15], the performance is one of the top rated methods for correlating salient maps and fixation maps.

The rest of this chapter is organized as follows: In Sect. 2, we present previous methods applied on digital paintings for restoration, authentication and style analysis. In Sect. 3 we present specific methods to visualize digital paintings based on visual saliency. Finally, in Sect. 4 we conclude our experiments and discuss possibilities for future work.

2 Digital Imaging for Cultural Heritage Preservation: Restoration, Authentication and Analysis

Even if image processing has been widely used in areas such as medical imaging, robotics and security, fewer applications have been developed concerning digital paintings. It is becoming increasingly important for experts or art historians to analyse painting style or to authenticate paintings. However, some studies prove that image processing algorithms can perform as well as human experts on applications dedicated to digital paintings [7]. Among them, the most common are: virtual restoration (Sect. 2.1), content authentication (Sect. 2.2) and the analysis of painting evolution in time and style (Sect. 2.3).

2.1 Restoration of Old Paintings

One of the most common processes consists in virtual painting restoration. For example in [8] the authors propose a technique to remove cracks on digitalized paintings. The first step detects cracks. In this process, cracks are mainly considered as dark areas with an elongated shape, so their detection are only performed on the luminance component of the image. It consists in filtering the image with the difference between the image's gray level morphological closing and the image itself. The authors suggest that a similar process can be used to detect bright cracks (like scratches on a photo) while replacing the morphological closing by an opening and computing the difference between the image and its opening. This process gives a gray level image with higher values for pixels that are most likely to belong to a crack. Then the image has a threshold filter applied to it in order to extract cracks from the rest of the image. Many strategies are considered from the simplest one: a global threshold whose value is computed thanks to the filtered image histogram to a more complex one: a spatially varying threshold. The author observes that some brush strokes may be misclassified as cracks, so they provided two techniques to distinguish them. The first one is semi-automatic and relies on a region growing algorithm where the seeds are chosen manually on pixels belonging to the class of cracks. In this way, pixels corresponding to a brush stroke, are not 8-connected to crack pixels, are removed from the resulting image. The second approach is based on an analysis of the Hue and Saturation components of cracks and brush strokes. A classification using a median radial basis function neural network is trained to separate cracks from brush strokes. As explained by the authors, these two approaches can be combined to give better results. Once cracks have been identified they need to be filled. The authors propose two methods, one using order statistic filters based on median, the other one based on controlled anisotropic diffusion. An illustration is presented in Fig. 1. This method gives good results even if some

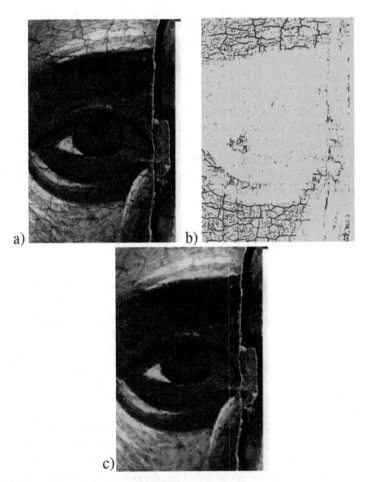

Fig. 1 (**a**) Zoom on the original painting containing cracks, (**b**) thresholded top hat transform containing mainly cracks, (**c**) the virtually restored painting with cracks filled with a median filter [8]

cracks remains (those not filtered by morphological tools, or when dark cracks occur in dark areas). It also seems, in their examples, that some edges are degraded, maybe because they are misinterpreted as cracks.

Other inpainting algorithms have been used to virtually restore paintings, for example Chinese paintings in [21, 39] or by using a more general restoration tool presented in [5]. An evaluation of the quality of such restorations has been proposed in [24] where 14 metrics were compared in order to evaluate 8 inpainting algorithms. The results showed first that exemplar-based inpainting algorithms worked better than partial differential equation ones, as the later tends to add blur when filling large areas; second that there is no ideal metric as they are really image-dependent.

2.2 Painting Identification and Authentication

Detecting cracks may also have another use, for example in painting identification and control of the evolution of ancient paintings. For example in [6] a part of the study was about painting authentication. Indeed, the painting *Mona Lisa* was stolen in 1911 and when the painting was returned to the Louvre Museum, they wanted to know if the painting was the original or a copy. The main theory was that the crack pattern is impossible to copy. So, based on three high resolution pictures taken at different periods (one before the theft in 1880, and two after in 1937 and 2005) the crack patterns were extracted in order to compare them and authenticate or not the painting. The authors proposed a method whereby they removed the content leaving on the cracks. To do so, images were first filtered by an isotropic low pass filter that removed almost all jpeg compression artifacts and the grainy aspect of the images. Then, in order to remove the craquelures two treatments were performed: one to remove dark cracks based on a gray level morphological closing and one to remove bright cracks based on an opening. These two processes provide a blurry image without cracks. An histogram specification was then used to match the gray level distributions of the original image and the filtered one. Then, subtracting the filtered image from the original one provided an image mainly composed of cracks. After a simple edge extraction algorithm provides a binary image of cracks (see Fig. 2). The three images of crack patterns were then geometrically rectified using an homography to be aligned and compared. The minor differences between the crack patterns allowed to confirm that the painting *Mona Lisa* was the original one. It also provided information about the best storage conditions of the painting as the cracks remained stable between 1937 and 2005.

2.3 Style Analysis

Another application using image processing algorithms is the analysis of painting styles. In [2] the work of several teams are presented on a large collection of 101 van Gogh's paintings. It includes various wavelet analysis, Hidden Markov Models,

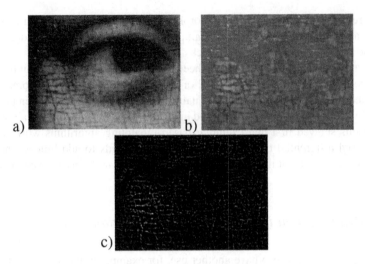

Fig. 2 (**a**) Zoom on the eye of Mona Lisa, (**b**) the filtered version containing cracks, (**c**) its edges [6]

feature extraction and classifiers to characterize the brushwork and authenticate van Gogh's paintings. In fact, many articles are focused on brushstroke analysis as they are often characteristic of a painter. In [29] the authors propose a two step procedure including a contour enhancement and a quantification of the brushstroke shape on small parts of a painting. This last step consists in filling closed curves, then skeletonizing and fitting a Nth order polynomial to the curve. A statistical analysis and a learning procedure on the polynomial coefficients granted a characterization of the painting style. In Fig. 3, the original painting and the extracted brushstrokes are presented. In [32], a large data set containing paintings from 91 artists from different styles is built to test artist and style categorization. They also tested saliency detection algorithms and compared them to human fixations. The two categorization process involve a variety of local and global visual features like color names, SIFT descriptor, three color SIFT descriptors and local binary pattern, etc. Then, a visual vocabulary is constructed using a bag-of-words framework and a classification is performed. The best accuracy results obtained in this paper with a combination of features is about 53% for artist identification and 62% for style identification. Results concerning saliency algorithms are also very promising as they give similar results to human fixations on paintings. This tends to prove that saliency is well suited for painting analysis. Other approaches of style analysis are presented in [3, 20]. In [20], the profile of an artist is characterized by a mixture of stochastic models (2D multi-resolution Hidden Markov Model). These models provide a reliable signature of artists even when there is no color in the painting, for example in Chinese ink paintings. A classification is then performed to compare or identify artists. Similarly, in [3], dual-tree complex wavelet transformation, Hidden Markov Tree modelling and Random Forest classifiers are used to perform a stylistic

Fig. 3 (**a**) The *Wheatfield with Crows* painting of Vincent van Gogh, (**b**) the brushstrokes extracted with [29] algorithm

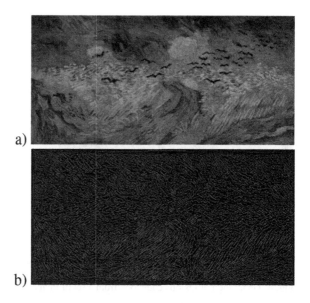

a)

b)

analysis of Vincent van Gogh's paintings. The authors applied these processes to date the paintings, but also to extract specific features that are characteristic of van Gogh's style. Another approach, presented in [33], uses small patches of texture (called textons) to characterize the brushstroke configuration. Their process learns a codebook of textons from a large number of paintings (Fig. 4), then a histogram is built representing the appearance frequency of each texton. The analysis of texton's distribution allows to establish van Gogh's paintings from those of other contemporary artists. The authors claimed that texton-based approach is more suitable for texture analysis than using classical image processing filters, since the latter introduces a smoothing that may remove some important features. Brushstrokes are not the only feature that help to identify an artist or an artistic movement. For example in [28], the authors focus their work on the analysis of pearls in paintings. The way pearls are represented explains how the nature is perceived by the painter and also gives informations on contemporary knowledge on optical theory. To analyse pearls, they used a spatiogram (an extension of histograms where spatial informations are kept). Each bin of the histogram is associated with three values which are the bin count, its spatial mean and spatial covariance. Four new metrics are also defined to characterize pearls thanks to their spatiograms, for example the mean distance between the spatiogram bin's centers. Experiments showed that these four metrics allowed to segregate artists only by observing their technique to paint pearls.

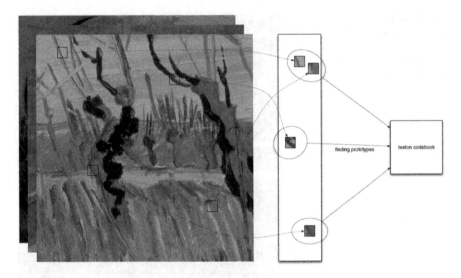

Fig. 4 Generation of textons codebook from a set of images [33]

3 Digital Painting Visualization Based on Visual Saliency

3.1 Human Perception of Digital Paintings

Painting analysis also explores the way paintings are perceived by humans. For example in [31, 34], a saliency map is used to model or interpret the way the human visual system (HVS) perceives visual art. In [31] the Itti and Koch's [15] saliency model was compared to the gaze behavior of human observers. In [34], the algorithm consists in a segmentation using a fuzzy C-Means of the painting, then features such as compacity, local contrast, edges and uniqueness are used to define each part of the segmented image. These criterions are combined into a saliency map using a weighted sum. A subjective testing strategy was tested with human observers and it proved that this saliency map is relevant to characterize zones of interest of paintings (see Fig. 5). Moreover, this is robust, regardless of the art movement they belong to.

In [38] a new metric called LuCo (for Luminance Contrast) is presented to quantify the artists intention to manipulate lightning contrast to draw visual attention to specific regions. It can be considered as a visual saliency measure dedicated to luminance features. A histogram containing Bayesian surprise values is computed for a set of patches across the painting. Then the LuCo score is computed as a skewness measure on the histogram (high values of LuCo indicating lightning effects).

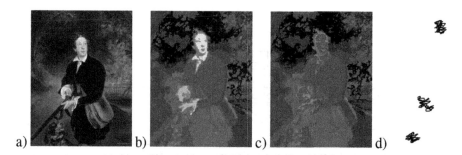

Fig. 5 (**a**) *Aleksey Konstantinovich Tolstoy* painting by Alexander Briullov, (**b**) resulting saliency map using algorithm presented in [34], (**c**) thresholded saliency map and (**d**) User defined saliency map for comparison

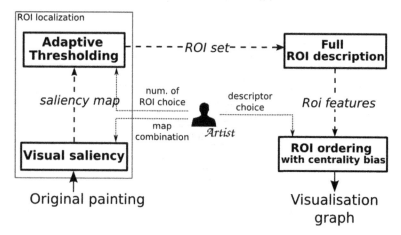

Fig. 6 Overview of the proposed automatic visualization method for digital paintings. The artist performs by: designing the final saliency map with custom weight, setting the number of regions to be in the visualization, selecting features to be interpreted in order

3.2 Visual Saliency-Based Visualization Method

In this section, the proposed method consists of three main steps which are presented in Fig. 6. First, a saliency map is created from an image so that ROI can be identified by a custom thresholding of map values. Next, the ROI are characterized by a set of features. Finally, the third step orders ROI visualization according to the artist's needs [17].

3.2.1 Adaptive ROI Localization Based on the Visual Saliency

The saliency map used in our method is a linear combination of several feature maps derived from color, intensity and orientation information according to the approach

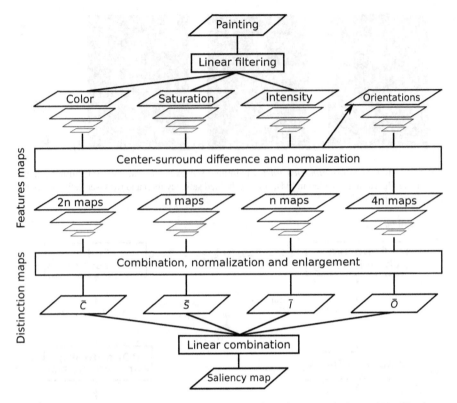

Fig. 7 Scheme of the proposed saliency system. $n = 2(L-4)$ where L is the number of levels on the multi-resolution pyramid

proposed by Itti [13]. As illustrated in Fig. 7, we integrated a new saliency map based on saturation, an important supplementary notion for paintings additionally to other maps provided by the Itti's framework. We can also observe in Fig. 7 that orientation is based on the maps of intensity. Linear filtering is used on a multi-resolution pyramid of the image in order to extract feature-based saliency maps by a center-surround algorithm [9, 14]. We used L dyadic pyramid levels, where L is defined as the number of possible sub-sampling given the original painting size. The local center-surround mechanism used to rate the conspicuity of a region is based on the subtractions of several layers of the pyramid. Subtractions are made between layers at level s and layers at level $s+\delta$ where $s \in [1, (L-4)]$ and $\delta \in \{3, 4\}$. Hence, $n = 2(L-5)$ subtraction results are provided.

For the results we have n maps for the intensity features $\overline{\mathscr{I}}$, n maps for the saturation features $\overline{\mathscr{S}}$, and $2n$ maps for the color features $\overline{\mathscr{C}}$ (half are for *blue-yellow* contrast and half for *red-green* contrast). The orientation features $\overline{\mathscr{O}}$ are calculated by filtering intensity maps resulting from the center-surround algorithm with Gabor filters oriented in four directions ($0°, 45°, 90°, 135°$) for $4n$ supplementary maps and a total of $T = 8n$ feature maps. For example, a 1024×1024 pixel painting will produce a 9-level pyramid and 64 maps ($n = 8$).

Each of the T maps is normalized through a feature combination strategy which relies on simulating local competition between neighboring salient locations. This process proved its accuracy over other strategies evaluated in [14]. Saliency maps $\overline{\mathscr{C}}, \overline{\mathscr{I}}, \overline{\mathscr{S}}$ and $\overline{\mathscr{O}}$, illustrated in Fig. 7, are obtained by the addition of sub-maps and are scaled to the size of the original image with bi-cubic interpolation. Finally, the four maps are used to produce a final saliency map $\mathscr{S}$. Weighting coefficients ω_i used for the feature combination are set up by artists, so that artwork can be interpreted according to the individual's sensitivity. Therefore, we define $\mathscr{S} = [\omega_1, \omega_2, \omega_3, \omega_4][\overline{\mathscr{C}}, \overline{\mathscr{I}}, \overline{\mathscr{S}}, \overline{\mathscr{O}}]^T$.

Once the saliency map $\mathscr{S}$ is produced, salient regions which are chosen to guide visualization paths and close-ups on digital paintings can be isolated. These regions could be directly segmented by thresholding the $\mathscr{S}$ map values, but the results obtained are not adapted to our objective as illustrated in Fig. 8a. Even if an optimal threshold value can be defined with constraints (e.g. by minimizing a cost function), thresholding does not allow to strictly control the number of regions, areas or the properties that we wanted in our framework. Therefore, we defined an adaptive thresholding approach which is guided by N the number of ROI expected as well as $\mathscr{A}_{min}$ and $\mathscr{A}_{max}$ the minimum and maximum areas that are authorized, respectively. Figure 8b shows that 3 regions can be found on the 1-dimension profile plotted by using multiple threshold, the second pic is omitted since it does not obey to area constraints contrary to Fig. 8a.

3.2.2 ROI Description

Isolated ROI are then labeled and characterized by a vector, denoted by **F**, composed of 15 features. This description prepares the final ordering step so that artists will choose and decide which combinations of features allow a proper ROI visualization sequence. This essential step provides the artist with a set of relevant characteristics which can be understood and used as an accurate guide. We have kept the four following classes of descriptors:

- Shape-based descriptors: area, perimeter, circularity, elongation and 16:9 compacity (expressing the space occupied by the ROI in a 16:9 bounding window),
- Position-based descriptors: center coordinates, orientation, absolute and relative distance from the center of gravity of the image and it's cardinal position,
- Color-based descriptors: mean hue, mean saturation and mean value,
- Texture-based descriptors: selected Haralick features such as energy, contrast, homogeneity and correlation [11].

Shape-based and position-based features usually involve simple morphological tools on binary images (thresholded image from $\mathscr{S}$) such as the principal component analysis.

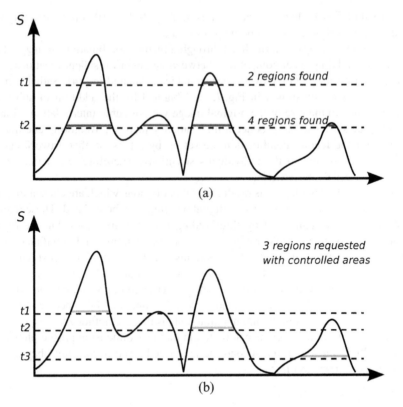

Fig. 8 The proposed adaptive thresholding method allows to control the number of regions to segment as well as the regions area properties. Examples of segmentation on an 1-dimensional profile of a saliency map with: (**a**) a classic thresholding method (2 threshold values), (**b**) the proposed adaptive thresholding method

One part of these descriptors is quantitative (those forming vector **F**) while others are only qualitative and only used to assist artists. Figure 9 illustrates the full description of a ROI in an image. Shape-based and position-based descriptors are the most appropriate for a wide audience, whereas texture-based descriptors have to be explicitly described for the application.

3.2.3 ROI Ordering

In order to create an animation from the digital painting, the described ROI have to be placed in an order that an experienced artist would use. Therefore, we propose that the artist balances each characteristic with weights $\omega_i \in \{\omega_i \in \mathbb{Z}, -\gamma \leq \omega_i \leq \gamma\}$. Descriptors are normalized and combined according to their weights to obtain a final score per ROI stored in the vector of scores **S**.

Feature	Value
Center:	(-26,-271)
Area:	33424 pixels
Perimeter:	1220 pixels
Orientation:	-3°
Relative orientation to center:	-34°
Circularity:	0.28
Elongation:	9.1
Energy:	0.022
Contrast:	96.4
Entropy:	8.3
Homogeneity:	0.119
Correlation:	0.98
Compacity:	0.34
Distance to center:	186 pixels
Relative distance to center:	17%
Hue:	35
Luminosity:	162
Saturation:	167

Fig. 9 Description of a sample region of interest (*left*) with various shape-based, position-based, color-based and textured-based features (*right*)

At this step, we choose to weight characteristics by a second coefficient ψ to take care of the eccentricity bias [35]. Indeed, the first ROI visualized should be influenced by it's proximity to the image center, while the following ROI should be influenced by the proximity of the previous ROI to avoid unpleasant backward and forward movements.

Therefore, the score S_n of each of the N regions is defined by:

$$S_n = \sum_i \psi_n \omega_i F_{ni}, \qquad (1)$$

where ψ_n is given by a gaussian weighting function $g(center, roi_n)$ which is related to a reference center and the center of a given region:

$$\psi = g(center, roi) = A \exp^{-\left(\frac{(center_x - roi_x)^2}{2\sigma_x^2} + \frac{(center_y - roi_y)^2}{2\sigma_y^2}\right)}, \qquad (2)$$

where

$$A = 1, \ \sigma_x = \sigma_y = 1. \qquad (3)$$

Transition ordering is given simply by sorting ROI scores, vector **S**, in decreasing order. First ROI in **S** is held and the rest of the ROI score's is updated with the new ψ weight and sorted again so that the second ROI can be established.

The transition graph is created by assigning ranks to ROI according to their position in the final vector. Graph links represent the transition between salient regions and the associated transition time expected. Currently, those times are defined by artists, but could also be computed from the features characterizing ROI and the relative distance between successive ROI (e.g. short time for a short distance, longer time for larger areas). The graph representation displays the benefits of allowing further constrained path computations (e.g. shortest path) and allows us to take part of the regions proximity into account.

3.2.4 Experimental Results

First, we present how our automatic visualization framework performs on several digital paintings. Then, we introduce a Mean Opinion Score study conducted using 18 volunteers on 36 randomly-based and 36 saliency-based generated videos from 6 digital paintings.

Results Analysis

The visual saliency system used in our method provides an appropriate identification of salient regions on digital paintings. The proposed method has been applied on several digital paintings. Figure 10 presents the feature-based saliency maps $\mathscr{C}$ Fig. 10b, $\mathscr{I}$ Fig. 10c, $\mathscr{S}$ Fig. 10d, and $\overline{\mathscr{O}}$ Fig. 10e computed from the painting

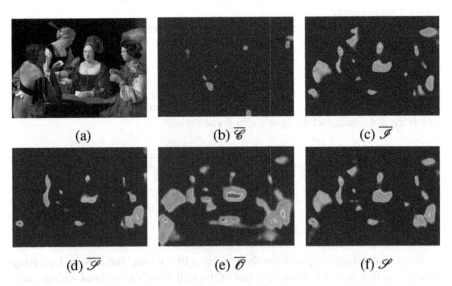

(a) (b) $\mathscr{C}$ (c) $\mathscr{I}$

(d) $\overline{\mathscr{S}}$ (e) $\overline{\mathscr{O}}$ (f) $\mathscr{S}$

Fig. 10 Examples of a saliency map obtained from (**a**) The original digital painting *The Cheat* of Georges de La Tour, (**b**) Color map $\mathscr{C}$, (**c**) Intensity map $\overline{\mathscr{I}}$, (**d**) Saturation map $\overline{\mathscr{S}}$, (**e**) Orientation map $\overline{\mathscr{O}}$, (**f**) Features combined in a final saliency map $\mathscr{S}$ with artist-set weightings of 0.1, 0.9, 0.4 and 0.2 (respectively for $\mathscr{C}, \overline{\mathscr{I}}, \overline{\mathscr{S}}$ and $\overline{\mathscr{O}}$)

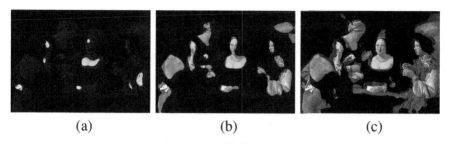

(a)   (b)   (c)

Fig. 11 Results of the ROI segmentation on the saliency map presented in Fig. 10f with the classic thresholding method. Different choices of threshold values are shown, respectively (**a**) 0.72, (**b**) 0.40 and (**c**) 0.15

from G. de La Tour *The Cheat*. The maps $\overline{\mathscr{I}}$ Fig. 10b, and $\overline{\mathscr{O}}$ Fig. 10e highlight particularly well the players face, gaze and cards, whereas the $\overline{\mathscr{C}}$ and $\mathscr{S}$ maps provide supplementary salient details for the color and texture of the clothes. A possible final saliency map $\mathscr{S}$ illustrated in Fig. 10f was built from an artist's weightings using the previous maps $(\overline{\mathscr{C}}, \overline{\mathscr{I}}, \mathscr{S}, \overline{\mathscr{O}})$. The features are combined in a final saliency map $\mathscr{S}$ with artist-set weightings of 0.1, 0.9, 0.4 and 0.2 (respectively for $\overline{\mathscr{C}}, \overline{\mathscr{I}}, \overline{\mathscr{S}}$ and $\overline{\mathscr{O}}$). This final map shows how the artists intentions can be kept to our system. Others results of saliency maps are provided in Fig. 14b on four digital paintings with custom weights on saliency features.

Then, from Fig. 10f, salient regions were isolated to produce the ROI sets presented in Figs. 11 and 12. Figure 12 illustrates the advantages raised by our proposed adaptive thresholding method, over a classical thresholding approach illustrated in Fig. 11. Controlling the number of regions segmented as well as their dimensions, is a difficult task, but by simply changing (manually or automatically) a single threshold value on the saliency map $\mathscr{S}$ as shown in Fig. 11a–c where the number of regions increased dramatically by decreasing the threshold value. The adaptive thresholding proposed provides regions with homogeneous sizes (we requested between 0.1 and 2% of the total image area) and with a controlled headcount (3, 5, 7, 9 regions where requested in Fig. 12a–d) ; these constraints are essential for the proposed framework. Note that increasing the number of requested regions will produce a set of regions which includes previous regions found by the process with a smaller requested number. Only the order of the detected regions will produce changes in the shape of regions due to the erasure step of the proposed procedure (see Sect. 3.2.1).

Such ROI were ordered according to scores defined by the artist's weighting on the ROI descriptors with weights $\omega_i \in \{\omega_i \in \mathbb{Z}, -5 \leq \omega_i \leq 5\}$. Figure 13a presents a possible corresponding transition graph from regions segmented in Fig. 12d. This path is defined by focusing only on the area, luminosity and entropy descriptors in the scoring step ($\omega = 2, 1, 4$ respectively). Another example of a path presented in Fig. 13b is defined by opting for the compacity ($\omega = 5$), perimeter ($\omega = 2$)

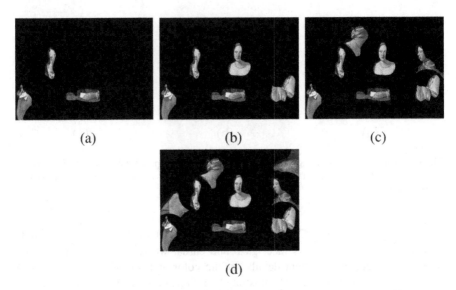

Fig. 12 Results of the ROI segmentation on the saliency map presented in Fig. 10f with the proposed adaptive thresholding method. Different choices of the region number requested are shown, respectively (**a**) 3, (**b**) 5, (**c**) 7 and (**d**) 9. Area constraints are set between 0.1 and 3% of the total image area

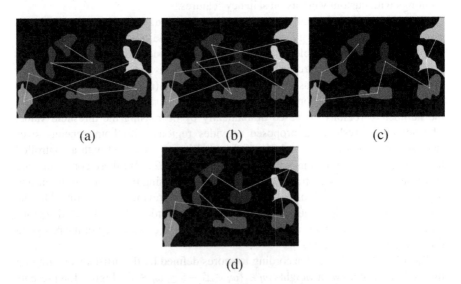

Fig. 13 Salient regions selected by thresholding the saliency map $\mathscr{S}$ obtained in Fig. 12d ordered by expert guidance to obtain two transition graphs resulting from different weightings: (**a**) area, $\omega = 2$, luminosity $\omega = 1$, entropy, $\omega = 4$ (**b**) compacity, $\omega = 5$, perimeter, $\omega = 2$, contrast, $\omega = 2$ and correlation, $\omega = -1$. The path in (**c**) used the same weightings as in the path in (**a**), as well as the path in (**d**) which used the same weightings that were used in the path (**b**), but with the consideration of the centrality/proximity bias

and contrast ($\omega = 2$) rather than the correlation ($\omega = -1$). Figure 13c, d illustrates the same paths with identical weights, but with the consideration of the centrality/proximity bias; this suggests the importance of considering this bias to obtain the most natural possible tracking, avoiding unnecessary back and forward movements.

Figure 14 illustrates an application of the proposed method on four digital paintings: *The Cheat (G. de La Tour), Massacre of the Innocents (P.P. Rubens), The Anatomy Lesson of Dr. Nicolaes Tulp (R. van Rijn), Mona Lisa (L. Da Vinci)*. The presented method suggests an appropriate interpretation of paintings according to the visual attention given by an observer, whose paths were validated by artistic experts. Note in Fig. 14c that the obtained paths present the most interesting parts of the digital paintings. Especially, the five salient regions found on the *Mona Lisa* painting by using our method (Fig. 14c) this corresponds to the main parts, that have been extensively discussed in classical art analysis (e.g. [40]): regions 1, 2 and 4 represent the *Mona Lisa's* details (heart, face/expression and hands) while regions 3 and 5 represent important background details. Salient regions found in *The Anatomy Lesson* highlight perfectly the different participants in the lesson: the master, the students and the corpse. Important parts of *The Cheat* are also revealed well, like the cheater's hidden cards.

Mean Opinion Score Evaluation

To assess the suitability of our visualization framework, we submitted a large set of generated videos to a Mean Opinion Score (MOS) evaluation. As reference, we compared MOS results between randomly generated videos and videos generated by our automatic visualization framework. Based on the six paintings (some are presented in Fig. 14), we created 72 short video clips, lasting 20 s each. From each painting, we derived six videos with a variable number of ROI (3–5) with ROI randomly located/sized and randomly ordered, as well as six automatically generated videos with a similar variable number of ROI.

Subjective quality assessment methods measure the overall perceived quality. They are carried out by humans. The most commonly used measure is the Mean Opinion Score (MOS) recommended by the International Telecommunication Union (ITU) [16]. It consists of having a group of subjects watching the processed sequences in order to rate their quality, according to a predefined quality scale. The most suitable way to assess image quality is subjective tests according to standardized protocols, which are defined in order to obtain correct, universal and reliable quality evaluations.

Eighteen neutral observers were questioned about the correct representation of the content of the digital paintings. Each volunteer watched a couple of randomly/automatically generated videos (with the same number of ROI) by painting and assigned a score $\in[1\text{–}5]$ (where 5 is the best score) to each clip (for a total of 216 views). Full size paintings were shown during 10 s before watching the clips. The size of the screen was 30 in. and the viewing distance was 2 m.

(a) Original   (b) Saliency Map   (c) Visualization Path

Fig. 14 (**a**) Digital paintings used to generate the videos of our Mean Opinion Score study (*from top to bottom: The Cheat (G. de La Tour), Massacre of the Innocents (P.P. Rubens), The Anatomy Lesson of Dr. Nicolaes Tulp (R. van Rijn) and the Mona Lisa (L. Da Vinci)*). (**b**) The corresponding saliency maps designed to obtain the segmentation. (**c**) The ordered regions forming visualization paths

To assess if the difference between both groups, random-based and saliency-based videos is significant, we chose the Wilcoxon signed rank test [25]. This test is appropriate because the samples are not independent. The results show that MOS values per painting are greater with the saliency-based method than the ones with the random-based method in most cases. As the standard deviations appear to be important, we assert the significant difference between the two groups random-based videos (MOS = 2.32 $\pm$ 1.03) and saliency-based videos (MOS = 3.59 $\pm$ 0.99) by the Wilcoxon signed rank test [25] ($V = 3820, p\text{-}value < 0.001$). This result suggests that our approach is well suited for selecting important regions to visualize digital paintings using a video method. Our framework performed particularly well on these paintings because it accurately localizes essential parts for the interpretation and comprehension of the paintings.

Note that randomly-based and saliency-based videos generated with 4 regions have the most separable MOS ($V = 566.5, p\text{-}value < 0.001$) compared to the 3 region groups ($V = 497, p\text{-}value < 0.001$) and the 5 region groups ($V = 388.5, p\text{-}value < 0.05$), see the density functions of scores obtained in Fig. 15. These results may be justified by the fact that in the 5 region groups, most of the paintings area is finally shown by the randomly-based as well as the saliency-based method so that MOS is less strongly separable between both groups. This tendency should increase with the number of regions used on the visualization path. By contrast, the groups with 3 regions are less strongly separable because of the potential proximity of the regions.

4 Conclusion

In this chapter we have shown that several methods have been developed in image processing, specifically for digital paintings. In the beginning we presented several methods that we applied on digital paintings for restoration, authentication and style analysis. We have proved that saliency is well suited for painting analysis for example.

In the second part of our experiment, we presented specific methods to visualize digital paintings based on visual saliency. In particular we developed a method which is able to automatically generate a video from a digital painting. The results of the proposed method suggests that our approach is well suited for selecting important regions to visualize digital paintings using video. Our framework performed particularly well on these paintings, because it accurately localizes essential parts for the interpretation and comprehension of the paintings.

We are convinced that it is very important to continue to develop such approaches in the future, in particular with the creation of museums on line collections based on virtual reality and augmented reality. To improve the quality of the automatic generation of video from digital painting, it is clear that it will be necessary to take into account gaze tracking.

Acknowledgements The authors would like to thank volunteers who accepted to participate in our opinion score campaign.

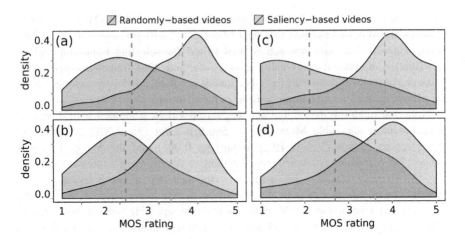

Fig. 15 Smoothed density functions of opinion scores collected over 218 videos by 18 volunteers. *Dashed-lines* indicate mean values. (**a**) Whole region number confound, (**b**) 3-regions (**c**), 4-regions and (**d**) 5-region groups

References

1. Aziz, M.Z., Mertsching, B.: Fast and robust generation of feature maps for region-based visual attention. IEEE Trans. Image Process. **17**(5), 633–644 (2008)
2. Berezhnoy, I.J., Brevdo, E., Hughes, S.M., Daubechies, I., Li, J., Postma, E., Johnson, C.R., Hendriks, E., Wang, J.Z.: Image processing for artist identification. IEEE Signal Process. Mag. **25**(4), 37–48 (2008)
3. Brevdo, E., Hughes S., Brasoveanu, A., Jafarpour, S., Polatkan, G., Daubechies, I.: Stylistic analysis of paintings using wavelets and machine learning. In: Proceedings of the 17th European Signal Processing Conference (EUSIPCO), Glasgow, Scotland (2009)
4. Condorovici, R.G., Vranceanu, R., Vertan, C.: Saliency map retrieval for artistic paintings inspired from human understanding. In: Proceedings of SPAMEC (2011)
5. Corsini, M., De Rosa, A., Cappellini, V., Barni, M., Piva, A.: Artshop: an art-oriented image processing tool for cultural heritage applications. J. Vis. Comput. Animat. **14**, 149–158 (2003)
6. Druon, S., Comby, F.: La Joconde – Essai Scientifique. Extraction des craquelures, Christian Lahanier, pp. 179–184 (2007)
7. Gallo, G., Stanco, F., Battiato, S.: Digital Imaging for Cultural Heritage Preservation: Analysis, Restoration and Reconstruction of Ancient Artworks. Taylor and Francis, Boca Raton, FL (2011)
8. Giakoumis, I., Nikolaidis, N., Pitas, I.: Digital image processing techniques for the detection and removal of cracks in digitized paintings. IEEE Trans. Image Process. **15**(1), 178–188 (2006)
9. Greenspan, H., Belongie, S., Goodman, R., Perona, P., Rakshit, S., Anderson, C.H.: Overcomplete steerable pyramid filters and rotation invariance. In: Proceedings of the IEEE Conference on Computer Vision and Pattern Recognition, pp. 222–228 (1994)
10. Guo, C., Zhang, L.: A novel multiresolution spatiotemporal saliency detection model and its applications in image and video compression. IEEE Trans. Image Process. **19**(1), 185–198 (2010)
11. Haralick, R.M., Shanmugam, K., Dinstein, I.: Textural features for image classification. IEEE Trans. Syst. Man Cybern. **3**(6), 610–621 (1973)

12. Harel, J., Koch, C., Perona, P.: Graph-based visual saliency. In: Proceedings of NIPS, pp. 545–552 (2006)
13. Itti, L.: Models of bottom-up and top-down visual attention. Ph.D. thesis, California Institute of Technology (2000)
14. Itti, L., Koch, C.: A comparison of feature combination strategies for saliency-based visual attention systems. J. Electron. Imaging **10**, 161–169 (1999)
15. Itti, L., Koch, C., Niebur, E.: A model of saliency-based visual attention for rapid scene analysis. IEEE Trans. Pattern Anal. Mach. Intell. **20**(11), 1254–1259 (1998)
16. ITU-T Recommendation (P.910): Subjective video quality assessment methods for multimedia applications (2000)
17. Kennel, P., Puech, W., Comby, F.: Visualization framework of digital paintings based on visual saliency for cultural heritage. Multimedia Tools Appl. **76**(1), 561–575 (2017)
18. Khan, F.S., Beigpour, S., Weijer, J., Felsberg, M.: Painting-91: a large scale database for computational painting categorization. Mach. Vis. Appl. **25**(6), 1385–1397 (2014)
19. Koch, C., Ullman, S.: Shifts in selective visual attention: towards the underlying neural circuitry. Hum. Neurobiol. **4**, 219–227 (1985)
20. Li, J., Wang, J.Z.: Studying digital imagery of ancient paintings by mixtures of stochastic models. IEEE Trans. Image Process. **13**(3), 340 (2004)
21. Lu, L.-C., Shih, T.K., Chang, R.-C., Huang, H.-C.: Multi-layer inpainting on Chinese artwork. In: Proceedings of IEEE International Conference on Multimedia and Expo (ICME) (2004)
22. McNamara, A., Booth, T., Sridharan, S., Caffey, S., Grimm, C., Bailey, R.: Directing gaze in narrative art. In: Proceedings of the ACM Symposium on Applied Perception, SAP'12, pp. 63–70. Association for Computing Machinery, New York (2012)
23. Niebur, E.: Saliency map. Scholarpedia **2**(8), 2675 (2007)
24. Oncu, A.I., Deger, F., Hardeberg, J.Y.: Evaluation of Digital Inpainting Quality in the Context of Artwork Restoration, pp. 561–570. Springer, Heidelberg (2012)
25. Oyeka, A., Ebuh, G.: Modified Wilcoxon signed-rank test. Open J. Stat. **2**, 172–176 (2012)
26. Pei, S.-C., Ding, J.-.J., Chang, J.-H.: Efficient implementation of quaternion fourier transform, convolution, and correlation by 2-d complex FFT. IEEE Trans. Signal Process. **49**(11), 2783–2797 (2001)
27. Pitzalis, D., Aitken, G., Autrusseau, F., Babel, M., Cayre, F., Puech, W.: TSAR: secure transfer of high resolution art images. In: Proceedings of EVA'08 Florence, Electronic Imaging and the Visual Art, France (2008)
28. Platia, L., Cornelis, B., Ruic, T., Piurica, A., Dooms, A., Martens, M., De Mey, M., Daubechies, I.: Spatiogram features to characterize pearls in paintings. In: Proceedings of IEEE ICIP'2011 (2011)
29. Postma, E.O., Berezhnoy, I.E., van den Herik, H.J.: Authentic: computerized brushstroke analysis. In: Proceedings of the 2005 IEEE International Conference on Multimedia and Expo, ICME, Amsterdam, The Netherlands, 6–9 July 2005
30. Quiroga, R.Q., Pedreira, C.: How do we see art: an eye-tracker study. Front. Hum. Neurosci. **5**, 98 (2011)
31. Redies, C., Fuchs, I., Ansorge, U., Leder, H.: Salience in paintings: bottom-up influences on eye fixations. Cogn. Comput. **3**(1), 25–36 (2011)
32. Shida, B., van de Weijer, J., Khan, F.S., Felsberg, M.: Painting-91: a large scale database for computational painting categorization. Mach. Vis. Appl. **25**, 1385–1397 (2014)
33. van der Maaten, L., Postma, E.: Identifying the real van gogh with brushstroke textons. White paper, Tilburg University, Feb 2009
34. Vertan, C., Condorovici, R.G., Vrânceanu, R.: Saliency map retrieval for artistic paintings inspired from human understanding. In: Proceedings of SPAMEC 2011, Cluj-Napoca, Romania, pp. 101–104 (2011)
35. Wolfe, J.M., Horowitz, T.S.: What attributes guide the deployment of visual attention and how do they do it? Nat. Rev. Neurol. **5**(6), 495–501 (2004)
36. Wu, B., Xu, L., Zeng, L., Wang, Z., Wang, Y.: A unified framework for spatiotemporal salient region detection. EURASIP J. Image Video Process. **2013**(1), 16 (2013)

37. Xu, L., Li, H., Zeng, L., Ngan, K.N.: Saliency detection using joint spatial-color constraint and multi-scale segmentation. J. Vis. Commun. Image Represent. **24**(4), 465–476 (2013)
38. Yang, S., Cheung, G., Le Callet, P., Liu, J., Guo, Z.: Computational modeling of artistic intention: quantify lighting surprise for painting analysis. In: Proceedings of the Eighth International Conference on Quality of Multimedia Experience (2016)
39. Zeng, Y.-C., Pei, S.-C., Chang, C.-H.: Virtual restoration of ancient Chinese paintings using color contrast enhancement and lacuna texture synthesis. IEEE Trans. Image Process. (Special Issue on Image Processing for Cultural Heritage) **13**(3), 416–429 (2004)
40. Zöllner, F.: Leonardo's Portrait of Mona Lisa del Giocondo. Gazette des Beaux-Arts **121**(1), 115–138 (1993)

Predicting Interestingness of Visual Content

Claire-Hélène Demarty, Mats Sjöberg, Mihai Gabriel Constantin,
Ngoc Q.K. Duong, Bogdan Ionescu, Thanh-Toan Do, and Hanli Wang

Abstract The ability of multimedia data to attract and keep people's interest
for longer periods of time is gaining more and more importance in the fields of
information retrieval and recommendation, especially in the context of the ever
growing market value of social media and advertising. In this chapter we introduce
a benchmarking framework (dataset and evaluation tools) designed specifically
for assessing the performance of media interestingness prediction techniques. We
release a dataset which consists of excerpts from 78 movie trailers of Hollywood-
like movies. These data are annotated by human assessors according to their degree
of interestingness. A real-world use scenario is targeted, namely interestingness is
defined in the context of selecting visual content for illustrating a Video on Demand
(VOD) website. We provide an in-depth analysis of the human aspects of this task,
i.e., the correlation between perceptual characteristics of the content and the actual
data, as well as of the machine aspects by overviewing the participating systems of
the 2016 MediaEval Predicting Media Interestingness campaign. After discussing
the state-of-art achievements, valuable insights, existing current capabilities as well
as future challenges are presented.

C.-H. Demarty (✉) • N.Q.K. Duong
Technicolor R&I, Rennes, France
e-mail: claire-helene.demarty@technicolor.com; quang-khanh-ngoc.duong@technicolor.com

M. Sjöberg
Helsinki Institute for Information Technology HIIT, Department of Computer Science,
University of Helsinki, Helsinki, Finland
e-mail: mats.sjoberg@helsinki.fi

M.G. Constantin • B. Ionescu
LAPI, University Politehnica of Bucharest, Bucharest, Romania
e-mail: mgconstantin@imag.pub.ro; bionescu@imag.pub.ro

T.-T. Do
Singapore University of Technology and Design, Singapore, Singapore

University of Science, Ho Chi Minh City, Vietnam
e-mail: thanhtoan_do@sutd.edu.sg

H. Wang
Department of Computer Science and Technology, Tongji University, Shanghai, China
e-mail: hanliwang@tongji.edu.cn

© Springer International Publishing AG 2017   233
J. Benois-Pineau, P. Le Callet (eds.), *Visual Content Indexing and Retrieval
with Psycho-Visual Models*, Multimedia Systems and Applications,
DOI 10.1007/978-3-319-57687-9_10

1 Introduction

With the increased popularity of amateur and professional digital multimedia content, accessing relevant information is now dependent on effective tools for managing and browsing, due to the huge amount of data. Managing content often involves filtering parts of it to extract what corresponds to specific requests or applications. Fine filtering is impossible however without a clear understanding of the content's semantic meaning. To this end, current research in multimedia and computer vision has moved towards modeling of more complex semantic notions, such as emotions, complexity, memorability and interestingness of content, thus going closer to human perception.

Being able to assess, for instance, the interestingness level of an image or a video has several direct applications: from personal and professional content retrieval, content management, to content summarization and story telling, selective encoding, or even education. Although it has already raised a huge interest in the research community, a common and clear definition of multimedia interestingness has not yet been proposed, nor does a common benchmark for the assessment of the different techniques for its automatic prediction exist.

MediaEval[1] is a benchmarking initiative which focuses on the multi-modal aspects of multimedia content, i.e., it is dedicated to the evaluation of new algorithms for multimedia access and retrieval. MediaEval emphasizes the multi-modal character of the data, e.g., speech, audio, visual content, tags, users and context. In 2016, the Predicting Media Interesting Task[2] was proposed as a new track in the MediaEval benchmark. The purpose of the task is to answer a real and professional-oriented interestingness prediction use case, formulated by Technicolor.[3] Technicolor is a creative technology company and a provider of services in multimedia entertainment and solutions, in particular, providing also solutions for helping users select the most appropriate content according to, for example, their profile. In this context, the selected use case for interestingness consists in helping professionals to illustrate a Video on Demand (VOD) web site by selecting some interesting frames and/or video excerpts for the posted movies.

Although the targeted application is well-defined and confined to the illustration of a VOD web site, the task remains highly challenging. Firstly, it raises the question of the subjectivity of interestingness, which may vary from one person to the other. Furthermore, the semantic nature of interestingness constrains its modeling to be able to bridge the semantic gap between the notion of interestingness and the statistical features that can be extracted from the content. Lastly, by placing the task in the field of the understanding of multi-modal content, i.e., audio and video, we push the challenge even further by adding a new dimensionality to the task. The

---

[1]http://www.multimediaeval.org/.

[2]http://www.multimediaeval.org/mediaeval2016/mediainterestingness/.

[3]http://www.technicolor.com.

choice of Hollywood movies as targeted content also adds potential difficulties, in the sense that the systems will have to cope with different movie genres and potential editing and special effects (i.e., alteration of the content).

Nevertheless, although highly challenging, the building of the task responds to the absence of such benchmarks. It provides a common dataset and a common definition of interestingness. To the best of our knowledge, the MediaEval 2016 Predicting Media Interestingness is the first attempt to cope with this issue in the research community. Even though still in its infancy, the task has, in this first year, been a source of meaningful insights for the future of the field.

This chapter focuses on a detailed description of the benchmarking framework, together with a thorough analysis of its results, both in terms of the performance of the submitted systems and in what concerns the produced annotated dataset. We identify the following main contributions:

- an overview of the current interestingness literature, both from the perspective of the psychological implications and also from the multimedia/computer vision side;
- the introduction of the first benchmark framework for the validation of the techniques for predicting the interestingness of video (image and audio) content, formulated around a real-world use case, which allows for disambiguating the definition of interestingness;
- the public release of a specially designed annotated dataset. It is accompanied with an analysis of its perceptual characteristics;
- an overview of the current capabilities via the analysis of the submitted runs;
- an in-depth discussion on the remaining issues and challenges for the prediction of the interestingness of content.

The rest of the chapter is organized as follows. Section 2 presents a consistent state of the art on interestingness prediction from both the psychological and computational points of view. It is followed by a detailed description of the MediaEval Predicting Media Interestingness Task, its definition, dataset, annotations and evaluation rules, in Sect. 3. Section 4 gives an overview of the different submitted systems and trends for this first year of the benchmark. We analyze the produced dataset and annotations, their qualities and limitations. Finally, Sect. 5 discusses the future challenges and the conclusions.

2   A Review of the Literature

The prediction and detection of multimedia data interestingness has been analyzed in the literature from the human perspective, involving psychological studies, and also from the computational perspective, where machines are taught to replicate the human process. Content interestingness has gained importance with the increasing popularity of social media, on-demand video services and recommender systems. These different research directions try to create a general model for human interest, go beyond the subjectivity of interestingness and detect some objective features that appeal to the majority of subjects. In the following, we present an overview of these directions.

2.1 Visual Interestingness as a Psychological Concept

Psychologists and neuroscientists have extensively studied the subjective perception of visual content. The basis of the psychological interestingness studies was established in [5]. It was revealed that interest is determined by certain factors and their combinations, like "novelty", "uncertainty", "conflict" and "complexity". More recent studies have also developed the idea that interest is a result of appraisal structures [58]. Psychological experiments determined two components, namely: "novelty-complexity"—a structure that indicates the interest shown for new and complex events; and "coping potential"—a structure that measures a subject's ability to discern the meaning of a certain event. The influence of each appraisal component was further studied in [59], proving that personality traits could influence the appraisals that define interest. Subjects with a high "openness" trait, who are sensation seeking, curious, open to experiences [47], were more attracted by the novelty-complexity structure. In opposition, those not belonging to that personality category, were influenced more by their coping potential. Some of these factors were confirmed in numerous other studies based on image or video interestingness [11, 22, 54, 61].

The importance of objects was also analyzed as a central interestingness cue [20, 62]. The saliency maps used by the authors in [20] were able to predict interesting objects in a scene with an accuracy of more than 43%. They introduced and demonstrated the idea that, when asked to describe a scene, humans tend to talk about the most interesting objects in that scene first. Experiments show that there was a strong consistency between different users [62]. Eye movement, another behavioral cue, was used by the authors in [9] to detect the level of interest shown in segments of images or whole images. The authors used saccades, the eye movements that continuously contribute to the building of a mental map of the viewed scene. The authors in [4] studied the object attributes that could influence importance and draw attention, and found that animated, unusual or rare events tend to be more interesting for the viewer.

In [65], the authors conducted an interestingness study on 77 subjects, using artworks as visual data. The participants were asked to give ratings on different scales to opposing attributes for the images, including: "interesting-uninteresting", "enjoyable-unenjoyable", "cheerful-sad", "pleasing-displeasing". The results show that disturbing images can still be classified as interesting, therefore negating the need of pleasantness in human visual interest stimulation. Another analysis [11] led to several conclusions regarding the influence on interest, namely: instant enjoyment was found to be an important factor, exploration intent and novelty had a positive effect and challenge had a small effect. The authors in [13] studied the influence of familiarity with the presented image on the concept of interestingness. They concluded that for general scenes, unfamiliar context positively influenced interest, while photos of familiar faces (including self photos) were more interesting than those of unfamiliar people.

It is interesting to observe also a correlation between different attributes and interestingness. Authors in [23] performed such a study on a specially designed and annotated dataset of images. The positively correlated attributes were found to be "assumed memorability", "aesthetics", "pleasant", "exciting", "famous", "unusual", "makes happy", "expert photo", "mysterious", "outdoor-natural", "arousing", "strange", "historical" or "cultural place".

2.2 Visual Interestingness from a Computational Perspective

Besides the vast literature of psychological studies, the concept of visual interestingness has been studied from the perspective of automatic, machine-based, approaches. The idea is to replicate human capabilities via computational means.

For instance, the authors in [23] studied a large set of attributes: RGB values, GIST features [50], spatial pyramids of SIFT histograms [39], colorfulness [17], complexity, contrast and edge distributions [35], arousal [46] and composition of parts [6] to model different cues related to interestingness. They investigated the role of these cues in varying context of viewing: different datasets were used, from arbitrary selected and very different images (weak context) to images issued from similar Webcam streams (strong context). They found that the concept of "unusualness", defined as the degree of novelty of a certain image when compared to the whole dataset, was related to interestingness, in case of a strong context. Unusualness was calculated by clustering performed on the images using Local Outlier Factor [8] with RGB values, GIST and SIFT as features, composition of parts and complexity interpreted as the JPEG image size. In case of a weak context, personal preferences of the user, modeled by pixel values, GIST, SIFT and Color Histogram as features, classified with a ν-SVR—Support Vector Regression (SVR) with a RBF kernel, performed best. Continuing this work, the author in [61] noticed that a regression with sparse approximation of data performed better with the features defined by Gygli et al. [23] than the SVR approach.

Another approach [19] selected three types of attributes for determining image interestingness: compositional, image content and sky-illumination. The compositional attributes were: rule of thirds, low depth of field, opposing colors and salient objects; the image content attributes were: the presence of people, animals and faces, indoor/outdoor classifiers; and finally the sky-illumination attributes consisted of scene classification as cloudy, clear or sunset/sunrise. Classification of interesting content is performed with Support Vector Machines (SVM). As baseline, the authors used the low-level attributes proposed in [35], namely average hue, color, contrast, brightness, blur and simplicity interpreted as distribution of edges; and the Naïve Bayes and SVM for classification. Results show that high-level attributes tend to perform better than the baseline. However, the combination of the two was able to achieve even better results.

Other approaches focused on subcategories of interestingness. For instance, the authors in [27] determined "social interestingness" based on social media ranking and "visual interestingness" via crowdsourcing. The Pearson correlation coefficient between these two subcategories had low values, e.g., -0.015 to 0.195, indicating that there is a difference between what people share on social networks and what has a high pure visual interest. The features used for predicting these concepts were color descriptors determined on the HSV color space, texture information via Local Binary Patterns, saliency [25] and edge information captured with Histogram of Oriented Gradients.

Individual frame interestingness was calculated by the authors in [43]. They used web photo collections of interesting landmarks from Flickr as estimators of human interest. The proposed approach involved calculating a similarity measure between each frame from YouTube travel videos and the Flickr image collection of the landmarks presented in the videos, used as interesting examples. SIFT features were computed and the number of features shared between the frame and the image collection baseline, and their spatial arrangement similarity were the components that determined the interestingness measure. Finally the authors showed that their algorithm achieved the desired results, tending to classify full images of the landmarks as interesting.

Another interesting approach is the one proposed in [31]. Authors used audio, video and high-level features for predicting video shot interestingness, e.g., color histograms, SIFT [45], HOG [15, 68], SSIM Self-Similarities [55], GIST [50], MFCC [63], Spectrogram SIFT [34], Audio-Six, Classemes [64], ObjectBank [41] and the 14 photographic styles described in [48]. The system was trained via Joachims' Ranking SVM [33]. The final results showed that audio and visual features performed well, and that their fusion performed even better on the two user-annotated datasets used, giving a final accuracy of 78.6% on the 1200 Flickr videos and 71.7% on the 420 YouTube videos. Fusion with the high-level attributes provided a better result only on the Flickr dataset, with an overall precision of 79.7 and 71.4%.

Low- and high-level features were used in [22] to detect the most interesting frames in image sequences. The selected low-level features were: raw pixel values, color histogram, HOG, GIST and image self-similarity. The high-level features were grouped in several categories: emotion predicted from raw pixel values [66], complexity defined as the size of the compressed PNG image, novelty computed through a Local Outlier Factor [8] and a learning feature computed using a ν-SVR classifier with RBF kernel on the GIST features. Each one of these features performed above the baseline (i.e., random selection), and their combination also showed improvements over each individual one. The tests were performed on a database consisting of 20 image sequences, each containing 159 color images taken from various webcams and surveillance scenarios, and the final results for the combination of features gave an average precision score of 0.35 and a *Top*3 score of 0.59.

2.3 Datasets for Predicting Interestingness

A critical point to build and evaluate any machine learning system is the availability of labeled data. Although the literature for automatic interestingness prediction is still at its early stages, there are some attempts to construct an evaluation data. In the following, we introduce the most relevant initiatives.

Many of the authors have chosen to create their own datasets for evaluating their methods. Various sources of information were used, mainly coming form social media, e.g., Flickr [19, 27, 31, 43, 61], Pinterest [27], Youtube [31, 43]. The data consisted of the results returned by search queries. Annotations were determined either automatically, by exploiting the available social media metadata and statistics such as Flickr's "interestingness measure" in [19, 31], or manually, via crowdsourcing in [27] or local human assessors in [31].

The authors in [19] used a dataset composed of 40,000 images, and kept the top 10%, ordered according to the Flickr interestingness score, as positive interesting examples and the last 10% as negative, non interesting examples. Half of this dataset was used for training and half for testing. The same top and last 10% of Flickr results was used in [31], generating 1200 videos retrieved with 15 keyword queries, e.g.,: "basketball", "beach", "bird", "birthday", "cat", "dancing". In addition to these, the authors in [31] also used 30 YouTube advertisement videos from 14 categories, such as "accessories", "clothing&shoes", "computer&website", "digital products", "drink". The videos had an average duration of 36 s and were annotated by human assessors, thus generating a baseline interestingness score.

Apart from the individual datasets, there were also initiatives of grouping several datasets of different compositions. The authors in [23], associated an internal context to the data: a strong context dataset proposed in [22], where the images in 20 publicly available webcam streams are consistently related to one another, thus generating a collection of 20 image sequences each containing 159 images; a weak context dataset introduced in [50] which consists of 2688 fixed size images grouped in 8 scene categories: "coast", "mountain", "forest", "open country", "street", "inside city", "tall buildings" and "highways"; and a no context dataset which consists of the 2222 image memorability dataset proposed in [29, 30], with no context or story behind the pictures.

3 The Predicting Media Interestingness Task

This section describes the Predicting Media Interestingness Task, which was proposed in the context of the 2016 MediaEval international evaluation campaign. This section addresses the task definition (Sect. 3.1), the description of the provided data with its annotations (Sect. 3.2), and the evaluation protocol (Sect. 3.3).

3.1 Task Definition

Interestingness of media content is a perceptual and highly semantic notion that remains very subjective and dependent on the user and the context. Nevertheless, experiments show that there is, in general, an average and common interestingness level, shared by most of the users [10]. This average interestingness level provides evidence to envision that the building of a model for the prediction of interestingness is feasible. Starting from this basic assumption, and constraining the concept to a clearly defined use case, will serve to disambiguate the notion and reduce the level of subjectivity.

In the proposed benchmark, interestingness is assessed according to a practical use case originated from Technicolor, where the goal is to help professionals to illustrate a Video on Demand (VOD) web site by selecting some interesting frames and/or video excerpts for the movies. We adopt the following definition of interestingness: *an image/video excerpt is interesting in the context of helping a user to make his/her decision about whether he/she is interested in watching the movie it represents*. The proposed data is naturally adapted to this specific scenario, and consists of professional content, i.e., Hollywood-like movies.

Given this data and use case, the task requires participants to develop systems which can automatically select images and/or video segments which are considered to be the most interesting according to the aforementioned definition. Interestingness of the media is to be judged by the systems based on visual appearance, audio information and text accompanying the data. Therefore, the challenge is inherently multi-modal.

As presented in numerous studies in the literature, predicting the interestingness level of images and videos often requires significantly different perspectives. Images are self contained and the information is captured in the scene composition and colors, whereas, videos are lower quality images in motion, whose purpose is to transmit the action via the movement of the objects. Therefore, to address the two cases, two benchmarking scenarios (subtasks) are proposed as:

- *predicting image interestingness*: given a set of key-frames extracted from a movie, the systems are required to automatically identify those images for the given movie that viewers report to be the most interesting in the given movie. To solve the task, participants can make use of visual content as well as external metadata, e.g., Internet data about the movie, social media information, etc.;
- *predicting video interestingness*: given the video shots of a movie, the systems are required to automatically identify those shots that viewers report to be the most interesting in the given movie. To solve the task, participants can make use of visual and audio data as well as external data, e.g., subtitles, Internet data, etc.

A special feature of the provided data is the fact that it is extracted from the same source movies, i.e., the key-frames are extracted from the provided video shots of the movies. Therefore, this will allow for comparison between the two tasks, namely to assess to which extent image and video interestingness are linked.

Furthermore, we proposed a binary scenario, where data can be either interesting or not (two cases). Nevertheless, a confidence score is also required for each decision, so that the final evaluation measure could be computed in a ranking fashion. This is more closely related to a real world usage scenario, where results are provided in order of decreasing interestingness level.

3.2 Data Description

As mentioned in the previous section, the video and image subtasks are based on a common dataset, which consists of Creative Commons trailers of Hollywood-like movies, so as to allow redistribution. The dataset, its annotations, and accompanying features, as described in the following subsections, are publicly available.[4]

The use of trailers, instead of full movies, has several motivations. Firstly, it is the need for having content that can be freely and publicly distributed, as opposed to e.g., full movies which have much stronger restrictions on distribution. Basically, each copyrighted movie would require an individual permission for distribution. Secondly, using full movies is not practically feasible for the highly demanding segmentation and annotations steps with limited time and resources, as the number of images/video excerpts to process is enormous, in the order of millions. Finally, running on full movies, even if the aforementioned problems were solved, will not allow for having a high diversification of the content, as only a few movies could have been used. Trailers, will allow for selecting a larger number of movies and thus diversifying the content.

Trailers are by definition representative of the main content and quality of the full movies. However, it is important to note that trailers are already the result of some manual filtering of the movie to find the most interesting scenes, but without spoiling the movie key elements. In practice, most trailers also contain less interesting, or slower paced shots to balance their content. We therefore believe that this is a good compromise for the practicality of the data/task.

The proposed dataset is split into *development data*, intended for designing and training the algorithms which is based on 52 trailers; and *testing data* which is used for the actual evaluation of the systems, and is based on 26 trailers.

The data for the video subtask was created by segmenting the trailers into video shots. The same video shots were also used for the image subtask, but here each shot is represented by a single key-frame image. The task is thus to classify the shots, or key-frames, of a particular trailer, into interesting and non interesting samples.

---

[4]http://www.technicolor.com/en/innovation/scientific-community/scientific-data-sharing/ interestingness-dataset.

3.2.1 Shot Segmentation and Key-Frame Extraction

Video shot segmentation was carried out manually using a custom-made software tool. Here we define a video shot as a continuous video sequence recorded between a turn-on and a turn-off of the camera. For an edited video sequence, a shot is delimited between two video transitions. Typical video transitions include sharp transitions or cuts (direct concatenation of two shots), and gradual transitions like fades (gradual disappearance/appearance of a frame to/from a black frame) and dissolves (gradual transformation of one frame into another). In the process, we discarded movie credits and title shots. Gradual transitions were considered presumably very uninteresting shots by themselves, whenever possible. In a few cases, shots in between two gradual transitions were too short to be segmented. In that case, they were merged with their surrounding transitions, resulting in one single shot.

The segmentation process resulted in 5054 shots for the development dataset, and 2342 shots for the test dataset, with an average duration of 1 s in each case. These shots were used for the video subtask. For the image subtask, we extracted a single key-frame for each shot. The key-frame was chosen as the middle frame, as it is likely to capture the most representative information of the shot.

3.2.2 Ground-Truth Annotation

All video shots and key-frames were manually annotated in terms of interestingness by human assessors. The annotation process was performed separately for the video and image subtasks, to allow us to study the correlation between the two. Indeed we would like to answer the question: Does image interestingness automatically imply video interestingness, and vice versa?

A dedicated web-based tool was developed to assist the annotation process. The tool has been released as free and open source software, so that others can benefit from it and contribute improvements.[5]

We use the following annotation protocol. Instead of asking annotators to assign an interestingness value to each shot/key-frame, we used a pair-wise comparison protocol where the annotators were asked to select the more interesting shot/key-frame from a pair of examples taken from the same trailer. Annotators were provided with the clips for the shots and the images for the key-frames, presented side by side. Also, they were informed about the Video on Demand-use case, and asked to consider also that "the selected video excerpts/key-frames should be suitable in terms of helping a user to make his/her decision about whether he/she is interested in watching a movie". Figure 1 illustrates the pair-wise decision stage of the user interface.

---

[5]https://github.com/mvsjober/pair-annotate.

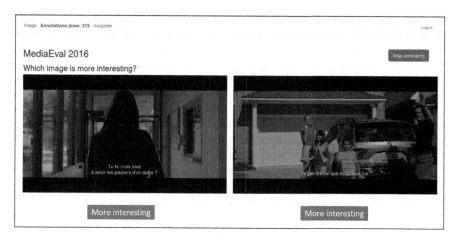

Fig. 1 Web user interface for pair-wise annotations

The choice of a pair-wise annotation protocol instead of direct rating was based on our previous experience with annotating multimedia for affective content and interestingness [3, 10, 60]. Assigning a rating is a cognitively very demanding task, requiring the annotator to understand, and constantly keep in mind, the full range of the interestingness scale [70]. Making a single comparison is a much easier task as one only needs to compare the interestingness of two items, and not consider the full range. Directly assigning a rating value is also problematic since different annotators may use different ranges, and even for the same annotator the values may not be easily interpreted [51]. For example, is an increase from 0.3 to 0.4 the same as the one from 0.8 to 0.9? Finally, it has been shown that pairwise comparisons are less influenced by the order in which the annotations are displayed than with direct rating [71].

However, annotating all possible pairs is not feasible due to the sheer number of comparisons required. For instance, n shots/key-frames would require $n(n - 1)/2$ comparisons to be made for a full coverage. Instead, we adopted the adaptive square design method [40], where the shots/key-frames are placed in a square design and only pairs on the same row or column are compared. This reduces the numbers of comparisons to $n(\sqrt{n} - 1)$. For example, for $n = 100$ we need to undergo only 900 comparisons instead of 4950 (full coverage). Finally, the Bradley-Terry-Luce (BTL) model [7] was used to convert the paired comparison data to a scalar value.

We modified the adaptive square design setup so that comparisons were taken by many users simultaneously until all the required pairs had been covered. For the rest, we proceeded according to the scheme in [40]:

1. Initialization: shots/key-frames are randomly assigned positions in the square matrix;
2. Perform a single annotation round according to the shot/key-frame pairs given by the square (across rows, columns);

3. Calculate the BTL scores based on the annotations;
4. Re-arrange the square matrix so that shots/key-frames are ranked according to their BTL scores, and placed in a spiral. This arrangement ensures that mostly similar shots/key-frames are compared row-wise and column-wise;
5. Repeat steps 2 to 4 until convergence.

For practical reasons, we decided to consider by default that convergence is achieved after five rounds and thus terminated the process when the five runs are finished. The final binary interestingness decisions were obtained with a heuristic method that tried to detect a "jumping point" in the normalized distribution of the BTL values for each movie separately. The underlying motivation for this empirical rule is the assumption that the distribution is a sum of two underlying distributions: non interesting shots/key-frames, and interesting shots/key-frames.

Overall, 315 annotators participated in the annotation for the video data and 100 for the images. The cultural distribution is over 29 different countries around the world. The average reported age of the annotators was 32, with a standard deviation around 13. Roughly, 66% were male, 32% female, and 2% did not specify their gender.

3.2.3 Additional Features

Apart from the data and its annotations, to broaden the targeted communities, we also provide some pre-computed content descriptors, namely:

Dense SIFT which are computed following the original work in [45], except that the local frame patches are densely sampled instead of using interest point detectors. A codebook of 300 codewords is used in the quantization process with a spatial pyramid of three layers [39].

HoG descriptors i.e., Histograms of Oriented Gradients [15] are computed over densely sampled patches. Following [68], HoG descriptors in a 2×2 neighborhood are concatenated to form a descriptor of higher dimension.

LBP i.e., Local Binary Patterns as proposed in [49].

GIST is computed based on the output energy of several Gabor-like filters (eight orientations and four scales) over a dense frame grid like in [50].

Color histogram computed in the HSV space (Hue-Saturation-Value).

MFCC computed over 32 ms time-windows with 50% overlap. The cepstral vectors are concatenated with their first and second derivatives.

CNN features i.e., the *fc7 layer* (4096 dimensions) and *prob layer* (1000 dimensions) of AlexNet [32].

Mid level face detection and tracking features obtained by face tracking-by-detection in each video shot via a HoG detector [15] and the correlation tracker proposed in [16].

3.3 Evaluation Rules

As for other tasks in MediaEval, participants were allowed to submit a total of up to 5 runs for the video and image subtasks. To provide the reader with a complete picture of the evaluation process in order to understand the achieved results, we replicate the exact conditions for the participants, here.

Each task had a required run, namely: for predicting image interestingness, classification had to be achieved with the use of the visual information only, no external data was allowed; for predicting video interestingness, classification had to be achieved with the use of both audio and visual information; no external data was allowed. External data was considered to be any of the following: additional datasets and annotations which were specifically designed for interestingness classification; the use of pre-trained models, features, detectors obtained from such dedicated additional datasets; additional metadata from the Internet (e.g., from IMDb). On the contrary, CNN features trained on generic datasets such as ImageNet were allowed for use in the required runs. By generic datasets, we mean datasets that were not explicitly designed to support research in interestingness prediction. Additionally, datasets dedicated to study memorability or other aspects of media were allowed, as long as these concepts are different from interestingness, although a correlation may exist.

To assess performance, several metrics were computed. The official evaluation metric was the mean average precision (MAP) computed over all trailers, whereas average precision was to be computed on a per trailer basis, over all ranked images/video shots. MAP was computed with the trec_eval tool.[6] In addition to MAP, several other secondary metrics were provided, namely: accuracy, precision, recall and f-score for each class, and the class confusion matrix.

4 Results and Analysis of the First Benchmark

4.1 Official Results

The 2016 Predicting Media Interestingness Task received more than 30 registrations and 12 teams coming from 9 countries all over the world submitted runs in the end (see Fig. 2). The task attracted a lot of interest from the community, which shows the importance of this topic.

Tables 1 and 2 provide an overview of the official results for the two subtasks (video and image interestingness prediction). A total of 54 runs were received,

---

[6]http://trec.nist.gov/trec_eval/.

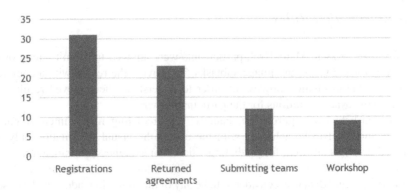

Fig. 2 2016 Predicting Media Interestingness task's participation at different stages

Table 1 Official results for image interestingness prediction evaluated by MAP

Team	Run name	MAP
TUD-MMC [42]	me16in_tudmmc2_image_histface	0.2336
Technicolor [56]	me16in_technicolor_image_run1_SVM_rbf	0.2336
Technicolor	me16in_technicolor_image_run2_DNNresampling06_100	0.2315
MLPBOON [52]	me16in_MLPBOON_image_run5	0.2296
BigVid [69]	me16in_BigVid_image_run5FusionCNN	0.2294
MLPBOON	me16in_MLPBOON_image_run1	0.2205
TUD-MMC	me16in_tudmmc2_image_hist	0.2202
MLPBOON	me16in_MLPBOON_image_run4	0.217
HUCVL [21]	me16in_HUCVL_image_run1	0.2125
HUCVL	me16in_HUCVL_image_run2	0.2121
UIT-NII [38]	me16in_UITNII_image_FA	0.2115
RUC [12]	me16in_RUC_image_run2	0.2035
MLPBOON	me16in_MLPBOON_image_run2	0.2023
HUCVL	me16in_HUCVL_image_run3	0.2001
RUC	me16in_RUC_image_run3	0.1991
RUC	me16in_RUC_image_run1	0.1987
ETH-CVL [67]	me16in_ethcvl1_image_run2	0.1952
MLPBOON	me16in_MLPBOON_image_run3	0.1941
HKBU [44]	me16in_HKBU_image_baseline	0.1868
ETH-CVL	me16in_ethcvl1_image_run1	0.1866
ETH-CVL	me16in_ethcvl1_image_run3	0.1858
HKBU	me16in_HKBU_image_drbaseline	0.1839
BigVId	me16in_BigVid_image_run4SVM	0.1789
UIT-NII	me16in_UITNII_image_V1	0.1773
LAPI [14]	me16in_lapi_image_runf1	0.1714
UNIGECISA [53]	me16in_UNIGECISA_image_ReglineLoF	0.1704
Baseline		0.16556
LAPI	me16in_lapi_image_runf2	0.1398

Table 2 Official results for video interestingness prediction evaluated by MAP

Team	Run name	MAP
UNIFESP [1]	me16in_unifesp_video_run1	0.1815
HKBU [44]	me16in_HKBU_video_drbaseline	0.1735
UNIGECISA [53]	me16in_UNIGECISA_video_RegsrrLoF	0.171
RUC [12]	me16in_RUC_video_run2	0.1704
UIT-NII [38]	me16in_UITNII_video_A1	0.169
UNIFESP	me16in_unifesp_video_run4	0.1656
RUC	me16in_RUC_video_run1	0.1647
UIT-NII	me16in_UITNII_video_F1	0.1641
LAPI [14]	me16in_lapi_video_runf5	0.1629
Technicolor [56]	me16in_technicolor_video_run5_CSP_multimodal_80_epoch7	0.1618
UNIFESP	me16in_unifesp_video_run2	0.1617
UNIFESP	me16in_unifesp_video_run3	0.1617
ETH-CVL [67]	me16in_ethcvl1_video_run2	0.1574
LAPI	me16in_lapi_video_runf3	0.1574
LAPI	me16in_lapi_video_runf4	0.1572
TUD-MMC [42]	me16in_tudmmc2_video_histface	0.1558
TUD-MMC	me16in_tudmmc2_video_hist	0.1557
BigVid [69]	me16in_BigVid_video_run3RankSVM	0.154
HKBU	me16in_HKBU_video_baseline	0.1521
BigVid	me16in_BigVid_video_run2FusionCNN	0.1511
UNIGECISA	me16in_UNIGECISA_video_RegsrrGiFe	0.1497
Baseline		0.1496
BigVid	me16in_BigVid_video_run1SVM	0.1482
Technicolor	me16in_technicolor_video_run3_LSTM_U19_100_epoch5	0.1465
UNIFESP	me16in_unifesp_video_run5	0.1435
UNIGECISA	me16in_UNIGECISA_video_SVRloAudio	0.1367
Technicolor	me16in_technicolor_video_run4_CSP_video_80_epoch9	0.1365
ETH-CVL	me16in_ethcvl1_video_run1	0.1362

equally distributed between the two subtasks. As a general conclusion, the achieved MAP values were low, which proves again the challenging nature of this problem. Slightly higher values were obtained for image interestingness prediction.

To serve as a baseline for comparison, we generated a random ranking run, i.e., samples were ranked randomly five times and we take the average MAP. Compared to the baseline, the results of the image subtask clearly confirm their performance, being almost all above the baseline. For the video subtask, on the other hand, the value range is smaller and a few systems did worse than the baseline. In the following we present the participating systems and analyze the achieved results in detail.

4.2 Participating Systems and Global Trends

Numerous approaches have been investigated by the participating teams to tackle both image and video interestingness prediction. In the following, we will firstly summarize the general techniques used by the teams and their key features (Sect. 4.2.1), and secondly present the global insights of the results (Sect. 4.2.2).

4.2.1 Participants' Approaches

A summary of the features and classification techniques used by each participating system is presented in Table 3 (image interestingness) and Table 4 (video interestingness). Below, we present the main characteristics of each approach. Unless otherwise specified, each team participated in both subtasks.

Table 3 Overview of the characteristics of the submitted systems for predicting image interestingness

Team	Features	Classification technique
BigVid [69]	denseSIFT+CNN+Style Attributes+SentiBank	SVM (run4)
		Regularized DNN (run5)
ETH-CVL [67]	DNN-based	Visual Semantic
		Embedding Model
HKBU [44]	ColorHist+denseSIFT+GIST+HOG+LBP (run1)	Nearest neighbor and SVR
	features from run1 + dimension reduction (run2)	
HUCVL [21]	CNN (run1, run3)	MLP (run1, run2)
	MemNet (run2)	Deep triplet network (run3)
LAPI [14]	ColorHist+GIST (run1)	SVM
	denseSIFT+GIST (run2)	
MLPBOON [52]	CNN, PCA for dimension reduction	Logistic regression
RUC [12]	GIST+LBP+CNN prob (run1)	Random Forest (run1)
	ColorHist+GIST+CNN prob (run2),	Random Forest (run2)
	ColorHist+GIST+LBP+CNN prob (run3)	SVM (run3)
Technicolor [56]	CNN (Alexnet fc7)	SVM (run1)
		MLP (run2)
TUD-MMC [42]	Face-related ColorHist (run1)	Normalized histogram-based
	Face-related ColorHist+Face area (run2)	confidence score
		NHCS+Normalized face
		area score (run2)
UIT-NII [38]	CNN (AlexNet+VGG) (run1)	SVM with late fusion
	CNN (VGG)+GIST+HOG+DenseSIFT (run2)	
UNIGECISA [1]	Multilingual visual sentiment ontology	Linear regression
	(MVSO)+CNN	

Table 4 Overview of the characteristics of the submitted systems for predicting video interestingness

Teams	Features	Classification technique	Multi-modality
BigVid [69]	denseSIFT, CNN Style Attributes, SentiBank	SVM (run1) Regularlized DNN (run2) SVM/Ranking-SVM (run3)	No
ETH-CVL [67]	DNN-based	Video2GIF (run1) Video2GIF+Visual Semantic Embedding Model (run2)	Text+Visual
HKBU [44]	ColorHist+denseSIFT+GIST +HOG+LBP (run1) features from run1 + dimension reduction (run2)	Nearest neighbor and SVR	No
LAPI [14]	GIST+CNN prob (run3) ColorHist+CNN (run4) denseSIFT+CNN prob (run5)	SVM	No
RUC [12]	Acoustic Statistics + GIST (run4) MFCC with Fisher Vector Encoding + GIST (run5)	SVM	Audio+Visual
Technicolor [56]	CNN+MFCC	LSTM-Resnet + MLP (run3) Proposed RNN-based model (run4, run5)	Audio+Visual
TUD-MMC [42]	ColorHist (run1) ColorHist+Face area (run2)	Normalized histogram-based confidence score (NHCS) run3) NHCS+Normalized face area score (run4)	No
UIT-NII [38]	CNN (AlexNet)+MFCC (run3) CNN (VGG)+GIST (run4)	SVM with late fusion	Audio+Visual
UNIFESP [1]	Histogram of motion patterns (HMP) [2]	Majority voting of pairwise ranking methods: Ranking SVM, RankNet RankBoost, ListNet	No
UNIGECISA [53]	MVSO+CNN (run2) Baseline visual features [18] (run3), Emotionally-motivated audio feature (run4)	SVR (run2) SPARROW (run3, run4)	Audio+Visual

BigVid [69] (Fudan University, China): explored various low-level features (from visual and audio modalities) and high-level semantic attributes, as well as the fusion of these features for classification. Both SVM and recent deep learning methods were tested as classifiers. The results proved that the high-level attributes are complementary to visual features since the combination of these features increases the overall performance.

ETH-CVL [67] (ETH Zurich, Switzerland): participated in the video subtask only. Two models were presented: (1) a frame-based model that uses textual side information (external data) and (2) a generic predictor for finding video highlights in the form of segments. For the frame-based model, they learned a joint embedding space for image and text, which allows to measure relevance of a frame with regard to some text such as the video title. For video interestingness prediction, the approach in [24] was used, where a deep RankNet is trained to rank the segments of a video based upon their suitability as animated GIFs. Note that RankNet captures the spatio-temporal aspect of video segments via the use of 3D convolutional neural networks (C3D).

HKBU [44] (Hong Kong Baptist University, China): used two dimensionality reduction methods, named Neighborhood MinMax Projections (NMMP) and Supervised Manifold Regression (SMR), to extract features of lower dimension from a set of baseline low-level visual features (Color Histogram, dense SIFT, GIST, HOG, LBP). Then nearest neighbor (NN) classifier and Support Vector Regressor (SVR) were exploited for interestingness classification. They found that after dimensionality reduction, the performance of the reduced features was comparable to that of their original features, which indicated that the reduced features successfully captured most of the discriminant information of the data.

HUCVL [21] (Hacettepe University, Turkey): participated in image interestingness prediction only. They investigated three different Deep Neural Network (DNN) models. The first two models were based on fine-tuning two pre-trained models, namely AlexNet and MemNet. Note that MemNet was trained on the image memorability dataset proposed in [36], the idea being to see if memorability can be generalized to the interestingness concept. The third model, on the other hand, depends on a proposed triplet network which comprised three instances with shared weights of the same feed-forward network. The results demonstrated that all these models provide relatively similar and promising results on the image interestingness subtask.

LAPI [14] (University Politehnica of Bucharest, Romania, co-organizer of the task): investigated a classic descriptor-classification scheme, namely the combination of different low-level features (HoG, dense SIFT, LBP, GIST, AlexNet fc7 layer features (hereafter referred as CNN features), Color Histogram, Color Naming Histogram) and use of SVM, with different kernel types, as classifier. For video, frame features were averaged to obtain a global video descriptor.

MLPBOON [52] (Indian Institute of Technology, Bombay, India): participated only in image interestingness prediction and studied various baseline visual features provided by the organizers [18], and classifiers on the development dataset. Principal component analysis (PCA) was used for reducing the feature dimension. Their final system involved the use of PCA on CNN features for the input representation and logistic regression (LR) as classifier. Interestingly, they observed that the combination of CNN features with GIST and Color Histogram features gave similar performance to the use of CNN features only. Overall, this simple, yet effective, system obtained quite high MAP values for the image subtask.

RUC [12] (Renmin University, China): investigated the use of CNN features and AlexNet probabilistic layer (referred as CNN prob), and hand-crafted visual features including Color Histogram, GIST, LBP, HOG, dense SIFT. Classifiers were SVM and Random Forest. They found that semantic-level features, i.e., CNN prob, and low-level appearance features are complementary. However, concatenating CNN features with hand-crafted features did not bring any improvement. This finding is coherent with the statement from MLPBOON team [52]. For predicting video interestingness, audio modality offered superior performance than visual modality and the early fusion of the two modalities can further boost the performance.

Technicolor [56] (Technicolor R&D France, co-organizer of the task): used CNN features as visual features (for both the image and video subtasks), and MFCC as audio feature (for the video subtask) and investigated the use of both SVM and different Deep Neural Networks (DNN) as classification techniques. For the image subtask, a simple system with CNN features and SVM resulted in the best MAP, 0.2336. For the video subtask, multi-modality as a mid-level fusion of audio and visual features, was taken into account within the DNN framework. Additionally, a novel DNN architecture based on multiple Recurrent Neural Networks (RNN) was proposed for modeling the temporal aspect of the video, and a resampling/upsampling technique was used to deal with the unbalanced dataset.

TUD-MMC [42] (Delft University of Technology, Netherlands): investigated MAP values obtained on the development set by swapping and submitting ground-truth annotations of image and video to the video and image subtasks respectively, i.e., using the video ground-truth as submission on the image subtask and the image ground-truth as submission on the video subtask. They concluded on the low correlation between the image interestingness and video interestingness concepts. Their simple visual features took into account the human face information (color and sizes) in the image and video with the assumption that clear human faces should attract the viewer's attention and thus make the image/video more interesting. One of their submitted runs, only rule-based, obtained the best MAP value of 0.2336 for the image subtask.

UIT-NII [38] (University of Science, Vietnam; University of Information Technology, Vietnam; National Institute of Informatics, Japan): used SVM to predict three different scores given the three types of input features: (1) low-level visual features provided by the organizers [18], (2) CNN features (AlexNet and VGG), and (3) MFCC as audio feature. Late fusion of these scores was used for computing the final interestingness levels. Interestingly, their system tends to output a higher rank on images of beautiful women. Furthermore, they found that images from dark scenes were often considered as more interesting.

UNIFESP [1] (Federal University of Sao Paulo, Brazil): participated only in the video subtask. Their approach was based on combining learning-to-rank algorithms for predicting the interestingness of videos by using their visual content only. For this purpose, Histogram of Motion Patterns (HMP) [2] were used. A simple majority voting scheme was used for combining four pairwise machine learned rankers

(Ranking SVM, RankNet, RankBoost, ListNet) and predicting the interestingness of videos. This simple, yet effective, method obtained the best MAP of 0.1815 for the video subtask.

UNIGECISA [53] (University of Geneva, Switzerland): used mid-level semantic visual sentiment features, which are related to the emotional content of images and were shown to be effective in recognizing interestingness in GIFs [24]. They found that these features outperform the baseline low-level ones provided by the organizers [18]. They also investigated the use of emotionally-motivated audio features (eGeMAPS) for the video subtask and showed the significance of the audio modality. Three regression models were reported to predict interestingness levels: linear regression (LR), SVR with linear kernel, and sparse approximation weighted regression (SPARROW).

4.2.2 Analysis of this Year'S Trends and Outputs

This section provides an in-depth analysis of the results and discusses the global trends found in the submitted systems.

Low-Level vs. High-Level Description The conventional low-level visual features, such as dense SIFT, GIST, LBP, Color Histogram, were still being used by many of the systems for both, image and video interestingness prediction [12, 14, 38, 44, 69]. However, deep features like CNN features (i.e., Alexnet fc7 or VGG) have become dominant and are exploited by the majority of the systems. This shows the effectiveness and popularity of deep learning. Some teams investigated the combination of hand crafted features with deep features, i.e., conventional and CNN features. A general finding is that such a combination did not really bring any benefit to the prediction results [12, 44, 52]. Some systems combined low-level features with some high-level attributes such as emotional expressions, human faces, CNN visual concept predictions [12, 69]. In this case, the resulting conclusion was that low-level appearance features and semantic-level features are complementary, as the combination in general offered better prediction results.

Standard vs. Deep Learning-Based Classification As it can be seen in Tables 3 and 4, SVM was mostly used by a large number of systems, for both prediction tasks. In addition, regression techniques such as linear regression, logistic regression, and support vector regression were also widely reported. Contrary to CNN features, which were widely used by most of the systems, deep learning classification techniques were investigated less (see [21, 56, 67, 69] for image interestingness and [56, 67, 69] for the video interestingness). This may be due to the fact that the datasets are not large enough to justify a deep learning approach. Conventional classifiers were preferred here.

Use of External Data Some systems investigated the use of external data to improve the results. For instance, Flickr images with social-driven interestingness labels were used for model selection in the image interestingness subtask by the Technicolor team [56]. The HUCVL team [21] submitted a run with a fine-tuning of the MemNet model, which was trained for image memorability prediction. Although memorability and interestingness are not the same concept, the authors expected that fine-tuning a model related to an intrinsic property of images could be helpful in learning better high-level features for image interestingness prediction. The ETH-CVL team [67] exploited movie titles, as textual side information related to movies, for both subtasks. In addition, ETH-CVL also investigated the use of the deep RankNet model, which was trained on the Video2GIF dataset [24], and the Visual Semantic Embedding model, which was trained on the MSR Clickture dataset [28].

Dealing with Small and Unbalanced Data As the development data provided for the two subtasks are not very large, some systems, e.g., [1, 56], used the whole image and video development sets for training when building the final models. To cope with the imbalance of the two classes in the dataset, the Technicolor team [56] proposed to use classic resampling and upsampling strategies so that the positive samples are used multiple times during training.

Multi-Modality Specific to video interestingness, multi-modal approaches were exploited by half of the teams for at least one of their runs, as shown in Table 4. Four teams combined audio and visual information [12, 38, 53, 56], and one team combined text with visual information [67]. The fusion of modalities was done either at the early stage [12, 53], middle stage [56], or late stage [38] in the processing workflows. Note that the combination of text and visual information was also reported in [67] for image interestingness prediction. The general finding here was that multi-modality brings benefits to the prediction results.

Temporal Modeling for Video Though the temporal aspect is an important property of a video, most systems did not actually exploit any temporal modeling for video interestingness prediction. They mainly considered a video as a sequence of frames and a global video descriptor was computed simply by averaging frame image descriptors over each shot. As an example, HKBU team [44] treated each frame as a separated image, and calculated the average and standard deviation of their features over all frames in a shot to build their global feature vector for each video. Only two teams incorporated temporal modeling in their submitted systems, namely Technicolor [56] who used long-short term memory (LSTM) in their deep learning-based framework, and ETH-CVL [67] who used 3D convolutional neural networks (C3D) in their video highlight detector, trained on the Video2GIF dataset.

4.3   In-Depth Analysis of the Data and Annotations

The purpose of this section is to give some insights on the characteristics of the produced data, i.e., the dataset and its annotations.

4.3.1 Quality of the Dataset

In general, the overall results obtained during the 2016 campaign show low values for MAP (see Figs. 1 and 2), especially for the video interestingness prediction subtask. To have a comparison, we provide examples of MAP values obtained by other multi-modal tasks from the literature. Of course, these were obtained on other datasets which are fundamentally different from the underlying data, both from the data point of view and also use case scenario. A direct comparison is not possible, however, they provide an idea about the current classification capabilities for video:

- ILSVR Challenge 2015, Object Detection with provided training data, 200 fully labeled categories, best MAP is 0.62; Object Detection from videos with provided training data, 30 fully labeled categories, best MAP is 0.67;
- TRECVID 2015, Semantic indexing of concepts such as: *airplane, kitchen, flags, etc.*, best MAP is 0.37;
- TRECVID 2015, Multi-modal event detection, e.g., *somebody cooking on an outdoor grill*, best MAP is less than 0.35.

Although higher than the obtained MAP for the Predicting Media Interestingness Task, it must be noted that for more difficult tasks such as multi-modal event detection, the difference of performance is not that high, given the fact that the proposed challenge is far more subjective than the tasks we are referring to.

Nevertheless, we may wonder, especially for the video interestingness subtask, whether the quality of the dataset/anotations partly affects the predicting performance. Firstly, the dataset size, although it is sufficient for classic learning techniques and required a huge annotation effort, it may not be sufficient for deep learning, with only several thousands of samples for both subtasks.

Furthermore, it may be considered to be highly unbalanced with 8.3 and 9.6% of interesting content for the development set and test set, respectively. Trying to cope with the dataset's unbalance has shown to increase the performance for some systems [56, 57]. This leads to the conclusion that, although this unbalance reflects reality, i.e., interesting content corresponds to only a small part of the data, it makes the task even more difficult, as systems will have to take this characteristic into account.

Finally, in Sect. 3.2, we explained that the final annotations were determined with an iterative process which required the convergence of the results. Due to limited time and human resources, this process was limited to five rounds. More rounds would certainly have resulted in better convergence of the inter-annotator ratings.

To have an idea of the subjective quality of the ground-truth rankings, Figs. 3 and 4 illustrate some image examples for the image interestingness subtask together with the rankings obtained by one of the best systems and the second worst performing system, for both interesting and non interesting images.

The figures show that results obtained by the best system for the most interesting images are coherent with the selection proposed by the ground-truth, whereas the second worst performing system offers more images at the top ranks which do not

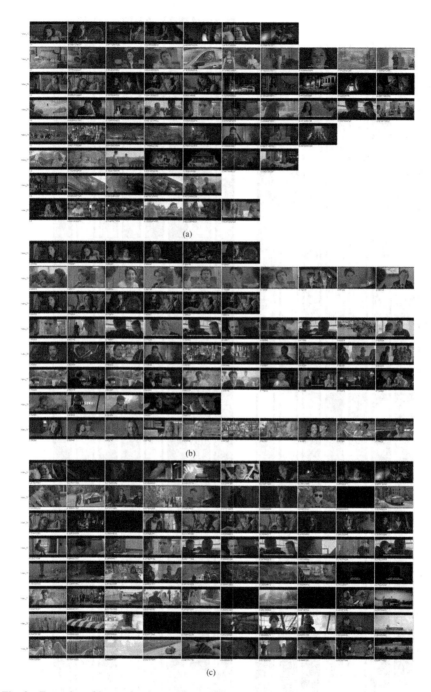

Fig. 3 Examples of interesting images from different videos of the test set. Images are ranked *from left to right* decreasing interestingness ranking. (**a**) Interesting images according to the ground-truth. (**b**) Interesting images selected by the best system. (**c**) Interesting images selected by the second worst performing system (Color figure online)

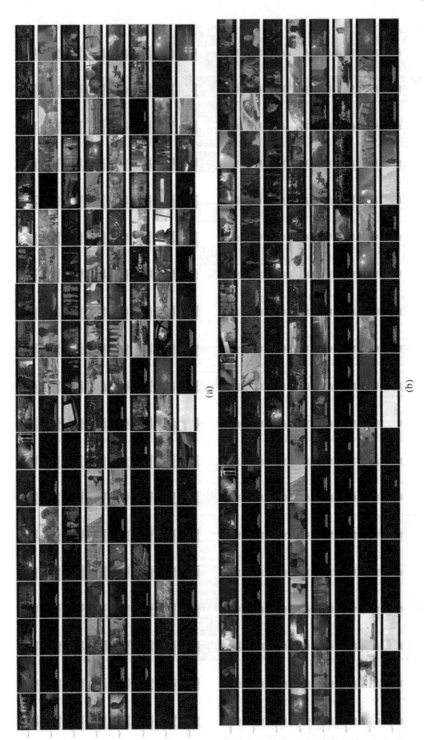

Fig. 4 Examples of non interesting images from different videos of the test set. Images are ranked *from left to right* increasing interestingness ranking. (**a**) Non interesting images according to the ground-truth. (**b**) Non interesting images selected by the best system (Color figure online)

really contain any information, e.g., black or uniform frames, with blur or objects and persons only partially visible.

These facts converge to the idea that both the provided ground-truth and the best working systems have managed to capture the interestingness of images. It also confirms that the obtained MAP values, although quite low, nevertheless correspond to real differences in the interestingness prediction performance.

The observation of the images which were classified as non interesting (Fig. 4) is also a source of interesting insights. According to the ground-truth and also to the best performing systems, non interesting images tend to be those mostly uniform, of low quality or without meaningful information. The amount of information contained in the non interesting images then increases with the level of interestingness. Note that we do not show here the images classified as non interesting by the second worst performing system, as we did for the interesting images, because there were too few (for the example 7 images out of 25 videos) to draw any conclusion.

We also calculated Krippendorff's alpha metric (α), which is a measure for inter-observer agreement [26, 37], to be $\alpha = 0.059$ for image interestingness and $\alpha = 0.063$ for video interestingness. This result would indicate that there is no inter-observer agreement. However, as our method (by design) produced very few duplicate comparisons it is not clear if this result is reliable.

As a last insight, it is worth noting that the two experienced teams [53, 67], i.e., the two teams that did work on predicting content interestingness before the MediaEval benchmark, did not achieve particularly good results on both subtasks and especially on the image subtask. This raises the question of the generalization ability of their systems on different types of content, unless this difference of performance comes from the choice of different use cases as working context. For the latter, this seems to show that, to different use cases correspond different interpretations of the interestingness concept.

4.3.2 Correlation Between the Two Subtasks

The Predicting Media Interestingness task was designed so that a comparison between the interestingness prediction for images and videos would be possible afterwards. Indeed, the same videos were used to extract both the shots and the key-frames to be classified in each subtask, each key-frame corresponding to the middle of shots. Thanks to this, we studied a potential correlation between image interestingness and video interestingness.

Figure 5 shows the annotated video ranking against their key-frame ranking for several videos in the development set. None of the curves exhibit a correlation (the coefficient of determination, *R-squared* or R^2, used while fitting a regression line to the data, exhibits values lower than 0.03), leading to the conclusion that the two concepts differ, in the sense that we cannot use video interestingness to infer the image interestingness and the other way round on this data and use case scenario.

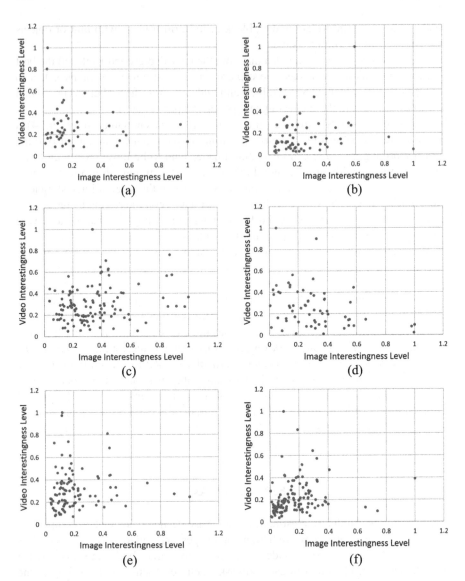

Fig. 5 Representation of image rankings vs. video rankings from the ground-truth for several videos of the development set. (**a**) Video 0, (**b**) Video 4, (**c**) Video 7, (**d**) Video 10, (**e**) Video 14, (**f**) Video 51

This conclusion is in line with what was found in [42] where the authors investigated the assessment of the ground-truth ranking of the image subtask against the ground-truth ranking of the video subtask and vice-versa. MAP value achieved by the video ground-truth on the image subtask was 0.1747, while for the image ground-truth on the video subtask, it was 0.1457, i.e., in the range, or even lower, than the random baseline for both cases. Videos obviously contain more information than a single image, which can be conveyed by other channels such as audio and motion, for example. Because of this additional information, a video might be globally considered as interesting while one single key-frame extracted from the same video will be considered as non interesting. This can explain, in some cases, the observed discrepancy between image and video interestingnesses.

4.3.3   Link with Perceptual Content Characteristics

Trying to infer some potential links between the interestingness concept and perceptual content characteristics, we did study how low-level characteristics such as shot length, average luminance, blur and presence of high quality faces influence the interestingness prediction of images and videos.

A first qualitative study of both sets of interesting and non interesting images in the development and test sets shows that most uniformly black and very blurry images were mostly classified as non interesting. So were the majority of images with no real information, i.e., close-up of usual objects, partly cut faces or objects, etc., as it can be seen in Fig. 4.

Figure 6 shows the distributions of interestingness values for both the development and test sets, in the video interestingness subtask, compared to the distributions of interesting values restricted to the shots with less than 10 frames. In all cases, it seems that the distributions of small shots can just be superimposed under the complete distributions, meaning that the shot length does not seem to influence the interestingness of video segments even for very short durations. On the contrary, Fig. 7 shows the two same types of distributions but for the image interestingness subtask and when trying to assess the influence of the average luminance value on interestingness. This time, the distributions of interestingness levels for the images with low average luminance seem to be slightly shifted toward lower interestingness

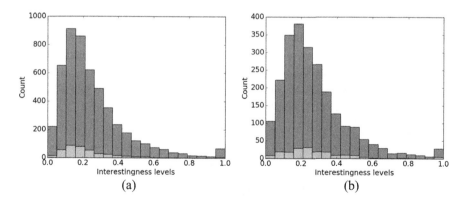

Fig. 6 Video interestingness and shot length: distribution of interestingness levels (in *blue*—all shots considered; in *green*—shots with length smaller than 10 frames). (**a**) Development set, (**b**) test set (Color figure online)

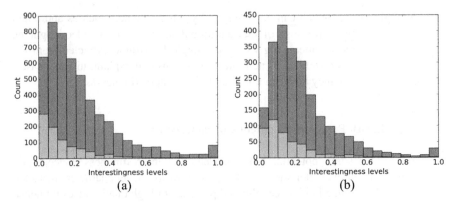

Fig. 7 Image interestingness and average luminance: distribution of interestingness levels (in *blue*—all key-frames considered; in *green*—key-frames with luminance values lower than 25). (**a**) Development set, (**b**) test set (Color figure online)

levels. This might lead us to the conclusion that low average luminance values tend to decrease the interestingness level of a given image, contrary to the conclusion in [38].

We also investigated some potential correlation between the presence of high-quality faces in frames and the interestingness level. By high-quality faces, we mean rather big faces with no motion blur, either frontal or profile, no closed eyes or funny faces. This last mid-level characteristic was assessed manually by counting the number of high-quality faces present in both the interesting and non interesting images for the image interestingness subtask. The proportion of high-quality faces on the development set was found to be 48.2% for the set of images annotated as interesting and 33.9% for the set of images annotated as non interesting. For the test set, 56.0% of the interesting images and 36.7% of the non interesting images contain high quality faces. The difference in favor of the interesting sets tends to prove that this characteristic has a positive influence on the interestingness assessment. This was confirmed by the results obtained by TUD-MMC team [42] who based their system only on the detection of these high quality faces and achieved the best MAP value for the image subtask.

As a general conclusion, we may say that perceptual quality plays an important role when assessing the interestingness of images, although it is not the only clue to assess the interestingness of content. Among other semantic objects, the presence of good quality human faces seems to be correlated with interestingness.

5   Conclusions and Future Challenges

In this chapter we introduced a specially designed evaluation framework for assessing the performance of automatic techniques for predicting image and video interestingness. We described the released dataset and its annotations. Content interestingness was defined in a multi-modal scenario and for a real-world, specific use case defined by Technicolor R&D France, namely the selection of interesting images and video excerpts for helping professionals to illustrate a Video on Demand (VOD) web site.

The proposed framework was validated during the 2016 Predicting Media Interestingness Task, organized with the MediaEval Benchmarking Initiative for Multimedia Evaluation. It received participation from 12 teams submitting a total of 54 runs. Highest MAP obtained for the image interestingness data was 0.2336, whereas for video interestingness prediction it was only 0.1815. Although a great deal of approaches were experimented, ranging from standard classifiers and descriptors, to deep learning and use of pre-trained data, the results show the difficulty of this task.

From the experience with this data, we can draw some general conclusions that will help shape future data in this area. Firstly, one should note that generating data and ground truth for such a subjective task is a huge effort and effective methods should be devised to reduce the complexity of annotation. In our approach we took advantage of a pair-wise comparison protocol which was further applied in an adaptive square fashion way to avoid comparing all possible pairs. This has limitation as it still requires a great number of annotators and resulted in a low inter-agreement. A potential improvement may consist on ranking directly series of images/videos. We could also think of crowd-sourcing the key-frames/videos returned by the participants' systems to extract the most interesting samples and evaluating the performances of the systems against these samples only.

Secondly, the source of data is key for a solid evaluation. In our approach we selected movie trailers, due to their Creative Commons licenses which allow redistribution. Other movies are in almost all cases closed content for the community. On the other hand, trailers are edited content which will limit at some point the naturalness of the task, but offer a good compromise given the circumstances. Future improvements could consist of selecting the data as parts of a full movie— a few Creative Commons movies are indeed available. This will require a greater annotation effort but might provide a better separation between interesting and non interesting content.

Thirdly, a clear definition of image/video interestingness is mandatory. The concept of content interestingness is already very subjective and highly user dependent, even compared to other video concepts which are exploited in TRECVID or ImageCLEF benchmarks. A well founded definition will allow for a focused evaluation and disambiguate the information need. In our approach, we define interestingness in the context of selecting video content for illustrating a web site, where interesting means an image/video which would be interesting enough to convince the user to watch the source movie. As a future challenge, we might want to compare the results of interestingness prediction for different use scenarios, or even test the generalization power of the approaches.

Finally, although image and video data was by design specifically correlated, i.e., images were selected as key-frames from videos, results show that actually predicting image interestingness and predicting video interestingness are two completely different tasks. This was more or less proved in the literature, however, in those cases, images and videos were not chosen to be correlated. Therefore, a future perspective might be the separation of the two, while focusing on more representative data for each.

Acknowledgements We would like to thank Yu-Gang Jiang and Baohan Xu from the Fudan University, China, and Hervé Bredin, from LIMSI, France for providing the features that accompany the released data, and Frédéric Lefebvre, Alexey Ozerov and Vincent Demoulin for their valuable inputs to the task definition. We also would like to thank our anonymous annotators for their contribution to building the ground-truth for the datasets. Part of this work was funded under project SPOTTER PN-III-P2-2.1-PED-2016-1065, contract 30PED/2017.

References

1. Almeida, J.: UNIFESP at MediaEval 2016 Predicting Media Interestingness Task. In: Proceedings of the MediaEval Workshop, Hilversum (2016)
2. Almeida, J., Leite, N.J., Torres, R.S.: Comparison of video sequences with histograms of motion patterns. In: IEEE ICIP International Conference on Image Processing, pp. 3673–3676 (2011)
3. Baveye, Y., Dellandréa, E., Chamaret, C., Chen, L.: Liris-accede: a video database for affective content analysis. IEEE Trans. Affect. Comput. **6**(1), 43–55 (2015)
4. Berg, A.C., Berg, T.L., Daume, H., Dodge, J., Goyal, A., Han, X., Mensch, A., Mitchell, M., Sood, A., Stratos, K., et al.: Understanding and predicting importance in images. In: IEEE CVPR International Conference on Computer Vision and Pattern Recognition, pp. 3562–3569. IEEE, Providence (2012)
5. Berlyne, D.E.: Conflict, Arousal and Curiosity. Mc-Graw-Hill, New York (1960)
6. Boiman, O., Irani, M.: Detecting irregularities in images and in video. Int. J. Comput. Vis. **74**(1), 17–31 (2007)
7. Bradley, R.A., Terry, M.E.: Rank analysis of incomplete block designs: the method of paired comparisons. Biometrika **39**(3-4), 324–345 (1952)
8. Breunig, M.M., Kriegel, H.P., Ng, R.T., Sander, J.: Lof: identifying density-based local outliers. In: ACM Sigmod Record, vol. 29, pp. 93–104. ACM, New York (2000)
9. Bulling, A., Roggen, D.: Recognition of visual memory recall processes using eye movement analysis. In: Proceedings of the 13th international conference on Ubiquitous Computing, pp. 455–464. ACM, New York (2011)
10. Chamaret, C., Demarty, C.H., Demoulin, V., Marquant, G.: Experiencing the interestingness concept within and between pictures. In: Proceeding of SPIE, Human Vision and Electronic Imaging (2016)
11. Chen, A., Darst, P.W., Pangrazi, R.P.: An examination of situational interest and its sources. Br. J. Educ. Psychol. **71**(3), 383–400 (2001)
12. Chen, S., Dian, Y., Jin, Q.: RUC at MediaEval 2016 Predicting Media Interestingness Task. In: Proceedings of the MediaEval Workshop, Hilversum (2016)
13. Chu, S.L., Fedorovskaya, E., Quek, F., Snyder, J.: The effect of familiarity on perceived interestingness of images. In: Proceedings of SPIE, vol. 8651, pp. 86,511C–86,511C–12 (2013). doi:10.1117/12.2008551, http://dx.doi.org/10.1117/12.2008551
14. Constantin, M.G., Boteanu, B., Ionescu, B.: LAPI at MediaEval 2016 Predicting Media Interestingness Task. In: Proceedings of the MediaEval Workshop, Hilversum (2016)

15. Dalal, N., Triggs, B.: Histograms of oriented gradients for human detection. In: IEEE CVPR International Conference on Computer Vision and Pattern Recognition (2005)

16. Danelljan, M., Hager, G., Khan, F.S., Felsberg, M.: Accurate scale estimation for robust visual tracking. In: British Machine Vision Conference (2014)

17. Datta, R., Joshi, D., Li, J., Wang, J.Z.: Studying aesthetics in photographic images using a computational approach. In: IEEE ECCV European Conference on Computer Vision, pp. 288–301. Springer, Berlin (2006)

18. Demarty, C.H., Sjöberg, M., Ionescu, B., Do, T.T., Wang, H., Duong, N.Q.K., Lefebvre, F.: Mediaeval 2016 Predicting Media Interestingness Task. In: Proceedings of the MediaEval Workshop, Hilversum (2016)

19. Dhar, S., Ordonez, V., Berg, T.L.: High level describable attributes for predicting aesthetics and interestingness. In: IEEE International Conference on Computer Vision and Pattern Recognition (2011)

20. Elazary, L., Itti, L.: Interesting objects are visually salient. J. Vis. **8**(3), 3–3 (2008)

21. Erdogan, G., Erdem, A., Erdem, E.: HUCVL at MediaEval 2016: predicting interesting key frames with deep models. In: Proceedings of the MediaEval Workshop, Hilversum (2016)

22. Grabner, H., Nater, F., Druey, M., Gool, L.V.: Visual interestingness in image sequences. In: ACM International Conference on Multimedia, pp. 1017–1026. ACM, New York (2013). doi:10.1145/2502081.2502109, http://doi.acm.org/10.1145/2502081.2502109

23. Gygli, M., Grabner, H., Riemenschneider, H., Nater, F., van Gool, L.: The interestingness of images. In: ICCV International Conference on Computer Vision (2013)

24. Gygli, M., Song, Y., Cao, L.: Video2gif: automatic generation of animated gifs from video. CoRR abs/1605.04850 (2016). http://arxiv.org/abs/1605.04850

25. Harel, J., Koch, C., Perona, P.: Graph-based visual saliency. In: Advances in Neural Information Processing Systems, pp. 545–552 (2006)

26. Hayes, A.F., Krippendorff, K.: Answering the call for a standard reliability measure for coding data. Commun. Methods Meas. **1**(1), 77–89 (2007). doi:10.1080/19312450709336664, http://dx.doi.org/10.1080/19312450709336664

27. Hsieh, L.C., Hsu, W.H., Wang, H.C.: Investigating and predicting social and visual image interestingness on social media by crowdsourcing. In: 2014 IEEE International Conference on Acoustics, Speech and Signal Processing (ICASSP), pp. 4309–4313. IEEE, Providence (2014)

28. Hua, X.S., Yang, L., Wang, J., Wang, J., Ye, M., Wang, K., Rui, Y., Li, J.: Clickage: towards bridging semantic and intent gaps via mining click logs of search engines. In: ACM International Conference on Multimedia (2013)

29. Isola, P., Parikh, D., Torralba, A., Oliva, A.: Understanding the intrinsic memorability of images. In: Advances in Neural Information Processing Systems, pp. 2429–2437 (2011)

30. Isola, P., Xiao, J., Torralba, A., Oliva, A.: What makes an image memorable? In: IEEE CVPR International Conference on Computer Vision and Pattern Recognition, pp. 145–152. IEEE, Providence (2011)

31. Jiang, Y.G., Wang, Y., Feng, R., Xue, X., Zheng, Y., Yan, H.: Understanding and predicting interestingness of videos. In: AAAI Conference on Artificial Intelligence (2013)

32. Jiang, Y.G., Dai, Q., Mei, T., Rui, Y., Chang, S.F.: Super fast event recognition in internet videos. IEEE Trans. Multimedia **177**(8), 1–13 (2015)

33. Joachims, T.: Optimizing search engines using clickthrough data. In: ACM SIGKDD international conference on Knowledge discovery and data mining, pp. 133–142. ACM, New York (2002)

34. Ke, Y., Hoiem, D., Sukthankar, R.: Computer vision for music identification. In: IEEE CVPR International Conference on Computer Vision and Pattern Recognition, vol. 1, pp. 597–604. IEEE, Providence (2005)

35. Ke, Y., Tang, X., Jing, F.: The design of high-level features for photo quality assessment. In: IEEE CVPR International Conference on Computer Vision and Pattern Recognition, vol. 1, pp. 419–426. IEEE, Providence (2006)

36. Khosla, A., Raju, A.S., Torralba, A., Oliva, A.: Understanding and predicting image memorability at a large scale. In: International Conference on Computer Vision (ICCV) (2015)
37. Krippendorff, K.: Content Analysis: An Introduction to Its Methodology, 3rd edn. Sage, Thousand Oaks (2013)
38. Lam, V., Do, T., Phan, S., Le, D.D., Satoh, S., Duong, D.: NII-UIT at MediaEval 2016 Predicting Media Interestingness Task. In: Proceedings of the MediaEval Workshop, Hilversum (2016)
39. Lazebnik, S., Schmid, C., Ponce, J.: Beyond bags of features: spatial pyramid matching for recognizing natural scene categories. In: IEEE CVPR International Conference on Computer Vision and Pattern Recognition, pp. 2169–2178 (2006)
40. Li, J., Barkowsky, M., Le Callet, P.: Boosting paired comparison methodology in measuring visual discomfort of 3dtv: performances of three different designs. In: Proceedings of SPIE Electronic Imaging, Stereoscopic Displays and Applications, vol. 8648 (2013)
41. Li, L.J., Su, H., Fei-Fei, L., Xing, E.P.: Object bank: a high-level image representation for scene classification & semantic feature sparsification. In: Advances in Neural Information Processing Systems, pp. 1378–1386 (2010)
42. Liem, C.: TUD-MMC at MediaEval 2016 Predicting Media Interestingness Task. In: Proceedings of the MediaEval Workshop, Hilversum (2016)
43. Liu, F., Niu, Y., Gleicher, M.: Using web photos for measuring video frame interestingness. In: Proceedings of the International Joint Conference on Artificial Intelligence, pp. 2058–2063 (2009)
44. Liu, Y., Gu, Z., Cheung, Y.M.: Supervised manifold learning for media interestingness prediction. In: Proceedings of the MediaEval Workshop, Hilversum (2016)
45. Lowe, D.: Distinctive image features from scale-invariant keypoints. Int. J. Comput. Vis. **60**, 91–110 (2004)
46. Machajdik, J., Hanbury, A.: Affective image classification using features inspired by psychology and art theory. In: ACM International Conference on Multimedia, pp. 83–92. ACM, New York (2010). doi:10.1145/1873951.1873965, http://doi.acm.org/10.1145/1873951.1873965
47. McCrae, R.R.: Aesthetic chills as a universal marker of openness to experience. Motiv. Emot. **31**(1), 5–11 (2007)
48. Murray, N., Marchesotti, L., Perronnin, F.: Ava: a large-scale database for aesthetic visual analysis. In: IEEE CVPR International Conference on Computer Vision and Pattern Recognition, pp. 2408–2415. IEEE, Providence (2012)
49. Ojala, T., Pietikainen, M., Maenpaa, T.: Multiresolution gray-scale and rotation invariant texture classification with local binary patterns. IEEE Trans. Pattern Anal. Mach. Intell. **24**(7), 971–987 (2002)
50. Oliva, A., Torralba, A.: Modeling the shape of the scene: a holistic representation of the spatial envelope. Int. J. Comput. Vis. **42**, 145–175 (2001)
51. Ovadia, S.: Ratings and rankings: reconsidering the structure of values and their measurement. Int. J. Soc. Res. Methodol. **7**(5), 403–414 (2004). doi:10.1080/1364557032000081654, http://dx.doi.org/10.1080/1364557032000081654
52. Parekh, J., Parekh, S.: The MLPBOON Predicting Media Interestingness System for MediaEval 2016. In: Proceedings of the MediaEval Workshop, Hilversum (2016)
53. Rayatdoost, S., Soleymani, M.: Ranking images and videos on visual interestingness by visual sentiment features. In: Proceedings of the MediaEval Workshop, Hilversum (2016)
54. Schaul, T., Pape, L., Glasmachers, T., Graziano, V., Schmidhuber, J.: Coherence progress: a measure of interestingness based on fixed compressors. In: International Conference on Artificial General Intelligence, pp. 21–30. Springer, Berlin (2011)
55. Shechtman, E., Irani, M.: Matching local self-similarities across images and videos. In: 2007 IEEE Conference on Computer Vision and Pattern Recognition, pp. 1–8. IEEE, Providence (2007)
56. Shen, Y., Demarty, C.H., Duong, N.Q.K.: Technicolor@MediaEval 2016 Predicting Media Interestingness Task. In: Proceedings of the MediaEval Workshop, Hilversum (2016)

57. Shen, Y., Demarty, C.H., Duong, N.Q.K.: Deep learning for multimodal-based video interestingness prediction. In: IEEE International Conference on Multimedia and Expo, ICME'17 (2017)
58. Silvia, P.J.: What is interesting? Exploring the appraisal structure of interest. Emotion 5(1), 89 (2005)
59. Silvia, P.J., Henson, R.A., Templin, J.L.: Are the sources of interest the same for everyone? using multilevel mixture models to explore individual differences in appraisal structures. Cognit. Emot. 23(7), 1389–1406 (2009)
60. Sjöberg, M., Baveye, Y., Wang, H., Quang, V.L., Ionescu, B., Dellandréa, E., Schedl, M., Demarty, C.H., Chen, L.: The mediaeval 2015 affective impact of movies task. In: Proceedings of the MediaEval Workshop, CEUR Workshop Proceedings (2015)
61. Soleymani, M.: The quest for visual interest. In: ACM International Conference on Multimedia, pp. 919–922. New York, NY, USA (2015). doi:10.1145/2733373.2806364, http://doi.acm.org/10.1145/2733373.2806364
62. Spain, M., Perona, P.: Measuring and predicting object importance. Int. J. Comput. Vis. 91(1), 59–76 (2011)
63. Stein, B.E., Stanford, T.R.: Multisensory integration: current issues from the perspective of the single neuron. Nat. Rev. Neurosci. 9(4), 255–266 (2008)
64. Torresani, L., Szummer, M., Fitzgibbon, A.: Efficient object category recognition using classemes. In: IEEE ECCV European Conference on Computer Vision, pp. 776–789. Springer, Berlin (2010)
65. Turner, S.A. Jr, Silvia, P.J.: Must interesting things be pleasant? A test of competing appraisal structures. Emotion 6(4), 670 (2006)
66. Valdez, P., Mehrabian, A.: Effects of color on emotions. J. Exp. Psychol. Gen. 123(4), 394 (1994)
67. Vasudevan, A.B., Gygli, M., Volokitin, A., Gool, L.V.: Eth-cvl @ MediaEval 2016: Textual-visual embeddings and video2gif for video interestingness. In: Proceedings of the MediaEval Workshop, Hilversum (2016)
68. Xiao, J., Hays, J., Ehinger, K., Oliva, A., Torralba, A.: Sun database: large-scale scene recognition from abbey to zoo. In: IEEE CVPR International Conference on Computer Vision and Pattern Recognition, pp. 3485–3492 (2010)
69. Xu, B., Fu, Y., Jiang, Y.G.: BigVid at MediaEval 2016: predicting interestingness in images and videos. In: Proceedings of the MediaEval Workshop, Hilversum (2016)
70. Yang, Y.H., Chen, H.H.: Ranking-based emotion recognition for music organization and retrieval. IEEE Trans. Audio Speech Lang. Process. 19(4), 762–774 (2011)
71. Yannakakis, G.N., Hallam, J.: Ranking vs. preference: a comparative study of self-reporting. In: International Conference on Affective Computing and Intelligent Interaction, pp. 437–446. Springer, Berlin (2011)

Glossary

BoVW   Bag-of-Visual-Words
BoW   Bag-of-Words
CBIR   Content-Based Image Retrieval
CNN   Convolutional Neural Networks
CVIR   Content-Based Video Retrieval
SVH   Human Visual System

© Springer International Publishing AG 2017
J. Benois-Pineau, P. Le Callet (eds.), *Visual Content Indexing and Retrieval
with Psycho-Visual Models*, Multimedia Systems and Applications,
DOI 10.1007/978-3-319-57687-9

Printed in the United States
By Bookmasters